THE STORY OF BUDDHISM

THE STORY OF BUDDHISM

A CONCISE GUIDE TO ITS HISTORY AND TEACHINGS

DONALD S. LOPEZ JR.

HarperOne
An Imprint of HarperCollins*Publishers*

HarperCollins books may be purchased for educational, business, or sales promotional use. For information please write: Special Markets Department, HarperCollins Publishers, 10 East 53rd Street, New York, NY 10022.

HarperCollins Web site: http://www.harpercollins.com

HarperCollins®, ®, and HarperOne™ are trademarks of HarperCollins Publishers.

Library of Congress Cataloging-in-Publication Data

Lopez, Donald S.
The story of Buddhism : a concise guide to its history & teachings / Donald S. Lopez.
p. cm.
Includes bibliographical references and index.
ISBN 978-0-06-009927-5
1. Buddhism. I. Title.

BQ4012 .L65 2001
294.3'09—dc21

00-054263

08 09 10 11 RRD(H) 10

For my parents

CONTENTS

ACKNOWLEDGMENTS

The dramatic growth in scholarship on Buddhism over the past half century, both in the quantity and the quality of that scholarship, has made it virtually impossible for a single scholar to claim knowledge of the entire tradition across its vast geographical and chronological sweep. I certainly cannot make such a claim. To write a book entitled *The Story of Buddhism,* therefore, it is essential to rely heavily on the work of others, and that is what I have done. The bibliography provides a list of the many books I have consulted in writing this book; I have not provided a list of the unpublished dissertations or scholarly articles I consulted since they are less accessible to the general reader, for whom this book is intended. In deference to this reader, I have also not provided footnotes in the text. However, at the end of each chapter I have provided a list for suggested reading where the topics explored in that chapter may be pursued in more depth.

The process of writing this book has left me with a deep sense of respect for the hundreds of scholars who have written about Buddhism over the last century. Their names are too numerous to list here. I would, however, like to thank Robert Sharf and Charles Hallisey for their comments and suggestions on the first draft of the manuscript.

PRONUNCIATION GUIDE

SANSKRIT AND PALI

The standard system for transliterating Sanskrit and Pali terms has been used here. Vowels occur in both long and short forms, with long vowels marked with a bar (macron) over the vowel. They are pronounced as follows:

ā like the a in la
ī like the ee in keep
ū like the u in super
a like the u in butter
e like the ay in bay
i like the i in it
o like the o in so
u like the ou in could

Some consonants without diacritical marks are not pronounced as one would expect in English:

c like ch in churn
th like t in too, but with more emphasis or aspiration
ph like p in port, but with more emphasis or aspiration; there is no f sound

Consonants with diacritical marks are pronounced as follows:

ñ like ny in Bunyan
ṛ like ri in rip
ś and ṣ are pronounced like sh in ship
ṭ, ḍ, ṇ are retroflex forms of t, d, and n and may be pronounced by curling the tongue against the roof of the mouth. Those who find this difficult may pronounce them as t, d, and n without penalty.
ḥ, ḷ, and ṅ are pronounced roughly as they would be in English.

CHINESE

The pinyin system for transliterating Chinese is used here. It is generally pronounced as might be expected, with the following conventions:

q is like ch in change
x is like sh in ship

JAPANESE

A bar (macron) over a vowel does not change the sound of the vowel but lengthens it.

TIBETAN

There is no generally accepted system for phonetically rendering Tibetan in English. Here a phonetic equivalent is provided, followed by a transliteration in the Wylie system. For example:

Tisong Detsen (Khri srong lde btsan)

INTRODUCTION

In northern India, the Fourteenth Dalai Lama rises at 4 A.M. and, having offered obeisance to the Buddha, sits down on his meditation cushion to contemplate his death. Knowing that death is certain, but the time of death uncertain, he prepares for death daily. He imagines an intricate process in which consciousness gradually retreats from the five senses to gather at his heart. Step by step, the four elements of earth, water, fire, and wind—the basic constituents of the material world and human body—lose the capacity to serve as a foundation for consciousness. First, the earth constituent dissolves, and the dying person loses the capacity to perceive forms clearly. Instead, a mirage appears, like that of water in a desert. Second, the water constituent dissolves, and the dying person is no longer able to hear sounds, seeing only what appears to be thick billowing smoke. With the third dissolution, that of the fire constituent, the dying person loses the ability to smell and perceives red sparks of light, like fireflies flickering in darkness. The last of the four elements, the wind constituent, dissolves next. The Dalai Lama imagines that his tongue will then lose the ability to taste, and his body will no longer be able to experience physical sensation or even to move. At this point, he will stop breathing, but he will not be dead. His mind will perceive a sputtering flame, like a burning Tibetan butter lamp.

According to Buddhist physiology, during the process of death, the winds—subtle energies that serve as the vehicles for consciousness—withdraw from a network of seventy-two thousand channels that course throughout the body. Among all these channels, the most important is the central channel, which runs from the genitals upward to the crown of the head, then curving down to end in the space between the eyes. Parallel to the central channel are the right and left channels, which wrap around it at seven points, creating constrictions that prevent winds from moving through the central channel. At these points of constriction there are also networks of smaller channels that radiate throughout the body. These points are called the seven wheels. The most important wheel is located at the heart.

At this point in the process of death, the sense consciousnesses have ceased to operate entirely. Next, all ordinary conceptions dissolve. The winds from the channels that course through the upper part of the body have now withdrawn from the right and left channels and have gathered at the crown of the head at the top of the central channel. When these winds descend through the central channel to the heart wheel, the dying person sees nothing but radiant white, like a clear autumn night sky before dawn, pervaded by moonlight. Shortly thereafter, the winds from the lower part of the body enter the central channel at the base of the spine and ascend toward the heart. This produces a vision of a bright red color, like a clear autumn sky pervaded by sunlight. Now the winds that have gathered above and below enter into the heart wheel, and the dying person seems to swoon, seeing everywhere a radiant blackness, like a clear autumn sky in the evening after the sun has set and before the moon has risen. Finally, in the last stage, the mind of clear light dawns, with the color of the sky at dawn, free from sunlight, moonlight, and darkness. This is death.

The Dalai Lama understands that if one is not able to recognize each of these stages as they occur, the mind of clear light will slip away and depart from the body, seeking a new place for rebirth. However, if he can remain mindful throughout the process, he will be able to bring death onto the path to enlightenment. When he encounters the mind of clear light, the most profound state of consciousness, he will dwell within it, passing through the radiant night to rise as a buddha in the clear light of dawn.

In Thailand, an audience gathers to watch a film. In it, a handsome prince named Vessantara is beloved by his kingdom because of his great generosity. He is married to a beautiful princess, named Maddī, who bears him two children, a boy and girl. One day a delegation arrives from a nearby kingdom that is suffering from drought. The king of that land has undertaken a fast in an effort to bring rain, but to no avail. They ask, therefore, that Vessantara give them one of the prized possessions of his land, a white elephant that brings rain wherever it goes. Vessantara agrees to their request. After the departure of the elephant, the people of Vessantara's kingdom complain that the source of their prosperity has been taken from them. They demand that Vessantara be punished. Vessantara's father refuses to imprison his son but eventually accepts the suggestion that he be banished, and Vessantara is sent into exile for the crime of giving a gift, but not before making a lavish gift to the people, providing clothing, food, and drink to all who need them. Maddī refuses to let him go alone, and she and the children accompany him to the forest.

En route to their forest hermitage, Vessantara gives away their carriage and horses. In the forest, they find the hut of an ascetic on Crooked Mountain, where they live contentedly for seven months amid flowers, songbirds, and friendly animals. But one night Maddī has a terrible dream that a strange man bursts into her hut and cuts out her heart. Calmed by Vessantara, she goes back to sleep. The next day, she sets out into the forest to collect food, leaving Vessantara to tend the children. While she is away, a brahmin arrives, the first human they have seen in seven months. But he makes an inhuman request, asking Vessantara to offer him not food and drink, but his son and his daughter. Vessantara immediately agrees. The children run away and hide, but their father finds them, and as they cling to his legs, their tears fall on his feet. But he does not change his mind, explaining to his children how giving gifts makes him happy. The brahmin leads the children away to be his servants, beating them as they go. The children escape and run back to their father, asking at least to be able to remain to bid farewell to their mother. But Vessantara does not relent, and his son asks him if his heart is made of stone. The children are once again led away into servitude, asking their father to give their toys to their mother to soothe her when she grieves. Vessantara is overcome with sorrow, thinking first to save the children but deciding in the end that a gift once given cannot be reclaimed. Watching in the distance as his children escape again from the brahmin, only to be run down and caught, he sheds hot tears of blood.

Maddī is overcome with despair when she returns home to find the children gone and searches for them throughout the night before fainting at Vessantara's feet. When she regains consciousness, she asks where the children have gone. He replies that he gave them to a brahmin as slaves but assures her that she is young enough to have more children. Eventually, another brahmin arrives, asking that Vessantara give him Maddī. Again, Vessantara agrees, and Maddī is led away without complaint, saying that Vessantara has the right to do with her as he pleases. The brahmin immediately reveals that he is, in fact, Indra, the king of the gods, come to test the limits of the prince's generosity. He returns Maddī to the prince and grants him eight wishes. Vessantara asks, among other things, that his father be glad to see him upon his return to the kingdom, that he ascend the throne to be a compassionate king, that he have a son, and that he never regret a gift.

He does not ask for the return of his children, who remain the slaves of the evil brahmin, made to serve him all day and sleep on the ground at night. The brahmin eventually takes them to the kingdom of Vessantara's father, who recognizes his grandchildren and purchases them from him. Learning from the children the whereabouts of their parents, the king expresses regret at having banished Vessantara and leads a procession to invite him to return. Vessantara and Maddī are overcome with joy to be reunited with their children. Vessantara agrees to return home and assume the throne, insisting that his gift of the elephant long ago had been proper. His first act as king is to free all captives, human and animal. Indra causes a rain of jewels that soon becomes waist deep. Vessantara distributes some of the jewels and saves the rest so that he might make more gifts in the future.

The Thai audience weeps as Vessantara gives away his children and then his wife and delights in the happy ending, although they already know the plot by heart. They also know that, upon his death, Vessantara will be reborn as the Buddha.

In Japan, the monk Tanno Kakudō rises each morning at 2 A.M. and dons a white robe and straw sandals, the traditional dress of the dead. He begins a solitary walk of twenty-two miles around Mount Hiei above Kyoto, stopping to pray at 270 shrines along the way. Tanno is a Buddhist monk of the Tendai sect, and he has made a vow to walk this route one thousand times, a feat accomplished by only eleven monks since 1945. According to tradition, if he cannot fulfill his vow to complete the "thousand-day walk," he must commit suicide.

During the first three years, he completed one hundred of these marathons, gaining such strength and stamina that he was able to complete the route, including the grueling fourteen-hundred-foot ascent at the end, in five and a half hours of steady walking, returning to his monastery by 7:30 A.M.. He would remove his straw sandals after each walk and hang them outside the temple door, requiring a new pair for each marathon. Increasing his pace, he completed four hundred circuits in the next two years. As the fame of his ordeal grew, people from a nearby village would kneel along the route, waiting for Tanno to touch them on their head and shoulders with his rosary as he passed. Only once along the route was he permitted to sit, pausing on a stone bench with a lotus blossom carved in its surface to visualize himself as a buddha and pray for the health and prosperity of the emperor and nation of Japan.

After completing seven hundred of the thousand circuits, Tanno faced his greatest ordeal, called the Great Fast. After attending his own funeral feast, he was locked inside the temple of the wrathful god Fudō, where he would recite one hundred thousand mantras over nine days. During that time, he was not allowed to eat, drink, or sleep. Such privation for seven days ordinarily results in death. Every night he was released from the temple in order to draw water from a nearby well, water that he had to use in various offerings but could not drink himself. On the first night, he required twelve minutes to return with two buckets of water suspended from a pole over his shoulder. On the ninth night, having now lost one-fourth of his body weight, he required one hundred minutes. Surviving this ordeal, he sat with the assembled monks and was declared now fit to pray for the welfare of the emperor and the nation. He was then offered a bowl of tea.

After only three weeks in which to recover from his fast, he undertook a more grueling pace, completing one hundred consecutive circuits of a longer route, thirty-five miles in length. This was followed by a yet more demanding route of fifty-two miles, each circuit requiring eighteen hours, allowing him only two hours of sleep. By the time he had completed 999 circuits, he had become national news, and television crews from around Japan came to record his final ascent on the final day. According to the tenets of his sect, upon the completion of the thousand-day walk, Tanno Kakudō became a living buddha.

These three cases appear to have very little in common. Although occurring simultaneously in a modern world of mass communication, they took place in different parts of the globe and in different languages. The Tibetan lama who sat on a cushion in meditation, the Thai audience who sat in chairs to watch a film, and the Japanese monk who paused in his morning marathon for a moment and sat on a stone bench embossed with a lotus blossom were unaware of one another and unfamiliar with one another's practices. Yet, each of the three accounts shares a single word, *buddha,* a term from the Sanskrit language of ancient India that means "awakened." An epithet rather than a given name, it was employed some twenty-five hundred years ago to describe one of the many itinerant teachers who wandered among the towns and villages along the river Ganges. This man, known simply as the Buddha, became one of the most famous figures in human history. We know very little about him; scholars even disagree on the date of his death by as much as a century. Yet some twenty-five hundred years later, a Tibetan lama living in exile in northern India, employees of businesses in Bangkok, a Japanese monk living on a mountain near Kyoto, and an American woman practicing Zen meditation in Michigan look back to him and call themselves Buddhists, tracing a direct link from the present back to an obscure Indian ascetic who died more than two millennia ago.

This link is traced back most often through the transmission of teachings. A teacher received instruction from his teacher, who received it from his teacher, moving back slowly over centuries and across oceans, deserts, and mountains to ancient India and into the presence of the Buddha himself. This retrospective route is more easily imagined in reverse. When we try to measure the movement of the Buddha's words from his time to ours, we are immediately confronted with problems. We do not know with certainty what language he spoke. We know that he left no writings, that what he taught was preserved in the memories of generations of his followers, not to be written down until some four centuries after his death. Thus, it is impossible to know precisely what the Buddha taught. Yet the authority of this man who authored no book was so great that works attributed to him have been composed in many languages and in many lands over many centuries. When Buddhists trace their lineage back to the Buddha, it is often through these texts, texts that often confound our desire for historical specificity.

The Buddha is reported to have exhorted his monks to "go and wander for the welfare of the multitudes, for the happiness of the multitudes, out of sympathy for the world, for the benefit, welfare, and happiness of gods and humans." And, indeed, the teachings of the Buddha were carried around the world, not as a disembodied truth descending on another culture from above, but rather as a more material movement—of monks, texts, relics, and icons—along trade routes and across deserts, mountains, and seas. Over the course of many centuries after the death of the Buddha, his words and his image made their way from India to the nations now named Bangladesh, Pakistan, Nepal, Sri Lanka, Afghanistan, Myanmar, Thailand, Laos, Cambodia, Malaysia, Indonesia, Vietnam, China, Taiwan, Tibet, Mongolia, Korea, and Japan. Over the past two centuries, Buddhism has become established in Europe, Australia, and the Americas. The languages in which the teachings were written included not only the classical Buddhist languages of Pali, Sanskrit, Chinese, and Tibetan, but also forgotten languages such as Khotanese, Sogdian, Tangut, and Tocharian B. Vast numbers of works were thus attributed to the Buddha. These in turn were commented upon, at great length. The words of the Buddha and his Indian commentators then had to be translated into new languages (with the translators remembered as heroes), where they in turn received further commentary. Remarkable numbers of texts were thus produced, which somehow had to be organized. These collections are referred to by the language in which they appear: the Pali canon, the Chinese canon, the Tibetan canon. And these so-called canons do not include many more local texts in various vernaculars that, because of time or circumstance, did not warrant inclusion. Buddhism has thus produced a vast literature, far beyond the capacity of a single person. One edition of the Tibetan canon, for example, contains 1,108 works that are traditionally regarded as spoken by the Buddha, or spoken with his sanction, and an additional 3,461 treatises by Indian Buddhist masters. Were the entire collection to be translated into English, it would fill some two hundred thousand pages. Not even the most erudite scholar is expected to know the names of all the works included, much less their contents.

This overwhelming ocean of texts, many long unread in languages long forgotten, inevitably changed through time and translation, presenting doctrines and practices at wild variance with one another, all claiming to originate from a man whose words can never be recovered. What holds it all together? The texts and practices that have been identified, by themselves or by others, as Buddhist, have varied widely across Asia and across history. These variations have been significant enough that what might be called Buddhist in Japan not to be recognized as Buddhist in Sri Lanka. Indeed, the mutual recognition of Buddhists from different regions of Asia has occurred with any frequency only over the past century with the identification of Buddhism as a "world religion," and even then Buddhists in one region have tended to claim that their Buddhism is more original or more pure or more efficacious than the Buddhism encountered elsewhere. Acknowledging the transformations that occur across time, across history, across culture, across language, would it not be more accurate, then, to speak not of *the* Buddhist tradition, but instead of many Buddhist traditions?

Such an approach has certain advantages if we wish to consider Buddhism as it has occurred across historical periods and across geographical regions. This Buddhism is not a coherent unity. But if one adopts a different perspective, a perspective that offers a different view of time, of history, and of people, then something that we might call Buddhism, in the singular, begins to appear. The Buddha taught, or so it is reported, that all beings in the universe are subject to rebirth without beginning, such that all beings in the universe were present, somewhere in the universe, when he taught the path to freedom in India twenty-five hundred years ago. Some who had the good fortune to hear his teachings and put them into practice were able to follow the path and free themselves from rebirth. Others, less fortunate, have continued to be reborn, again and again. They missed the opportunity to sit in the circle of the Buddha's disciples. But the Buddha claimed, or so it is reported, not to have invented a new path, or to have discovered a path that was previously unknown, but simply to have uncovered a path that had been long forgotten. The path had been taught by other buddhas in the distant past and would be taught by other buddhas in the distant future. He was but one of many buddhas. These compassionate beings would appear in the world again. And in the meantime, the teachings of the buddha who lived in India twenty-five hundred years ago, our Buddha, would remain in the world. No matter that, when reading Buddhist texts, we find many different paths and many different descriptions of the state of freedom from rebirth. No matter that there are even different predictions of how long the Buddha's teaching will remain in the world before it is forgotten. In this sense, the particulars of time and place and language seem less important. If everyone has been reborn countless times in the past, everyone has already been reborn in countless places and has spoken countless languages. And if the Buddha is regarded as a skillful teacher who, recognizing the different interest and capacities of his listeners, teaches different things to different people according to their needs, then the contradictions in the teaching are perhaps simply apparent. The Buddha, however he is understood and whatever he is recorded to have said, provides the reference point for what is called Buddhism.

A book with the title *The Story of Buddhism* might be written in any number of ways. One might take a historical approach, consulting the ancient archaeological remains of Buddhism in India before turning to the chronicles of the kingdoms that came to embrace the teachings of the Buddha. Here, one would note that, in the histories of many Buddhist lands, few events are considered more important than the installation of the first image of the Buddha or the founding of the first monastery. One might take a political approach, examining the role of Buddhist monks as advisers of kings and emperors. Here, one would note that Buddhism tended to arrive first at court, delivered by emissaries (sometimes Buddhist monks) who offered texts and images to the throne, along with claims of their extraordinary powers. One might take an economic approach, examining how what began as a brotherhood of beggars became a wealthy and powerful institution, providing all manner of financial services. Here, one would examine the economy of karma, whereby material gifts to monks and nuns meant to provide for their physical sustenance would be exchanged for spiritual merit to provide for the well-being of laypeople in this lifetime and the next. One might take a sociological approach, considering the ways in which Buddhist monasteries provided for some a haven for those unable to succeed in the world, for others a conduit to influence and fame that would have been unavailable through other means. Here, one would examine the role of women in Buddhism; the Buddha is reported to have taken the revolutionary step of accepting women into his order, yet he is said to have done so with great reluctance, predicting that by his deed the duration of his teaching had been curtailed. One might adopt a literary approach, examining the fascinating network of images, narratives, and tropes that connect Buddhist texts across the centuries. Here, one would note the development of the biography of the Buddha and the ways in which this increasingly stylized biography came to serve as a model for the lives of subsequent saints. One might adopt a philosophical approach, comparing the diverging tenets of all manner of scholastic traditions, each of which was at great pains to demonstrate how its doctrines derived from the Buddha himself. Here, it would be important to note that the scholars who wrote sophisticated discourses on the immaterial nature of the Buddha also offered prayers and incense to his image. One might take an art historical approach, tracing the roles of art and architecture across Asia. Here, one would note that in their studies of Buddhist art in India, scholars have long been intrigued by a number of early stone carvings in which the Buddha is not present but absent. The carvings depict scenes in which obeisance is being paid to the footprints of the Buddha or to a tree. In one scene, considered to depict the Buddha's departure from the palace, a riderless horse is shown. Such works have led to the theory that early Buddhism was aniconic, that is, that there was a prohibition against depicting the Buddha in bodily form; he could only be represented with certain symbols. The argument is based in part on another absence, with the lack of any prescriptions for depicting the Buddha in early texts taken as evidence that such depictions were proscribed. This view has been challenged by those who offer a different interpretation of many of the scenes regarded as evidence of aniconism. Perhaps the carvings do not depict events from the life of the Buddha but rather show pilgrimages to and worship of important sites from the life of the Buddha, such as the Bodhi tree.

It is important to note that writing a single volume work entitled *The Story of Buddhism* is a distinctively modern and, until rather recently, non-Buddhist thing to do. Even the term *Buddhism* is of recent vintage. In seventeenth-century Europe, only four religions were identified in the world: Christianity, Judaism, Mohammedism, and Paganism (also known as Idolatry). The history of the academic study of religion is in one sense a process of replacing Paganism with a larger list of isms: Hinduism, Confucianism, Taoism, Shintoism, Sikhism, and, of course, Buddhism. Hinduism is a term derived from *hind,* a Persian word for the Indus River Valley, an area now located in Pakistan and populated by Muslims. Hinduism has no correlate in Sanskrit, its sacred language. Buddhism is a somewhat more complicated case. We really cannot say with certainty what the Buddha himself called what it was he said. As noted above, none of what are regarded by the faithful as his words were written down until some four centuries after he passed into *nirvāṇa.* However, when they were written down, we find him referring to what he taught as the *dharma vinaya. Dharma* is famously untranslatable; nineteenth-century translators used to render *dharma* as "law." More recently it is often translated as teachings or doctrine. *Vinaya* refers to the rules of monastic discipline. Thus, the Buddha divided what he taught into, perhaps, a set of doctrines and a set of rules. The corpus of his teachings came to be referred to in Sanskrit as *buddhadharma,* the teaching or doctrine of the Buddha, and his followers as *bauddha,* Buddhist. Thus, an adjective, *bauddha,* that may be accurately rendered as "Buddhist," existed in Sanskrit, even if there was little consensus over precisely what it encompassed.

But the term *Buddhism* has only recently been adopted by Buddhists. In Sri Lanka, what we might call Buddhism is simply referred to as the *sāsana,* the teaching. In Tibet, it is most commonly referred to as *nang pa'i chos,* the religion of the insiders. In China, it is *fo jiao,* the teaching of the Buddha (*fo* used to be pronounced as *budh* in Chinese). In Japan, it is *butsudo,* the way of the Buddha. Over the history of these traditions, apart from a general recognition of India as the birthplace of the Buddha, there is little sense of the referents of these various names being a single entity that we might call Buddhism. They were, instead, like a variety of dialects, not always mutually comprehensible.

If there was little cognizance among the Buddhists of belonging to a single pan-Asian tradition, there was confusion among the European travelers who encountered them. Only in 1801 does the *Oxford English Dictionary* record the use of the term *Boudhism,* changed to *Buddhism* in 1816 in the phrase of a contributor to the *Asiatic Journal:* "The name and peculiarities of Buddhism have a good deal fixed my attention." In 1829 Edward Upham published *The History and Doctrine of Budhism,* the first work in English with the word, albeit lacking one *d,* in its title. But even at the end of the nineteenth century, the referent was not always clear, and the spelling of the term was, in one famous case, intentionally altered. Madame Blavatsky, founder of the Theosophical Society, remembered as a key figure in the Buddhist revival in Sri Lanka, distinguished between the corrupt practices of Asian Buddhists, which she called Buddhism, and a more esoteric science of enlightenment, called Budh-ism, a synonym of Theosophy.

It is only with the invention of the category of religion, with its obligatory constituents of a founder, sacred scriptures, and fixed body of doctrine, that Buddhism comes to be counted as a world religion. Even then, it was judged by many Europeans as a rival to Christianity. During the nineteenth century, monks from a variety of traditions came to speak of a single pan-Asian Buddhism in an attempt to counter the attacks of Christian missionaries and colonial officials. One of the early attempts to unite Buddhism under a single creed (and a single flag) was made not by an Asian Buddhist but by a Theosophist, Colonel Henry Steel Olcott. In 1891 he formulated a set of fourteen rather bland principles ("1. Buddhists are taught to show the same tolerance, forbearance, and brotherly love to all men, without distinction; and an unswerving kindness toward members of the animal kingdom"), principles that, with some effort, he persuaded a variety of Sri Lankan, Burmese, and Japanese Buddhist leaders to endorse.

Also during the nineteenth century, Buddhism became a subject of academic inquiry in Europe and America, focused primarily on the study of texts. Since that time, scholarly knowledge of Buddhism has expanded and changed and continues to change. The date of the Buddha's birth remains a topic of active scholarly debate; the circumstances that led to the rise of the movement (or movements) known as the Mahāyāna, the "Great Vehicle," continue to be explored, as does the degree of its importance in India; cases of direct plagiarism of Hindu tantric texts by Buddhists (simply substituting the word *Śiva* with the word *Buddha*) are being discovered; birch bark scrolls inscribed with the Buddhist texts continue to be unearthed (such as those acquired by the British Library in 1994); previously unknown works (at least in Europe and America) are being translated into English; meditation is being reconsidered, both in terms of the extent of its practice historically as well as its function as a form of private and motionless ritual; the events of the first centuries after the death of the Buddha and prior to the writing down of his teachings remain a source of active speculation and study, considering, for example, what prompted the act of writing. And scholars continue to speculate about the reasons why, apart from the obvious factors such as Muslim invasions, Buddhism seemed to disappear from India, the land of its birth, around the twelfth century. If it did not entirely disappear, what remained, and why?

Thus, knowledge of Buddhism is always changing, and, in important ways, Buddhism changes in the process. This book attempts to reflect the current state of that knowledge and to avoid the errors and prejudices of the past. At the same time, this book, like all books, is a product of its time. In the history of Buddhist scholarship, this is a period in which there is less interest in Buddhist philosophy and more emphasis on Buddhist practice, less interest in Buddhism as a global entity and more interest in its local manifestations, less interest in the practices of elites, especially monastics, and more interest in the practices of ordinary monks, nuns, and laypeople. There is less interest in scholastic debates and more interest in social history. There is less interest in doctrine and more interest in ritual. These prejudices are inevitably present here, but with at least the hope of some recognition of their presence and an attempt at some semblance of balance, given the impossible task of encompassing Buddhism in one hundred thousand words.

My primary aim is to focus on Buddhist practice, in the broad sense of the term. Rather than portray Buddhism as a philosophy or a way of life, as it is so often characterized in the West, I prefer to view Buddhism as a religion to which ordinary people have turned over the centuries for the means to confront, control, or even escape the exigencies of life. The Buddha named what he spoke as the dharma, a word that used to be rendered as "law," now more commonly as "teaching" or "doctrine." But *dharma* has many meanings; traditional commentators provide ten. It is derived from the Sanskrit root meaning "to hold," and Buddhist monks are fond of saying that the dharma is what holds one back from falling into suffering. Precisely what it is that constitutes the dharma is a question that has absorbed Buddhist thinkers for centuries, but this functional sense of the dharma as a means of protection from suffering and for the promotion of well-being, both now and in the future, remains a constant across the Buddhist world and across Buddhist history.

What is encompassed by this dharma is indeed vast. It can include chanting the Buddha's name, circumambulating his relics, prostrating before his image, copying, reading, or reciting his words, painting his image, taking and maintaining vows, offering food and robes to monks and nuns, writing arcane commentaries, sitting in meditation, exorcising demons, visualizing oneself as the Buddha, placing flowers before a book, burning oneself alive.

My task here is to present these various activities within a context of doctrine and practice. I have not, for the most part, traced their historical origins or their evolution over time and between cultures. I have tried to avoid engaging in my own extended analysis, seeking instead to describe some of the manifestations of Buddhism in such a way that their own logic will be clear. In an effort to achieve this, I do not begin, as most books do, with a retelling of the life of the Buddha. I follow, instead, a more traditional approach. Buddhist histories generally start at the beginning, with the creation of the universe. The appearance of the Buddha in the world is regarded by Buddhists as the most auspicious event in history. In order to understand how this might be so, it is necessary to understand the nature of the world that the Buddha entered, in terms not only of its physical topography, but also of its location in time. The Buddha's first words as an infant were that this was his final birth. The momentous nature of this claim, even when not made by a newborn child, can be appreciated only if one has some understanding of the Buddhist theory of reincarnation. The Buddha claimed that, whether buddhas come or go, the nature of the universe remains the same. Hence, I describe the nature of the universe prior to his appearance.

The second and longest chapter of the book is devoted to the Buddha. Here I tell the story of the life of the Buddha as it is most commonly told, beginning with his birth as a prince and ending with his entry into nirvāṇa as the enlightened one eighty years later. Along the way, I discuss what is traditionally considered to be his first sermon on the four noble truths: the apparently simple formula according to which life is qualified by suffering, that suffering has a cause, that there is a state beyond suffering, and that there is a path to that state. Indeed, in this chapter, and throughout the book, I try to provide a mixture of history, legend, and doctrine, an approach that is often found in Buddhist literature. In the case of the Buddha, his teaching is often meant to serve as a substitute for his presence.

The basic narrative of the life of the Buddha is remarkably similar across the Buddhist world, but there is a vast range of opinion concerning the precise meaning of the events of that life, and especially about what the Buddha taught from the night of his enlightenment to his passage into nirvāṇa forty-five years later. Some would claim that the Buddha never ceased teaching the dharma during that time; others would claim that he uttered not a single word. Even after he was gone, the Buddha remained alive in the world in the form of relics that were entombed and worshiped and, later, in the form of images. From the life of the Buddha, I turn, then, to the various persons he has been understood to be and to have been. For a central element in the life of the Buddha is his previous lives, not simply his immediately preceding life as Prince Vessantara, whose delight in giving caused him to give away even his children and his wife, but his many previous lives, sometimes as an animal, when he was a bodhisattva, one who has promised to become a buddha and has set out on the path to buddhahood, a path that encompasses many millions of lifetimes. Some forms of Buddhism declare that there are at this moment many bodhisattvas ready to offer their aid to any and all who call upon them. Some forms of Buddhism declare that all beings will one day set out on the bodhisattva path and hence that all beings will become buddhas. This is possible, they declare, because all beings are endowed with something called the buddha nature.

A Buddhist is generally defined as someone who seeks refuge in the three jewels: the Buddha, the dharma, and the saṅgha. Chapter 3 is devoted to the dharma. Rather than seeking to survey the vast range of Buddhist doctrine, I consider here some of the strategies that Buddhist thinkers have employed to control the vast repository of doctrine they inherited. In order for the dharma to be controlled, it had to be classified, a process that involved facing the contradictions that occurred when so many texts claimed to be the word of the Buddha. From these rather philosophical concerns, I turn to some of the more practical uses of the word of the Buddha and the various forms of protection it has provided to those who follow its admonitions.

Saṅgha means "community," and the saṅgha, the third of the three jewels, is variously interpreted. Sometimes it means the community of those who have followed the path of the Buddha and achieved nirvāṇa. Sometimes it means the community of monks and nuns. Most broadly, it refers to the community of followers of the

Buddha. Here, I consider the saṅgha in two chapters. Chapter 4 examines the world of monks and nuns. The first followers of the Buddha renounced family life in order to seek the path to nirvāṇa. They lived on the donations of others, going from door to door each morning on their begging rounds. The group eventually became large enough to require a code of conduct, with individual rules formulated, according to tradition, by the Buddha himself on the occasion of a particular transgression. Some deeds, such as murder or breaking the vow of chastity, required permanent expulsion. Lesser offenses needed only to be confessed in order to be expiated. The community of monks, which is said to have slept outdoors in the early years, soon came to require more permanent shelters, and these structures, donated by lay supporters, became the first monasteries.

Both in the case of begging for food and in the case of the donation of shelter, one observes the strong reliance of monks on the laity. But the laity received something in return, namely the merit accrued from giving gifts to a virtuous person. Indeed, monks do not thank laypeople for the food they receive; laypeople thank monks for providing them with the opportunity for giving. The order of nuns was said to have been established by the Buddha himself, creating an order for women whose husbands had abandoned them to become monks. The fact that the Buddha conceded that women have the capacity to achieve enlightenment and created the opportunity for them to do so has been called a revolutionary act, given the condition of women in India at the time. Yet nuns were burdened by rules and regulations far more stringent than those for monks, and the order of nuns eventually died out in many parts of the Buddhist world.

Chapter 5 is devoted to the group that has always constituted the majority of Buddhists and whose support is essential for the survival of monks and nuns: laypeople. Buddhist laypeople have generally considered themselves incapable of doing the things that monks and nuns do and thus have devoted themselves instead to their support, in the hope of accruing the merit that will allow them to become monks and nuns, ideally as disciples of the next buddha, in a future lifetime. In the meantime, laypeople generally seek a pleasant rebirth in heaven for themselves and for their family members and, to that end, engage in all manner of charitable activities, often directed toward monks and nuns, but also directed toward others: a common form of Buddhist merit making is the freeing of animals bound for slaughter. Much lay practice is associated with death rituals where, again, monks are called on to serve as intermediaries between the realm of the living and the realm of the dead.

The ultimate aim of Buddhism, however, is to escape death entirely through achieving enlightenment, and the final chapter considers several of the ways in which this state has been sought. Meditation serves as only one of several techniques employed in pursuit of enlightenment. Some would claim that enlightenment requires the accumulation of merit over many lifetimes. Others would claim that enlightenment is possible in this very lifetime. Some would claim that enlightenment is a gradual process of purifying the mind of defilements. Others would claim that we are already enlightened and simply need to recognize it. Some would claim that enlightenment requires monumental effort. Others would claim that enlightenment is benevolently bestowed by the Buddha.

No single volume can do justice to Buddhism. I can only hope to give some sense of the contours of the world of Buddhism here. In order to trace these contours, I have relied above all on Buddhist stories. Most Buddhists throughout history have not engaged in meditation. Many monks have not known the four noble truths. But everyone, monk and nun, layman and laywoman, knows stories about the Buddha, about the bodhisattvas, about famous monks and nuns. These stories, sometimes miraculous, sometimes humorous, sometimes both, have provided the most enduring means for the transmission of the dharma, more enduring even than grand images carved in stone. Each retelling of a story is slightly different from the one before, with embellishments and omissions, yet always able to be told again, its plot providing a coherence to the myriad constituents of experience, from which we may derive both instruction and delight. And so I begin my story of Buddhism.

I

THE UNIVERSE

The universe has no beginning. It is the product of karma, the law of the cause and effect of actions, according to which virtuous actions create pleasure in the future and nonvirtuous actions create pain. It is a natural law, accounting for all the happiness and suffering in the world. The beings of the universe have been reborn without beginning in six realms, as gods, demigods, humans, animals, ghosts, and hell beings. Their actions create not only their individual experiences of pleasure and pain, but also the domains in which they dwell. The physical universe is thus the product of the individual and collective actions of the inhabitants of the universe. Buddhist practice is directed largely at performing deeds that will bring happiness in the future, avoiding deeds that will bring pain, and counteracting the future effects of misdeeds done in the past. And there are some who seek the ultimate goal of freedom from the bonds of karma and the universe it has forged.

The workings of karma are understood over the course of lifetimes without beginning, and thus Buddhists speak not only of days and months and years, but also of aeons. The cosmological systems of Indian Buddhism describe a universe that passes through four periods: creation, abiding, destruction, and nothingness. The physical universe is created during the first period, which begins when the faint wind of the past karma of beings starts to blow in the vacuity of space at the end of the previous period of nothingness. Beings come to inhabit the world during the period of abiding. During the period of destruction, the physical universe is incinerated by the heat of seven suns. This is followed by a period of nothingness, after which the fourfold cycle begins again.

According to a widely known creation myth, the first humans in the present period of abiding had a life span of eighty thousand years. Free from the marks of gender, they were able to fly and were illuminated by their own light; there was no need for a sun or moon. They also did not require food. At that time, the surface of the earth was covered by a white frothy substance. One day one of the beings descended to earth and dipped the tip of its finger into the substance and then touched the finger to its tongue. The taste was sweet. Soon everyone was eating the white substance, which would naturally replenish itself. But the introduction of this food into their bodies soon caused them to lose their natural luster, and the sun and moon appeared to illumine the sky. The added weight of their bodies soon made it impossible for them to fly. The white substance evolved into a naturally growing huskless rice that would be ready to harvest again the day after it was picked. But as the beings ate more and more of the rice, it became necessary for them to somehow eliminate the waste that was accumulating in their bodies, and the anus and genitals developed. One couple soon discovered an additional use for the genitals and engaged in sexual intercourse for the first time. The others were scandalized, pelting them with mud. Soon, to hide their shameful activities, people began to build houses. Growing too lazy to pick the rice each day, they began to take more than they needed and hoard it in their homes. As a result, the rice developed husks and required more and more time to grow. Soon people began to steal from one another, requiring the election of a king who would enforce a system of laws. And this is how human society began.

In this myth we see the story of a fall, from a state of luminous freedom to slavery to the land. From the single fateful act of tasting the white, sticky substance came first the sun and the moon, then the need to eat food, then gender, then sexuality, then settlements, then society. According to Buddhist cosmology, things have continued to decline, with the human life span decreasing to one hundred years, at which point the Buddha appeared in history. There are numerous predictions as to how long his teaching will remain in the world, ranging from five hundred to five thousand (or even twelve thousand) years. The life span of humans will continue to drop over many millennia, until it reaches only ten years, a time of pestilence, famine, and war, with armies of children fighting bloody battles. At this point, the life span will begin to increase, growing slowly back again to eighty thousand. The world will be like a heaven, with wish-granting trees bearing their fruit and society free from the need for any form of government. It is when the human life span is at its apex of eighty thousand years (some five billion years from now) that the next buddha, Maitreya, will appear. After twenty cycles in which the human life span ranges from eighty thousand to ten, this universe will be destroyed.

In the meantime, humans inhabit a flat world that has at its center the square Mount Meru, its four faces made of gold, silver, lapis lazuli, and crystal. The mountain is surrounded by seven concentric ranges, beyond which there is a great ocean, with island continents located in the four cardinal directions. Humans inhabit the southern continent, called Jambudvīpa (Rose Apple Island), facing the lapis side of Mount Meru, which makes the sky and ocean blue.

Six realms are located in this world, populated by beings who are born there as a result of their karma. Together, these six constitute the Desire Realm, so called because the beings who populate it are driven by desire. The first and highest is the realm of gods. These are abodes of pleasure, ranging from pleasure gardens filled with the sound of celestial music, the scent of jasmine, the taste of ambrosia, and the touch of beautiful women, to sublime immaterial states of deep concentration distinguished by various levels of mental bliss. The lowest of the heavens is that of the kings of the four directions, who reign over their respective slopes of Mount Meru. Each month they go forth into the world of humans to observe their conduct, which they report back to the gods of the next heaven, located on the flat summit of the mountain. It is called the Heaven of the Thirty-Three and is populated by the gods of ancient India, ruled by Indra. This is an instance, to be repeated throughout the Buddhist world, of subsuming and subordinating local deities into the Buddhist pantheon. Other heavens float above Mount Meru in the sky. Above the heavens of the Desire Realm are the Form Realm and the Formless Realm, places of sublime rebirth that result from achieving deep states of meditation in the previous life. In the Form Realm, the beings remain attached to beautiful forms but are free from manifest desire. The highest heavens, if they can be called that, are in the Formless Realm, whose gods exist without form as deep states of concentrated consciousness, absorbed in infinite space, infinite consciousness, nothingness, and neither existence nor nonexistence. But even here, beings are bound in the cycle of rebirth.

Gods live very long lives, but they are not immortal. The death of gods in the heavenly realms is attended by six signs: their natural luster fades, their grand throne becomes uncomfortable, their bodies begin to perspire, the garlands of flowers around their necks begin to wilt, their servants are reluctant to approach them, their palace becomes dusty. At that moment, it is said that the god has a vision of his or her next lifetime, and because a god will almost inevitably be reborn in a lower realm (because gods squander their time in heaven intoxicated by pleasure), this is the most intense suffering in the cycle of rebirth. This cycle is called *saṃsāra,* literally meaning "wandering" in Sanskrit. The second category (omitted in some presentations) is the class of demigods, deities less powerful than gods but more powerful than humans. They are jealous of the gods and engage in warfare with them. The third place of rebirth is as a human, already familiar to us. The realms of gods, demigods, and humans are regarded as fortunate places of rebirth within the cycle.

The other three realms, of animals, ghosts, and hell beings, are considered unfortunate, containing, as they do, increasingly intense and varied forms of suffering. Animals are said to suffer the particular fate of having to spend their lives in the pursuit of food, while also seeking to avoid becoming food. Unlike humans, for animals it is the taste of their flesh, the texture of their skin, or the scent of their musk that may serve as the cause of their death. The next realm is that of ghosts, some of whom inhabit the human world, invisible to all but the spiritually advanced. Ghosts suffer from hunger and thirst (thus, the term *hungry ghosts*). They are constantly seeking food and drink, and when they find them, they encounter obstacles. A river, upon their approach, may turn into burning sand or into a current of pus and blood. Ghosts are depicted as having huge abdomens and tiny limbs. Their throats are sometimes the size of the eye of a needle, sometimes tied in a knot. When they are able to ingest food, it turns into spears and balls of molten lead. The origin of the category of ghost is unclear, but their depiction in Buddhist iconography suggests a human suffering from acute starvation, with a bloated abdomen supported precariously by a skeletal frame. The Sanskrit term rendered here as "ghost," *preta,* means "departed," suggesting that these ghosts are the wandering spirits of departed ancestors whose families have failed to make the proper offerings for their sustenance in the next life. Buddhist monks and nuns, who (at least theoretically) have renounced the responsibilities of family life, have traditionally taken it as their task to feed the hungry ghosts.

Buddhist texts describe an extensive and harrowing complex of hells. There are eight hot hells, eight cold hells, four neighboring hells, and a number of trifling hells. The eight hot hells are lands made of burning iron, located one below another deep beneath the surface of the earth, where the denizens undergo a variety of tortures over a protracted lifetime. The first, and least severe, is called the Reviving Hell, where one is born with weapons in hand, engaged in mortal combat. Upon being killed, a voice from the sky shouts, "Revive," and the whole process begins again. According to a more detailed description, the hell has a number of different regions, reserved for those who have committed specific misdeeds. Those who have killed birds without remorse find themselves in a pit filled with a mixture of excrement and molten copper. Having no form of sustenance, they are forced to eat it. But the excrement is filled with maggots that, once inside the body, consume it from the inside until nothing remains. The lifetime in this hell is described as follows: "If fifty human years were a day, and thirty of these were a month, and twelve of those were a year, then five hundred of those years would be one day in this hell, and one would live five hundred years of such days." This, the shortest of the infernal life spans, might be calculated as 1.62×10^{12} years. The other hot hells entail various forms of burning, sometimes being cast into cauldrons of molten metal, sometimes being impaled on spears by demons. In the hell reserved for adulterers, males see a beautiful woman at the top of a tree beckoning them to climb up. As they climb, the leaves of the tree are transformed into razors and knives that lacerate their bodies. Arriving at the treetop, they find that the woman is gone.

Looking down, they see her at the foot of the tree, calling to them. Climbing down, they suffer the same injuries, only to find the woman at the top of the tree. They continue to climb up and down the tree in pursuit of the object of their desire for ten trillion years. In the most tortuous of the hells, reserved for those who have committed particularly heinous crimes, such as parricide, one's body is indistinguishable from fire. The cold hells are barren wastelands of snow and ice, cast in eternal darkness. The names of the cold hells, Bursting Blisters, Moaning, Chattering, Split like a Lotus, give some sense of the suffering experienced there. Upon release from the hot or cold hells, one passes through the neighboring hells, whose names are also evocative: Burning Ashes, Mud of Corpses, Road of Razors, Burning River.

REALITY

Buddhist texts make repeated reference to the difference between the way things appear and the way things are, to how believing what one perceives with the senses leads only to suffering, while understanding the way things really are leads to freedom from suffering. Hence, the Buddhist universe is not simply the topography of heavens and hells, but the reality that lies behind them. This reality is not regarded as an innovation of the Buddha, but rather as a fact that the Buddha discovered, just as previous buddhas had discovered it in the past and future buddhas will discover it in the future. The Buddha declared that, whether or not buddhas appear in the world, the nature of things remains the same.

The hallmark of Buddhist thought is the doctrine of no-self. Some of the philosophical schools of ancient India spoke of the existence of an eternal self that passed from lifetime to lifetime, taking on and leaving behind a body, much as we don and doff our clothes each day. Beings are enslaved in the cycle of rebirth because they fail to recognize this silent self as their true nature, identifying instead with constituents of the fleeting world. To see the self is to become who one has always truly been.

The Buddhist doctrine of no-self seems to stand in direct contradiction, declaring that a permanent, indivisible, autonomous self is an illusion and that the belief in such a self is the cause of all suffering. The Buddha provided a detailed analysis of the constituents of mind and body, most commonly dividing them into five groups, called the aggregates. The first is form, which includes not only visible forms seen by the eyes but also imperceptible subtle matter, as well as sounds, odors, tastes, and tangible objects. The other four aggregates are mental. Feeling is the factor that accompanies every moment of consciousness and is of three types: pleasurable, painful, and neutral, with pleasure defined as that which one wishes to encounter again when it ceases, pain as that which one wishes to be separated from when it arises, and neutrality, to which one is indifferent. All feelings of pleasure and pain, all happiness and suffering, are the effects of past actions, the fruition of karmic seeds planted in the past by virtuous and nonvirtuous deeds of body, speech, and mind. The third factor is discrimination, the innate mental ability to distinguish between objects. Like feeling, it accompanies all moments of consciousness, allowing them to differentiate one object from another and to recognize an object seen in the past. Setting aside the fourth aggregate for a moment, the fifth of the five aggregates is consciousness. In Buddhism, there are six forms of consciousness. The eye consciousness perceives colors and shapes, the ear consciousness perceives sounds, the nose consciousness perceives smells, the tongue consciousness perceives flavors, the body consciousness perceives tangible objects, and the mental consciousness perceives "phenomena," that is, anything that exists. The fourth aggregate, called conditioning factors, is something of a "none of the above" category, encompassing a disparate set of factors that do not fit into the other five categories, including what we would call emotions, both positive (such as nonattachment, effort, and conscientiousness) and negative (such as anger, pride, resentment, and jealousy). There are also factors here that can be either virtuous or nonvirtuous, depending on one's intention: sleep, contrition, investigation, and analysis. In the category of conditioning factors we find concepts that are neither material nor mental (such as time, impermanence, number, and similarity).

The Buddhist claim is that these five aggregates are the inventory of what we call the person and that it is a complete inventory; no parts are missing. Of particular significance is the fact that each of the aggregates and all of their subcategories are impermanent, none lasting more than an instant. Nothing, therefore, is worth clinging to. One can search exhaustively through all the aggregates, and one will not be able to find anything that does not disintegrate the moment after it comes into existence. The most important conclusion to be drawn is that there is no self among the aggregates. Indeed, mind and body function perfectly without a doer of deeds and a thinker of thoughts. What we call the person is simply a process, a chain of causes and effects, driven by the engine of karma. To perceive a self amid this process, to posit an owner whose possessions extend to the mind and the body and then out into the world, driven by desire and protected by hatred, is simply to forge more links in the chain of rebirth. To put an end to suffering, it is necessary to perceive an absence, to see that the self that seems so real was never there in the first place.

It is often asked how rebirth is possible if there is no self. Long ago a Buddhist monk answered the question with another question: "Can a flame move from one candle to another?" His point was that although it is possible to light one candle with another, the same flame does not move between them. The flame is, scientifically speaking, a process of oxidation, changing every instant, yet it appears to move from one candle to another. The person is simply a process of mental and physical constituents, among which is the process called consciousness. Consciousness, although changing every moment, persists as a continuum over time. Death is simply the movement of consciousness, ever changing, from one physical foundation. Rebirth is the movement of consciousness, ever changing, to a different physical foundation (which is itself impermanent), like lighting one candle with another.

With the development of various schools in the centuries after the Buddha's death, the doctrine of no-self came to be widely interpreted. Perhaps in testimony to the tenacity of the belief in self, one group, called the Vātsīputrīyas, posited the existence of something they termed the "inexpressible self," which travels from one lifetime to the next. A Chinese pilgrim in India in the seventh century reported that a Vātsīputrīya sect was the largest of the Buddhist schools. Although we cannot credit their philosophy of self as the reason for their popularity, it is useful to note two points: first, that the doctrine of no-self was widely interpreted throughout the history of Buddhist thought, and second, that such interpretations were the purview of a tiny group of scholars whose views on the subject remained unknown to the vast majority of Buddhists. That the Vātsīputrīyas could hold what seems to us such a heretical view and yet remain widely popular suggests that, despite the claims of the philosophers, the doctrine of no-self is less central to the lives of Buddhists than we are often led to imagine. Furthermore, the doctrine of no-self in much of its philosophical elaboration seemed to apply only to the person; the five aggregates, although impermanent, were presented as having some kind of reality, whether as the objects of raw sense perception, as one school argued, or as partless particles of matter that combined to form gross objects.

Some four hundred years after the Buddha's death and the rise of a movement referred to as the Mahāyāna, the "Great Vehicle," discourses of the Buddha began to appear that called themselves "perfection of wisdom" sūtras. These sūtras came to be known by their length, hence the *Perfection of Wisdom in Eight Thousand Stanzas,* the *Perfection of Wisdom in Twenty-Five Thousand Stanzas,* the *Perfection of Wisdom in One Hundred Thousand Stanzas,* the *Perfection of Wisdom in One Letter.* Like many other Mahāyāna sūtras, the perfection of wisdom texts were not systematic treatises that set forth philosophical points and doctrinal categories in a straightforward manner. Instead, they strike the modern reader as having something of the nature of revelations, bold pronouncements proclaimed with certainty rather than speculative arguments developed in a linear fashion. The perfection of wisdom that the sūtras repeatedly praised, rather than presented, was the knowledge of emptiness (*śūnyatā*). To see that all phenomena are empty is to see the truth. This emptiness was often presented in a series of negations, negations that made reference to Buddhist categories that heretofore were said to have some reality. Thus, referring to the five aggregates, the *Heart Sūtra* says, "In emptiness, there is no form, no feeling, no discrimination, no conditioning factors, no consciousness." In order to become a buddha it was necessary to see everything in the universe, from the form aggregate to the omniscient mind of the Buddha, to be empty; as the sūtras repeatedly declared, not to see anything is to see everything.

The systematization of this absence, called emptiness, was not to be found in the anonymous perfection of wisdom sūtras but was accomplished by a later generation of authors whose names are known to us. The most famous of all is Nāgārjuna. We know very little about his life. Traditional biographies state that he was born four hundred years after the Buddha and lived for six hundred years. Modern scholarship places him in the first or second century of the common era. His role in the early development of the Mahāyāna is suggested by the fact that traditional biographies credit him with retrieving the *Perfection of Wisdom in One Hundred Thousand Stanzas* from a jeweled casket at the bottom of the sea, where it had been held in safekeeping by the king of the dragons since the time of the Buddha.

Nāgārjuna's most famous work, both in India (based on the number of commentaries that survive) and in the West, is his *Treatise on the Middle Way* (*Madhyamakaśāstra*). It is a verse work in twenty-six chapters that begins with the famous obeisance to the Buddha, "Homage to the perfect Buddha, most excellent of teachers, who taught that what arises dependently has no cessation, no production, no annihilation, no permanence, no coming, no going, no difference, no sameness, is free of elaborations, and peaceful." Among the topics that he subjects to analysis are motion, vision, karma, suffering, liberation, the four truths, and buddhahood, demonstrating that each is empty.

The *Treatise on the Middle Way* is an often cryptic work, written in a turgid poetic style. Unlike many works in its genre, it lacks a prose commentary by the author in which the dense phrases are expanded. The fact that it has inspired so many commentaries over the centuries suggests that it is often ambiguous, such that the precise meaning of emptiness remains elusive. Nonetheless, a number of key points can be identified.

In his first sermon, the Buddha had prescribed a middle way between the extremes of self-indulgence and extreme asceticism.

Apparently drawing on his experience as a prince and later as a renunciate, he counseled against a life devoted to the gratification of the senses as well as a life in which the body is subjected to privation. Instead, a course between these two, controlling the senses but sustaining the body, provides the best approach to enlightenment. Nāgārjuna also prescribes a middle way, but of a philosophical variety, a middle way between the extremes of existence and nonexistence. Precisely what neither existence nor nonexistence might mean was the subject of debate by later commentators, but Nāgārjuna provides a clue when he equates the terms *emptiness, dependent origination,* and *the middle way.*

Dependent origination has two meanings in Buddhist thought. The first refers to a twelvefold sequence of causation: ignorance, action, consciousness, name and form, sources, contact, feeling, attachment, grasping, existence, birth, aging and death. In some accounts this sequence is said to have constituted the Buddha's enlightenment. Nonetheless, it remains one of the more vexing categories of Buddhist thought, one whose origins and precise meaning continue to elude scholars. Several traditional commentaries explain it as a description of the process of rebirth, with some organizing the twelve links over the course of a single lifetime and others dividing the twelve over three lifetimes. The second meaning of *dependent origination* is a more general one, the notion that everything comes into existence in dependence on something else. It is this second meaning that Nāgārjuna equates with emptiness and the middle way.

The manner in which dependent origination can serve as a synonym for emptiness is clarified by one of Nāgārjuna's interpreters, who defines *self* as that which does not depend on something else. In this sense, the notion of self is extended beyond persons to encompass all phenomena. Anything that exists autonomously, independently, or objectively can be said to have "self." Nāgārjuna's claim, as one might suspect, is that such a self is also an illusion, to believe in such a self is ignorance, and to understand that such a self does not exist is wisdom, indeed, the perfection of wisdom. Emptiness, therefore, is not the negation of existence but rather is the absence of a particular kind of existence, an existence that is independent of any other factors. If nothing exists independently, then everything exists dependently and lacks, or in other words is empty of, independent existence. It is in this sense that *dependent origination* and *emptiness* are synonyms. Together, they represent a middle way between the extremes of existence and nonexistence, which are glossed by some commentators as the extremes of independent existence and utter nonexistence.

The *Treatise on the Middle Way* is largely devoted to demonstrating that the basic categories of experience—motion, the sense faculties, fire, and fuel—as well as the basic categories of Buddhism—the four truths, nirvāṇa, and the Buddha himself—are empty because they are somehow dependent, depending for their existence either on their causes or on their parts or on the human mind that names them. For example, Nāgārjuna demonstrates that motion does not occur because it cannot be located either on the path already traversed, the path being traversed, or the path not yet traversed: motion cannot be present where it is already past; it would be redundant for motion to be present on the path currently being traversed; and motion cannot be present on the portion of the path that lies ahead. Writing always in verse, Nāgārjuna rarely qualifies his negations; he does not specify that he is refuting only the independent existence of the object under scrutiny and not its very existence. But he is sensitive to the charge of nihilism, having a hypothetical opponent charge that the doctrine of emptiness denies all existence, making everything and anything impossible. Nāgārjuna replies that, on the contrary, it is emptiness that allows for possibility. He states, "For whom emptiness is possible, everything is possible." What he seems to mean is that if things were indeed as autonomous, independent, objective, and real as we ignorantly conceive them to be, existence would be static and unchanging, concretized to the point of paralysis. It is emptiness that allows for change and transformation, most importantly the transformation of the mind from ignorance to wisdom, from saṃsāra to buddhahood. If the afflictions were endemic to the mind, such transformation would be impossible. As he says in another work traditionally attributed to him, the *Hymn to the Sphere of Reality* (*Dharmadhātustava*), "When a fireproof garment, stained by various stains, is placed in fire, the stains are burned but the garment is not. In the same way, the mind of clear light is stained by desire. The stains are burned by the fire of wisdom; the clear light is not."

Yet Nāgārjuna must account for the world; he must impart some status to the universe and its constituents. To do so, he introduces the doctrine of the two truths: ultimate truths and conventional truths. Ultimate truths are so called because they are the objects of the ultimate consciousness, the mind perceiving reality directly. The ultimate truth is emptiness. Some readings of Nāgārjuna and his commentators suggest that these truths are plural in the sense that each phenomenon in the universe is qualified by emptiness, its own absence of independent existence, and thus has its own emptiness. This does not entail a qualitative difference among these many emptinesses but rather that emptiness, the ultimate truth, is to be found as the true nature of each of the objects of our experience.

But what is the status of these objects, if they are ultimately empty? Nāgārjuna calls them conventional truths. They include everything other than emptiness that exists in the universe, from a form to the omniscient mind of the Buddha. The term *conventional truth* is in a sense a misleading translation of the Sanskrit term, which has a more pejorative sense, meaning according to one etymology, "truth for those obscured by ignorance." If a truth is something that exists as it appears, then conventional truths are not true; a chair, for example, appears in our unanalyzed experience to exist objectively and autonomously, encompassing its parts. But the chair is in fact empty of such independent existence. Therefore, the chair appears in one way but actually exists in another and so is not true. Only the ignorant would believe that things exist in the way that they appear. Yet this false appearance of conventional truths does not render them utterly nonexistent. As Nāgārjuna says, without conventional truths, the ultimate cannot be known. Indeed, the category of the conventional encompasses all of the salubrious components of the Buddhist path, including the Buddha. The relation between the two truths would then seem to be one between an object (the conventional truth) and its true nature (the ultimate truth). The *Heart Sūtra* famously declares, "Form is empty. Emptiness is form." Commentators have taken this as an expression of the relation between the two truths. Form, the first of the five aggregates and a conventional truth, is empty. Emptiness, the ultimate reality, is not to be found apart from the objects of ordinary experience; it is the very nature of form.

It should be noted, however, that the exposition of emptiness set forth by Nāgārjuna and his commentators (who were not always in agreement) was just one of the many Buddhist views of the nature of reality that developed in India. It was by no means the most popular; as mentioned above, a Chinese pilgrim reported that the Vātsīputrīyas, who spoke of an "inexpressible self," claimed many adherents. In the Theravāda tradition, the two truths were interpreted to mean something akin to ordinary and technical languages. When the Buddha said "this is a man" or "this is a woman," he was speaking in the conventional sense; when he said "this is impermanent" or "this is an aggregate," he was speaking in the ultimate sense. Nāgārjuna was certainly widely read and commented upon in Tibet, less so in East Asia. His influence has been somewhat exaggerated by the fact that his *Treatise on the Middle Way,* and one of its commentaries, is preserved in Sanskrit and has been much studied by modern scholars.

A competing view of reality to that of the middle way, or Madhyamaka, of Nāgārjuna was the Yogācāra view, associated with the fourth-century Indian scholar Asaṅga. Sometimes referred to as "mind only," it denies the existence of external objects. One of the arguments for the subjective nature of experience is the discrepancy in the way that two people may perceive the same object. In the Buddhist case, the experiences of beings from different realms in saṃsāra are compared. What might appear as a glass of water to a human appears as ambrosia to a god, as a home to a fish, as burning sand to a ghost, and as molten lead to a hell being. Who is to say what it really is? For the Yogācāra, there is no public, objective experience of a single world. Instead, each person perceives his or her own world, created by karma. They speak of a form of consciousness called the substratum (*ālayavijñāna*), where all the seeds of one's past deeds are deposited. One by one, these seeds come to fruition, simultaneously creating a consciousness and its object; the object does not exist prior to its perception by consciousness. As that experience ceases, another seed will fructify, creating another experience of subject and object. Each being in the universe, therefore, inhabits a private world. It is as if the universe were populated by countless cinemas, each occupied by a single person, each eternally viewing a different film projected by consciousness, each eternally suspending disbelief. For the Yogācāra, ignorance and suffering result from believing the movie to be real, from mistaking the projections to be an external world, from thinking that what appear to be external objects are independent of consciousness, and then running after them, desiring some and hating others. For the Yogācāra, wisdom is the insight that everything is of the nature of consciousness and the product of one's own projections. With this insight, desire and hatred, attachment and aversion, naturally cease, for their objects are seen to be illusions. With the achievement of enlightenment, the substratum consciousness is transformed into the mirrorlike wisdom of a buddha.

The Madhyamaka and Yogācāra are but two of a wide range of descriptions of reality that developed across the Buddhist world. In China, one finds not only the familiar notion of the presence of reality in the constituents of ordinary experience, referred to as "the interpenetration of principle and phenomena," but also the more far-reaching claim that each phenomenon contains within itself every other phenomenon in the universe, described in the metaphor of a vast net bearing a jewel at every knot, each jewel containing within itself the reflection of all the other jewels. In Zen, there is the saying "mountains are mountains," referring to the dictum that before one begins the practice of Zen, mountains are mountains; during the practice of Zen, mountains are not mountains; after the practice of Zen, mountains are mountains.

THE END

Unlike so many other traditions, the Buddhist scriptures contain no classic account of an end time, an apocalypse, an eschaton. Certainly we can locate predictions of wars between the forces of good and evil and descriptions of the cosmic cycles, of how the physical universe comes into existence, of how, through karma, the world comes to be populated, how that world persists through cycles of fortune and misfortune, calculated by the wax and wane of the human life span, and how, finally, the physical universe is destroyed and the cosmos passes into a period of involution, with the inhabitants of the world retreating into the heavens. But according to Indian Buddhist cosmology, that period of cosmic involution is only temporary, and a new cycle of creation, abiding, and disintegration will begin. But this is not what we usually mean when we talk about an apocalypse, in which the world is destroyed once and for all, or an eschaton, in which the final purpose of human existence and of creation is fulfilled.

Indeed, we find in Buddhist literature a rather pronounced reluctance to deal with beginnings or ends. In the accounts of the Buddha's enlightenment experience under the tree, it is said that he had a vision of all of his past lives going back over billions of aeons, but never does it say that he beheld the beginning, that he experienced that primal moment of creation that is a seemingly ubiquitous element of myth and ritual, not only in the so-called primitive religions, but in Vedic traditions of India as well. The Buddha warned that to refuse to follow the religious path until one knows whether or not the world is eternal is to be like the man who refused to have a poison arrow extracted from his body until he knew whether the person who shot the arrow was tall, short, or of medium height. The Buddha described all such questions as "a jungle, a wilderness, a puppet-show, a writhing and a fetter, and coupled with misery, ruin, despair, and agony."

Indeed, the Buddha refused to answer the question of whether the universe has an end. But how does one interpret silence? The fourth-century Indian commentator Vasubandhu explained that the Buddha would not answer in the affirmative or the negative because he would be misunderstood: to say that saṃsāra is endless would suggest that there is no liberation, and to say that saṃsāra ends would suggest that individual effort is unimportant. The fourteenth-century Tibetan commentator Tsong kha pa suggested that the Buddha knew that saṃsāra would never end, as if he refrained from delivering that particular piece of bad news so as to spare the world needless despair.

In India, both positions were presented; there were those who held that saṃsāra is endless and those who held that saṃsāra will end. Those who held that saṃsāra is endless compared it to the limitless sky, which, although impinged on the horizon by mountains that seem to rise up to violate its domain, can never be obscured by them. Even though buddhas have appeared throughout history to liberate innumerable sentient beings, the buddhas are like the great mountains that rise and fall; they can never block out the sky. In this model, saṃsāra appears as a constant, almost as nature. It is portrayed as neither positive nor negative and cannot ultimately be opposed. It functions rather as the unlimited stage for the drama of suffering and the drama of enlightenment.

The second Indian model is presented in the more familiar Buddhist vocabulary of cause and effect, of contagion and antidote. Saṃsāra is ultimately the product of ignorance, the belief in self, and the antidote to that ignorance is the understanding that there is no self. Thus, saṃsāra will end when wisdom has utterly displaced ignorance. The metaphor here is not of mountains and the sky but of stains on gold; the stains can be removed, leaving the gold untainted. Gold can be stained but it cannot rust. Whereas other metals lose their luster to rust and are permanently corroded in the process, the stains on gold are only superficial; beneath them is pure gold, and that purity can be uncovered. It is not surprising, then, that many of the arguments that saṃsāra will someday end seem to pivot on an oft-cited declaration, "The nature of the mind is clear light; the stains are adventitious." That is, the defilements that give rise to the cycle of birth, aging, sickness, and death are superficial, accidental, incidental, added on, implying what might seem to be a surprisingly substantialist position for a Buddhist thinker, that the nature of consciousness persists after the defilements have been expunged because the mind is somehow more real than the defilements.

If the defilements, the negative mental states of craving, hatred, pride, jealousy, ignorance, are not innate but are, in a sense, accidental, then they can be removed. But there must be a mechanism for their removal, and this mechanism, of course, is the Buddhist path. But that path, and the nature of the universe through which it leads, remains unknown until a being appears in the world who, over the course of many lifetimes, has perfected himself to the point that he gains an insight that has been long forgotten. Having gained that insight, he proclaims it to the world. Such a being is called a buddha. Some twenty-five hundred years ago, it is said, a being destined soon to be a buddha was residing in a heaven above Mount Meru. Having determined that the time was right for him to complete the task he had set for himself aeons ago when he promised to find a way to escape from suffering and then to show that way to the world, he surveyed the continent of Jambudvīpa, seeking the appropriate city, the appropriate clan, the appropriate parents for his final birth. He then made his descent.

Suggested Reading

Hopkins, Jeffrey. *Meditation on Emptiness.* London: Wisdom Publications, 1983.

Jamgön Kongtrul Lodrö Tayé. *Myriad Worlds: Buddhist Cosmology in Abhidharma, Kālacakra, and Dzog-chen.* Ithaca: Snow Lion Publications, 1995.

Lopez, Donald S., Jr. *The Heart Sūtra Explained: Indian and Tibetan Commentaries.* Albany: State University of New York Press, 1988.

Matsunaga, Daigan, and Alicia Matsunaga. *The Buddhist Concept of Hell.* New York: Philosophical Library, 1972.

Nattier, Jan. *Once upon a Future Time: Studies in a Buddhist Prophecy of Decline.* Berkeley: Asian Humanities Press, 1991.

Sadakata, Akira. *Buddhist Cosmology: Philosophy and Origins.* Tokyo: Kōsei Publishing, 1997.

2

THE BUDDHA

The Buddha was born the son of a king, in what is today southern Nepal. The date of his birth is unknown. Many scholars have set the date at 563 B.C.E., although other sources suggest that he was born as much as a century later. According to traditional biographies, his mother dreamed that a white elephant had entered her womb. Ten lunar months later, as she strolled in a garden, the child emerged, not by the usual route, but from under her right arm. Unlike other infants, he was able to walk and talk immediately. A lotus flower blossomed under his foot at each step, and he announced that this would be his last lifetime. The child was named Siddhārtha, "he who achieves his aim"; his clan name was Gautama. Convinced that his son was unusual, the king summoned the court astrologers to predict the boy's future. Seven agreed that he would become either a great king or a great renunciate; one astrologer said that there was no doubt, the child would become a great renunciate. His father set out to prevent this possibility. Apparently assuming that depression is what leads to the religious life, he endeavored to shield his son from any and all things that might make him unhappy. He gave him three palaces: one for winter, one for summer, one for the rainy season. He provided him with the best of everything, surrounded him with beautiful women, and ensured that he not be exposed to old age, sickness, or death. His son excelled at everything he tried, becoming skilled in all the sciences and arts, including the arts of love. At the age of sixteen he married a beautiful princess.

The prince was so content in his sheltered domain that he seemed not to have become curious about the outside world for twenty-nine years. Only then did he ask his father to allow him to take a chariot ride through the city. His father initially refused but eventually relented, but not without first sending out his troops to remove all the sick, old, and ugly people from the royal route and stationing musicians in the trees to serenade the prince as he rode. Somehow (whether it was the work of the gods or of fate), one old person escaped the soldiers' scrutiny, standing bent and wizened as the prince passed by. Not knowing what this was that stood before him, the prince asked his charioteer to explain. He was told that this was an old man. The prince asked whether this was the old man, the only one in the world, or if there were others like him. When he was told that everyone—the prince, his father, his wife, and his kinsmen—would all one day become old and bent, the prince reacted, the texts report, like a bull when lightning strikes in the meadow. He commanded his driver to take him back to the palace at once.

The prince eventually summoned the courage for three more trips beyond the palace walls. On the first he saw a sick person, on the second he saw a corpse being carried to the cremation ground, on the third he saw a renunciate beneath a tree, absorbed in serene meditation. Having been exposed, in turn, to the existence of old age, sickness, death, and the fact that there are those who seek a state beyond them, he went to his father and asked permission to leave the city and retire to the forest. His father refused and offered his son anything if he would stay. The prince asked that his father promise that he would never die, become ill, grow old, or lose his fortune. His father answered that these things were beyond his powers. The prince retired to his harem, where he was entertained by beautiful women. But he was unmoved, and as the night wore on the women fell asleep in all manner of inelegant postures, disheveled and drooling. The prince was disgusted by the scene, declaring that women are by nature impure, and resolved to go forth in search of a state beyond birth and death.

Upon being informed that his wife had given birth to a son, he was not overjoyed, saying instead, "An impediment has been born. A fetter has arisen." The child was, accordingly, named Rāhula, "fetter." But before the prince left the palace, he crept into his wife's chamber to look upon his infant son. He resisted the urge to hold him, knowing that to do so would awaken his wife and prevent his departure from the world. It is this last look, looking at but not touching what he was to leave behind, that forms one of the most poignant moments in the narrative. (In another version of the story, Rāhula had not yet been born on that fateful night. Instead, the prince's final act as a householder was to conceive his son, whose gestation period extended over the six years of his father's searching. Rāhula was born on the night that his father achieved enlightenment.)

The prince set out for the unknown, leaving the world he knew behind, exchanging his royal robes for the clothes of his servant, giving up the royal cuisine for whatever passers-by would place in his begging bowl. Wandering for six years, he became the disciple of master meditators who taught him how to achieve deep states of blissful concentration. He quickly equaled the attainments of his teachers and recognized that the goals they had achieved remained within saṃsāra. Next, he joined a band of five ascetics dedicated to the most extreme forms of self-mortification. The prince also became adept at this, surviving on one grain of rice and one drop of water a day. But one day, while bathing in a river, he fainted from weakness and came to the conclusion that mortification of the flesh was not the path to freedom. So he accepted a dish of rice and yogurt from a young woman who mistook his gaunt visage for a ghost to whom the local village made offerings. He ate the meal and then cast the dish into the river, saying, "If I am to become a buddha today, may the dish float upstream." The plate floated upstream for some distance before disappearing into a whirlpool, descending down to the palace of a serpent king, where it landed on top of the dishes used by the previous buddhas, making a clicking sound.

Seeing that he had abandoned their regimen, his five companions, still convinced of the efficacy of asceticism, abandoned him in scorn. Now left alone, the prince determined that he would sit down under a tree and not rise until he had found what he had sought for so long. That night, on the full moon of May, six years after he had left his palace, he meditated all night. He was attacked by Māra, the god of desire, who recognized that the prince was seeking to put an end to craving and thereby free himself from Māra's control. Māra attacked him with a conflagration of nine storms—storms of wind, rain, rocks, weapons, live coals, burning ashes, sand, mud, and darkness—but the prince remained serene and meditated on love, turning the hail of fury into a shower of blossoms. Next Māra sent his three beautiful daughters, Lust, Thirst, and Discontent, to tempt the prince, but he remained unmoved. Seeking to determine what kind of woman he would be attracted to, they appeared first as virgins, then as women in the prime of their youth, then as middle-aged women, and finally as old women. When the prince remained unmoved, they tried to return to their youthful forms but were unable to because the prince had so resolved. In desperation, Māra challenged the prince's right to occupy the spot of earth upon which he sat, claiming that it belonged to him instead. The prince, seated in the meditative posture, stretched out his right hand and touched the earth, asking the goddess of the earth to confirm that a great gift that he had made as Prince Vessantara in his previous life had won him the right to sit beneath the tree. She assented with a tremor, and Māra withdrew.

Now the prince meditated through the night. During the first watch of the night, he had a vision of all of his past lives, recalling where he had been reborn, what he had been named, which caste he had belonged to, what food he had eaten. He saw the persistence of the person, both in its plenitude and paucity, multiplied through its continuity across aeons of evolution and dissolution, rising on the rope of memory to the karmic present. It was these constituents of social identity—place, name, family, caste, food, pleasure, pain, and death—that he had abandoned as he went forth from the house and the responsibilities of the householder, giving up a permanent dwelling place, renouncing his former abode. His vision of his past lives amounted to an insight into his personal identity as it is found in saṃsāra, the cycle of birth and death.

During the second watch of the night, he saw the workings of the law of karma, how beings rise and fall, succeed and fail, as a consequence of their deeds. In the third watch of the night, the hours before dawn, he was transformed. Accounts differ as to precisely what it was that he understood, and, indeed, Buddhist schools throughout history have looked back to this night to claim their particular view of reality to have been discovered by the prince. Yet all agree that he became a buddha, an awakened one, one who has roused himself from the slumber of ignorance. The implication, of course, is that the rest of the world remains asleep.

His first vision of his entire past enhances the potency of the vision of the third watch, in which he saw (at least according to many accounts), in the instantaneous present, that this person is a mere projection, that before and behind the chain of causation there is no agent, no person, no self, that the liberating identity beyond saṃsāra is no self. The personal continuity recollected in the vision of his past abodes is proved a fiction by the vision of the third watch, where there is no self to be seen. The prince saw the past and present order of the world in the first two watches of the night. When he saw that that ordered world has no essence, he was awakened. This tension, in the paradigmatic event of the tradition, between personal identity and identitylessness, between saṃsāra and nirvāṇa, between continuity and cessation, between the historical and ahistorical, is played out throughout Buddhist philosophy.

The experience of that night was sufficiently profound for the prince, now the Buddha, to remain in the vicinity of the tree for seven weeks, savoring his enlightenment. One of those weeks was rainy, and the serpent king came and spread his hood above the Buddha to protect him from the storm. Later, two merchants approached him and offered him food. In return, the Buddha plucked some hairs from his head and gave them to the merchants. It is noteworthy that the Buddha's first gift to the world was not the gift of the dharma, but the gift of a relic.

He was unsure as to what to do next, since he felt that what he had understood was so profound that it would be difficult for others to comprehend. The god Brahmā descended from his heaven to entreat him to teach. He showed him a lotus pond and pointed out that some of the lotuses were under water, some were at the level of the water, and some had risen above the water and blossomed, untouched by the water. In the same way, there are humans at different levels of development, some of whom would benefit from his teaching. That a god would make this request of the Buddha suggests that the gods remained subject to the cycle of rebirth from which the Buddha was now free; they depended on him to show them the path to liberation. The incident also shows the way in which Buddhism subordinated the Indian gods to the authority of the Buddha. A similar process would be repeated throughout Asia, as all manner of local deities and spirits were incorporated into Buddhist pantheons.

The Buddha decided to teach and concluded that the most suitable students were his first teachers of meditation, but he was informed by a deity that they had died. He thought next of his five old comrades in the practice of asceticism. His achievement of enlightenment carried with it supernormal powers, and the Buddha determined that they were residing in a deer park in Sarnath, outside Banaras. He set out on foot, meeting along the way a wandering ascetic with whom he exchanged greetings, explaining to the man that he was the sole enlightened one, unsurpassed even by the gods. The man responded with indifference.

Nearing the deer park, the five ascetics noted his approach and, still stung by his apparent indulgence, conspired to ignore him. But as he approached his charisma compelled them to rise and greet him. They asked the Buddha what he had understood since they left him, and he taught what has come to be known as the "four noble truths." In fact, this is a misleading translation. The term translated as "noble" is *āryan,* a Sanskrit word, ruined by Hitler, meaning "superior." The Indo-European peoples who appeared in northern India around 1500 B.C.E. called themselves Aryans. The Buddha is said to have redefined the word to mean superiority of character and insight (specifically someone who has seen nirvāṇa) rather than superiority of blood and birth. Thus, his first teaching concerns four things that are truths for those who have seen nirvāṇa but that are not known to be true by the unenlightened; a more accurate rendering would thus be "four truths for the [spiritually] noble."

THE FOUR TRUTHS

The first truth is the truth of suffering. According to the Buddhist psychological systems, suffering is a feeling that may afflict the body or the mind. The Buddha identified the obvious sufferings that humans undergo: birth, aging, sickness, death, losing friends, gaining enemies, not finding what one wishes for, encountering what one does not wish for. But he is also said to have identified a more subtle form of pain: pleasure. He observed that pain and pleasure are qualitatively different, that a painful experience will remain painful unless one acts to counteract the pain, but a pleasurable experience will naturally become painful eventually. Indeed, there is no pleasurable worldly activity—listening to music, eating food, drinking wine, making love—that will remain pleasurable indefinitely. Each source of pleasure will eventually become a source of pain. Conventional wisdom to practice moderation, to know "when to stop," acknowledges this fact. Pleasure is therefore compared to the relief felt when a heavy burden is shifted from one shoulder to another. After a while, the other shoulder will begin to hurt, at which point the burden will be shifted back. The Buddha referred to feelings of pleasure as sufferings of change because they will naturally turn into pain unless one consciously desists. There is a third, even more subtle, form of suffering. This is called the suffering of conditioning, referring to the fact that all beings are so conditioned by their past deeds as to be susceptible to suffering in the next moment. Once it is acknowledged that the person is a process of physical and mental constituents, and once it is acknowledged that those constituents are impermanent and thus subject to change at any moment, there is no way to ensure that suffering will not occur in the next moment. This form of suffering is so subtle that it goes unnoticed by the ignorant, like a wisp of cotton in the palm of the hand, but is considered the most immediate form of suffering by the enlightened, like a wisp of cotton in the eye.

The second truth is the truth of origin, in which a series of causes are traced back to their root. The immediate cause of suffering is karma, the seeds of virtuous and nonvirtuous deeds done in the past. In Buddhism, karma is something like a natural law, according to which virtuous deeds cause pleasure and nonvirtuous deeds cause pain. Indeed, every feeling of pleasure or pain we experience is said to be the result of some deed done in the past. That deed could have occurred in the present lifetime or thousands of lifetimes ago. It is this doctrine that has resulted in Buddhism sometimes being labeled as fatalistic. Buddhist thinkers hold that all forms of suffering, from the annoyance of a hangnail to the suffering of war, are the direct products of past deeds. They would say, however, that although experience is, in that sense, given, our response to experience is free. Indeed, it is our free response to the events of our lives (those events caused by karma) that creates future karma, which in turn determines the future.

Buddhist practice, whether for laypeople or monks and nuns, is largely centered around performing virtuous deeds and avoiding nonvirtue. These categories are not vaguely construed but are closely specified, as is so often the case in Buddhist thought, in a list. The standard formulation is of ten nonvirtuous deeds. Three are physical: killing, stealing, sexual misconduct. Four are verbal: lying, divisive speech, harsh speech, and senseless speech. Three are mental: covetousness, harmful intent, wrong view. It is noteworthy that negative karma may be accumulated as a result not only of words and deeds, but also of thoughts. Most of the ten are straightforward, some are not. Sexual misconduct, for example, involves having sexual relations against the other person's will or with someone who has a vow of celibacy. It extends to include such things as having sexual relations during the daytime or in the presence of an image of the Buddha. Senseless speech seems to include all forms of speech motivated by desire, hatred, or ignorance that are not classed as lying, divisive speech, or harsh speech. These include gossip, bragging, loquaciousness, lamentation, singing, and reading bad commentaries, that is, much of human discourse. Wrong view comprises a range of non-Buddhist philosophical positions but in this context refers most importantly to the belief that actions do not have effects; this rejection of the law of karma is said to be particularly grave since it leads to the indiscriminate performance of the other nine nonvirtues.

Each deed has a different weight, depending both on the object of the deed and the strength of the motivation. Killing a human is therefore more consequential than killing an animal, killing an elephant more consequential than killing an ant. Intention is of prime importance in Buddhist theories, so that rubbing the back of one's neck to find one has inadvertently killed a gnat does not constitute a deed of killing. Yet a soldier in an army bears the karma of murder even if he himself kills no one in the battle because he is part of the group responsible for the death. Of all possible sins, five are identified as the most heinous, resulting in rebirth in the most tortuous hell. They are (1) patricide, (2) matricide, (3) killing an arhat, (4) maliciously wounding the Buddha, and (5) causing schism in the community of monks and nuns. These five deeds are not hypothetical. The last three were committed by the Buddha's evil cousin, Devadatta. His negative karma was so great that he did not even live out his life before being reborn in hell but was swallowed by the earth.

What is particularly pernicious about the law of karma is that it is not the weight of one's deeds in the present life that determines one's future fate, despite the fact that it is quite common in Buddhist depictions of hell to find the condemned standing before the Lord of Death, who holds aloft a pair of scales. Instead, any "complete action" (an action that fulfills certain criteria of intention and execution) from any of one's innumerable past lives can serve as the cause for an entire future lifetime. Thus, each being in the universe bears the seeds for countless future births in saṃsāra. The deeds of the present life are nonetheless crucial, for it is one's state of mind at the moment of death that "selects" from the vast repository the particular seed that serves as the cause of the next lifetime. Thus, Buddhists are fond of saying that if you wish to know what you were like in the past, look at your present body. That is, one's status as a human is the sign of having performed an ethical act in the past, and the specific conditions of one's body—one's beauty, health, and station—are all the result of past deeds. If you want to know what you will be in the future, look at your present mind. That is, your predominant state of mind, whether it is inclined toward virtue or nonvirtue, will be manifest at the moment of death, when the seed for your next life will bear its fruit.

The vast store of karmic seeds carried by each being in the universe creates the apparently infinite possibility for future rebirth. Simply stopping action is therefore not a viable solution to the dilemma of birth and death. The Buddha postulated that it was necessary instead to put an end to the cause of action. These causes he identified as the *kleśa,* a term perhaps best rendered as "afflictions." These are negative states of mind such as pride, doubt, jealousy, spite, miserliness, distraction, and resentment. Primary among these are the "three poisons," desire, hatred, and ignorance. These are the states of mind that motivate the performance of the nonvirtuous deeds that in turn produce suffering. Buddhist texts describe at length which of the afflictions motivates which of the nonvirtues. Stealing can be motivated by desire or hatred, for example, sexual misconduct by desire, hatred, or ignorance.

Of the three poisons, the most fundamental, and hence the root cause of all suffering, is ignorance. Ignorance in Buddhism does not refer to a lack of knowledge but to an active misconception about the nature of things. The various misconceptions under which humans operate are sometimes summarized as the four perverse views: seeing the impermanent as permanent, the ugly as beautiful, the painful as pleasurable, and no-self as self. To counteract these views, Buddhist texts are replete with descriptions designed to generate a sense of revulsion toward the world, it being noted, for example, that hair, teeth, and fingernails that seem so pleasing when attached to the body become immediately repulsive when they become detached from the body. One also finds detailed descriptions of the process of digestion, sufficiently graphic to turn the most dedicated gourmand away from the table. The stomach is described as a cesspool and the body as a source of four secretions (bile, phlegm, pus, and blood; the Buddha is said to lack the first three). By developing a sense of revulsion toward food, one comes to see that what one once thought was beautiful is in fact ugly.

But such measures are forms of suppression. To uproot desire entirely, one must overcome the final and most fundamental of the four perverse views. The most powerful form of ignorance is to see self where there is no self. The doctrine of no-self is certainly the most famous and the most widely elaborated in Buddhist thought. It seems that the Buddha rejected the doctrines current among other renunciate philosophers of his day who saw the key to liberation from suffering in the recognition of an eternal self or soul. For the Buddha, it was the belief in self, the belief that among the various constituents of mind and body there is something that lasts longer than an instant, that is the cause of all suffering. The belief in self engenders the desire that soothes the self and the hatred that protects it. Desire and hatred then inspire the performance of nonvirtuous deeds, which in turn produce the negative karma that create suffering. Ignorance is thus the root cause of suffering. Consequently, if ignorance could be eliminated, suffering would end.

The third truth describes not the path to the elimination of suffering but the goal itself, described as cessation. This cessation, the state of the utter absence of suffering, is better known as nirvāṇa. Generally etymologized as "blowing out," nirvāṇa is not technically a place but instead an absence, the absence of suffering in the present and the absence of any possibility of suffering in the future. All suffering has been destroyed because the causes of suffering, the afflictions, have been destroyed. Indeed, enlightenment is sometimes said to consist of the twofold knowledge of the destruction of the afflictions and the impossibility of the afflictions arising again in the future. The Buddha passed into nirvāṇa upon his death. When we examine this momentous event from the vantage point of Buddhist doctrine, it seems that at that moment the Buddha ceased to exist. His enlightenment at the age of thirty-five had destroyed the seeds for all future rebirth. Because he was from that moment utterly free of ignorance, it was impossible for him to experience desire or hatred and so could not perform deeds motivated by them. He therefore produced no further karma for the remainder of his life. When the karma that served as the cause for his lifetime ran its course, there were no more causes, either from a past life or from his present life, for future rebirth.

Two types of nirvāṇa are thus described. The first is called the "nirvāṇa with remainder." This is the nirvāṇa that the Buddha achieved under the Bodhi tree, when he destroyed all the seeds for future rebirth. But the karma that had created his present life was still functioning and would do so until his death, like a watch that has been wound but will eventually stop. Thus, his mind and body during the rest of his life are what was left over, the remainder, after he realized nirvāṇa. The second type is called the "nirvāṇa without remainder," or final nirvāṇa. This is the nirvāṇa that the Buddha passed into upon his death. But where did he go?

A Theravāda text tells of a monk named Yamaka who announced that the Buddha taught that a monk who has destroyed desire, hatred, and ignorance no longer exists after his death. His position was reported to Śāriputra, who went to see the monk, explaining that it is wrong to say that the monk ceases to exist when he enters nirvāṇa because the monk does not exist prior to entering nirvāṇa. To speak of the monk as someone who exists in one moment and does not exist in the next, to speak of the cessation of the monk, is to assume that there is a monk, that there is a self, that the monk, and hence the person, is something more than a collection of momentary constituents, an aggregation of physical and mental components, a series of causes and effects, coming into and going out of existence in each instant. Nirvāṇa is not, therefore, the destruction of anything or a place where someone goes but is, instead, the absence that is created when all the causes of what might, for the sake of convenience, be called the person, have been destroyed, when the last effect has been produced and there are no causes left. This tension between the notion of the person as an agent, capable of winning salvation, and the notion of the person as a fiction, indeed a dangerous fiction that is the source of all woe, would persist in one form or another throughout the developments of Buddhist thought in Asia. It would be stated perhaps most powerfully in the *Diamond Sūtra,* where the buddha-to-be, called a bodhisattva, is said to vow to lead all beings into the final nirvāṇa, knowing that there are no beings to be led to the final nirvāṇa.

The fourth truth is the path to nirvāṇa, the means of putting an end to suffering. The path is described in many different ways, with recourse, as always, to various lists. One of the most common delineations of the path is in terms of the three trainings: in ethics, meditation, and wisdom, each of which is considered essential to the attainment of nirvāṇa.

Ethics (*śīla*) in this context refers to desisting from nonvirtuous deeds of body and speech. The various vows that Buddhists take will be discussed in detail in the chapters on monastic life and lay practice. In the context of the path, it is commonly stated that it is impossible to control one's mind—the essential task of meditation—until one is able to control the coarser operations of body and speech. One must therefore vigilantly refrain from nonvirtuous deeds such as killing, stealing, sexual misconduct, lying, divisive speech, harsh speech, and senseless speech. Such restraint, especially when it occurs through keeping a vow, also serves to produce positive karma, necessary for progress along the path.

Meditation (*samādhi*) in this context refers to a state of concentration in which the mind remains focused on a chosen object for an extended period of time. Such mental stability occurs only as the result of extensive training, for the mind in its ordinary state is out of control, described variously in Buddhist texts as a wild elephant and a drunken monkey. The random and unintentional movement of thought from one subject to another must be brought under control through the practice of meditation. Here meditation, contrary to popular conceptions, is not a state of blissful trance but is instead a laborious process of choosing an object of concentration, focusing the mind on the object, and vigilantly bringing the mind back to the object whenever it wanders off. Buddhist texts wryly observe that in the early stages of practice, distraction is interrupted by occasional moments of meditation. Forty objects of concentration are traditionally set forth, to be prescribed depending on which of the afflictions predominates. Those who are hateful should meditate on love, those attached to the body should meditate on impermanence, those who are prideful should meditate on causation, those who are distracted should meditate on the breath. The ever-deepening states of concentration that result from sustained focus on the chosen object are delineated in great detail in Buddhist texts, resulting in a state of concentration sometimes identified as serenity (*śamatha*). At this point, the meditator is able to place the mind on the object and keep it there indefinitely, with only the slightest effort. It is only at this point that the mind has been turned into a suitable instrument with which to investigate the nature of reality.

That reality is the absence of self, and it is the understanding that there is no self that constitutes salvific wisdom (*prajñā*), the third of the three trainings. This understanding is not easily gained. The belief in self has been so deeply ingrained over countless lifetimes in the past that the claim that there is no self seems at first to be counterintuitive. In order to overcome the belief in self, therefore, it is necessary to gain more than an intellectual understanding of its nonexistence. One must gain a direct and nonconceptual realization.

Stated more technically, it is impossible to destroy the seeds for future suffering and rebirth until one understands the lack of self at a deep level of concentration, specifically the level of serenity. This is not to suggest that a conceptual understanding of no-self is without benefit. In many traditions of Buddhist practice, such an understanding is an essential prerequisite to any deeper realization. Texts speak in fact of three types of wisdom. The wisdom arising from hearing refers to the level of understanding that one can gain through study; hearing in this context refers specifically to listening to teachings but also extends to include reading. The second type is the wisdom arising from thinking. Here, thinking refers to what one would normally call meditation: the understanding that results from a careful and systematic investigation carried out while seated in the formal meditative posture. The third and highest form of wisdom is the wisdom arising from meditation, where meditation refers specifically to understanding conjoined with the deep level of concentration known as serenity. Using this concentrated mind to understand the absence of self produces a state called insight (*vipaśyanā*). It is only at this level that the seeds of suffering are destroyed, but it is impossible (at least according to the gradualist approach) to arrive at this level of wisdom without passing through the other two.

The precise content of meditation on no-self varies among Buddhist traditions but generally entails a systematic search among the components of the body and the mind, seeking to find that autonomous and substantial entity that we imagine the self to be. This practice is described in chapter 6. The assumption, of course, is that a thorough investigation of the body and the mind will conclude ultimately that there is no such self to be found, that the person is a collection of impermanent moments of mind and body, constantly breaking up like a hard rain on a stone courtyard. This very absence of self is the true nature of the person, and a deep understanding of the absence of self leads to the state of the absence of suffering called nirvāṇa.

In the early traditions (and in present-day Theravāda), one is said to pass through four stages in the path to nirvāṇa. The first is called the stream-enterer, marked by the initial realization of the absence of self at the level of deep concentration. This initial vision of nirvāṇa destroys all seeds for future rebirth as an animal, ghost, or hell being. One has entered the stream leading to nirvāṇa and will be reborn a maximum of seven more times. The second stage is that of the once-returner, who, as the name suggests, will be reborn in the Desire Realm at most one more time before either entering nirvāṇa or being reborn in a heaven of the Form Realm, whence he or she will enter nirvāṇa. The third stage is called the never-returner, who has destroyed all the seeds that would cause returning, that is, being reborn, in the Desire Realm. The final stage is that of the arhat, a term that means one who is worthy of worship. The arhat will enter nirvāṇa upon death. If one thinks of nirvāṇa as cessation, then an arhat is one who achieves the cessation of the afflictions of desire and hatred and then achieves the cessation of the aggregates at death. These four stages may encompass several lifetimes, or they may be completed in one, as the Buddha did when he passed through the four stages in a single evening as he sat under the Bodhi tree, rising the next morning as an arhat. It was considered possible for laypeople to pass through the four stages, although in the Theravāda tradition it was stated that a layperson who became an arhat had to be ordained as a monk or nun within seven days or die; the body of a layperson, unpurified by monastic vows, was considered incapable of supporting such a state of enlightenment.

Another articulation of the fourth truth, the truth of the path, is the eightfold path, although this list is less important than many world religions textbooks would lead one to believe. The eight elements are correct action, correct speech, correct livelihood, correct view, correct mindfulness, correct meditation, correct intention, and correct effort. These eight fit neatly under the three trainings, with correct action, correct speech, and correct livelihood falling under the training in ethics; correct effort, correct mindfulness, and correct meditation falling under the training in meditation; and correct view and correct intention falling under the training in wisdom.

The order of the four truths is the subject of much commentary. The four occur in two pairs, and in each the effect is preceded by the cause. Suffering is the effect of origin, and cessation is the effect of the path. The first pair is to be abandoned, the second pair is to be adopted. The fact that the truths appear out of chronological sequence, with the effect coming before its cause, is explained through recourse to a medical model, in which the Buddha, in setting forth the truths, is following the procedure of a physician. The physician's first task is to recognize that illness is indeed present and to identify it. This is precisely what the Buddha does in observing that existence is qualified by suffering. The second step is to make a diagnosis, to determine the source of the malady. In the second truth, the truth of origin, the Buddha explains the sequence of causes, both immediate and mediate, that give rise to suffering. The physician's next task is to determine whether the disease is fatal or whether a subsequent state of health is possible; that is, the physician makes a prognosis. The third truth is the postulation of a state free from suffering, called cessation or nirvāṇa. Once the prognosis is made, the physician must prescribe the cure, the course of action that will lead from sickness to health. The fourth and final truth of the path is said to be the Buddha's prescription.

The doctrine of the four truths illustrates the centrality of the notion of causation in Buddhist thought. Indeed, if it is possible to identify a particular contribution of the Buddha to the philosophies of his day, it would be the thoroughgoing emphasis on causation as an inexorable force whose devastating effects can be escaped by understanding its operation. That is, everything is an effect of a cause. If the cause can be identified and destroyed, the effect is also destroyed. This is the meaning of the first two truths and why they seem at first to be placed out of sequence. The first truth, suffering, is the effect. Suffering must be recognized as such and its pernicious quality acknowledged. It is then that the cause of suffering can be identified, and this is the second truth, the truth of origin. And within the second truth itself a sequence of suffering is set forth: the immediate cause of suffering is negative karma, which in turn is caused by desire and hatred, which in turn are caused by ignorance. If the root cause, ignorance, can be destroyed, the massive tree of suffering is uprooted, never to grow again.

This insight seems to have been regarded as revolutionary, as the story of Śāriputra's conversion illustrates. Śāriputra was a disciple of another renunciate teaching the path to liberation when he encountered one of the Buddha's original disciples, Aśvajit, on the road. He noticed Aśvajit's serene countenance and stopped to ask him who his teacher might be. Aśvajit replied that his teacher was the Buddha. When Śāriputra went on to ask what it was that the Buddha taught, Aśvajit demurred, explaining that he had only recently renounced the life of a householder and was incapable of presenting the teaching in full; he could only give a summary. Śāriputra would not be put off, however, and asked Aśvajit to provide him with the spirit of the Buddha's teaching. Aśvajit said, "For those things that have causes, the Tathâgata has set forth the causes. And he has also set forth their cessation. The great renunciate has so spoken." According to the story, by simply hearing these words, which to our ears may hardly seem inspiring, Śāriputra gained the first stage of insight into nirvāṇa and became a stream-enterer. He went on to become the wisest of the Buddha's disciples. And Aśvajit's summation became perhaps the most famous statement in all of Buddhist literature. Indeed, what may have begun, according to the story, as something simply to satisfy a persistent questioner so that Aśvajit could continue on his way, became a slogan and eventually a mantra, its very recitation said to have healing powers. These words were often enshrined in a stūpa, serving as a substitute for a relic of the Buddha.

Śāriputra repeated this statement to his companion, Maudgalyāyana, who also became a stream-enterer upon hearing it. Together, they became disciples, indeed, the two chief disciples of the Buddha, with Śāriputra renowned for his wisdom and Maudgalyāyana for his magical powers. Maudgalyāyana could perform intercelestial travel as easily as a person bends his arm, and the tradition is replete with the tales of his travels, flying to the Himalayas to find a medicinal plant to cure the ailing Śāriputra and bringing a sprig from the Bodhi tree to be planted at the Jetavana monastery, even taking the form of an eagle to defeat a great serpent whose vast hood had cast the entire world into darkness. Yet Maudgalyāyana's supernormal powers, unsurpassed in the world, were insufficient to overcome the law of cause and effect and the power of his own karma, as the famous tale of his death displays.

A group of naked ascetics resented the fact that the people of the kingdom of Magadha had shifted their allegiance and patronage from them to the Buddha and his followers, and they blamed Maudgalyāyana, who had reported that in his celestial and infernal travels he had observed deceased followers of the Buddha in heaven and the followers of other teachers in hell. They hired a group of bandits to assassinate the monk. When he discerned their approach, the eighty-four-year-old monk made his body very tiny and escaped through the keyhole. He eluded them in different ways for six days, hoping to spare them from committing the deed of immediate retribution of killing an arhat. On the seventh day, Maudgalyāyana temporarily lost his supernormal powers, the residual karmic effect of having brought about the death of his parents in a distant previous lifetime. The bandits beat him mercilessly until his bones had been smashed to the size of grains of rice and left him for dead. He then soared into the air and into the presence of the Buddha, where he paid his final respects and passed into nirvāṇa at the Buddha's feet.

THE LAST DAYS OF THE BUDDHA

The Buddha spent the forty-five years after his enlightenment traveling with a group of disciples from city to city, from village to village, across northeastern India, teaching the dharma to those who would listen, occasionally debating with (and according to the Buddhist sources always defeating) masters from other sects and gaining followers from all social classes. Those who decided to go forth from the household and become his disciples joined what came to be known as the *saṅgha*, the community of monks and nuns. Their practice is described in chapter 4. The majority of the Buddha's followers did not renounce the world, however, and remained in lay life. The Buddha also provided teachings for them, described in chapter 5. He taught the dharma both to the rich and to the poor, to the powerful and the destitute, to gods and humans, and even to nonhumans. The demoness Hārītī kidnapped and devoured several children every day in the city of Rājagṛha. The Buddha therefore kidnapped her favorite among her five hundred children and hid him in his begging bowl. When Hārītī finally found him and demanded his return, the Buddha asked her to consider how the mothers of the city felt upon the loss of their only children, when Hārītī was so upset at losing only one of her five hundred. Hārītī agreed to desist yet needed another source of sustenance. The Buddha instructed the monks to make daily offerings to Hārītī and her sons. Chinese travelers to ancient India report seeing a statue of Hārītī, holding an infant, in the dining halls of monasteries.

But not all were converted. Some launched intrigues against the Buddha and persecuted his followers. And some were unable to benefit from his presence. Ānanda, the Buddha's cousin and personal attendant, once asked the Buddha to approach an old woman and teach her the dharma. When the Buddha stood before her, she turned her back; when he stood behind her, she turned forward; when he stood above her, she lowered her head. Finally she covered her face with her hands. The Buddha explained that there are some people whose past karma prevents them from even seeing the Buddha, much less benefiting from his teaching. Yet three times each day and night the Buddha surveyed the world with his omniscient eye to locate those that he might benefit, often traveling to them, using his supernormal powers to do so.

Others came to the Buddha. A young mother, distraught with grief, brought her dead infant to the Buddha. Knowing of his great powers, she begged him to bring her child back to life. He promised to do so, saying that he only required a single mustard seed from a household that had known no suffering. The woman set out from door to door, asking for a mustard seed and hearing from each family a different tale of sorrow. She slowly understood the universality of suffering, laid her child to rest, and became a nun, eventually achieving nirvāṇa.

Shortly before his own death, the Buddha remarked to Ānanda, apparently in passing, that a buddha can, if requested, extend his life span for thousands of years. The Buddha reiterated this point a second and then a third time, but Ānanda, distracted by Māra, failed to request that he do so. Māra then appeared and reminded the Buddha of his promise to him, made shortly after his enlightenment, to pass into nirvāṇa when he had completed his instructions in the dharma. The Buddha agreed to pass away three months hence, at which point the earth quaked. Ānanda was roused from his meditation and asked the Buddha the reason for the tremor. He was told that there are eight reasons for an earthquake, one of which was when a buddha relinquishes the will to live. Ānanda immediately implored him not to do so, but the Buddha explained that the time for such requests had passed and criticized him for missing the earlier suggestion; had he asked then, the Buddha would have consented. The Buddha even reminded him that he had mentioned this power of a buddha fifteen times in the past, and each time Ānanda had said nothing.

At the age of eighty the Buddha accepted a meal from a blacksmith, instructing the smith to serve only him and to bury the rest of the meal without offering it to others. The Buddha contracted dysentery shortly thereafter and lay down on his right side between two trees, which immediately blossomed out of season. He instructed the monk who was fanning him to step to one side, explaining that he was blocking the view of the deities who had assembled to witness his passing. He asked the five hundred disciples who had assembled whether they had any last question or doubt. When they remained silent, he asked a second time, and then a third. He then declared that none of them had any doubt or confusion, that they all had achieved at least the level of stream-enterer and thus were destined to achieve nirvāṇa. The Buddha then entered into meditative absorption, passing from the lowest level to the highest, then from the highest to the lowest, before entering the fourth level of concentration, whence he passed into nirvāṇa.

The scene of the Buddha's passage into nirvāṇa is one of the most widely depicted in Buddhist art, with the Buddha lying peacefully on his right side, surrounded by all manner of humans, deities, and animals. Those who have become arhats are distinguished by the serene expressions on their faces; they know that all conditioned things are transitory. The others, the gods, the not yet enlightened monks, the laity, and the animals—even the mighty tiger—weep openly. The reason for their sorrow is often said to be their sense of loss at not being able to hear, and thus benefit from, the Buddha's teachings again. But one finds evidence of a more personal reverence of the Buddha. Even in the apparently stoic tradition of the Theravāda, the most heartfelt devotion is expressed by the most serene of monks. When Śāriputra is about to take his final leave of the Buddha, going home to teach his stubborn mother before he must die, he embraces the Buddha's legs and says, "I have practiced the ten perfections for one innumerable aeon and one hundred thousand aeons so that I might worship these feet."

The Buddha is said to have instructed his followers to cremate his body and distribute the relics that remained among various groups of his followers, who were to enshrine them in hemispherical reliquaries called stūpas. His body lay in a coffin for seven days before being placed on a funeral pyre. No one, however, was able to set the pyre ablaze. The Buddha's chief disciple, Mahākāśyapa, had been away at the time of his death. Upon his arrival, only he was able to light the pyre. The relics were initially entrusted to one group, until armed men from seven other regions arrived and demanded the relics. In order to avert bloodshed, a monk intervened and divided the relics into eight portions. Ten sets of relics were said to have been enshrined, eight from portions of his remains, one from the ashes left from the pyre, and one from the bucket that was used to distribute the remains into eight parts. The king Aśoka (discussed in chapter 5) is said to have gathered up the relics more than a century later and enshrined them in eighty-four thousand stūpas.

The stūpa would become a reference point denoting the Buddha's presence in the landscape. Early texts and the archaeological records link stūpa worship with the Buddha's life and especially the key sites in his career. A standard list of eight shrines is recommended for pilgrimage and veneration, located at the places of his birth, his enlightenment, his first turning of the wheel of dharma, and his death, as well as four cities where he performed miracles. For example, a stūpa was located in Sāṃkāśya, where the Buddha descended to the world after teaching the dharma to his mother (who died seven days after his birth) in the Heaven of the Thirty-Three. However, stūpas are also found at places that were sacred for other reasons, often associated with a local deity. Stūpas were constructed for past buddhas and for prominent disciples of the Buddha. Indeed, stūpas dedicated to disciples of the Buddha may have been especially popular because the monastic rules stipulate that donations to such stūpas became the property of the monastery, whereas donations to stūpas of the Buddha remained the property of the Buddha, who continued to function as a legal resident of most monasteries in what was called "the perfumed chamber." Like the Buddha, the stūpa was regarded as a legitimate recipient of gifts, and rules prohibited these gifts from being converted to money and used for other purposes.

Throughout the history of Buddhism and across the Buddhist world, relics have been considered potent objects and have generated strong reactions in their devotees and their disparagers. In 873 C.E., the Chinese emperor ordered that a portion of a finger bone of the Buddha be transported to the capital. According to a contemporary report, its arrival caused an outpouring of the most dramatic devotions. A soldier amputated his left arm and held it before the relic, while others cut off their hair and bit off their fingers. Stūpas, then, were not considered to contain bits of ash and bone but were said to contain the Buddha himself; the relics, deemed indestructible, were described as infused with the virtues of a buddha. It is, therefore, somewhat misleading to describe the stūpa as a substitute for the Buddha; it was said that to see the stūpa is to see the Buddha. The vicinity of a stūpa (or of a sacred site associated with the life of the Buddha, such as Bodhgaya, the site of his enlightenment) was considered an auspicious site for the entombment of the ashes of both monks and laity; hundreds of minor stūpas have been discovered around such sites. The stūpa, through the power of the Buddha it contained, was believed to have the power to deliver into heaven the dead whose names were inscribed there.

The potency of relics was even acknowledged by enemies of the dharma. In 1561, the Portuguese conquered the kingdom of Sri Lanka and captured its Buddhist king. The Portuguese viceroy sailed back to his headquarters in Goa, on the western coast of India, with his prisoner in velvet-covered chains. He also carried a greater prize, indeed, the kingdom's most precious treasure, a tooth of the Buddha, mounted in gold. The king of Pegu in Burma heard of this great theft and sought its return. He sent a delegation to Goa, offering a vast sum of gold to the Portuguese in return for the tooth. The Portuguese, their treasury depleted, were inclined to accept the offer until the archbishop intervened, protesting that returning the tooth would further encourage idolatry among the heathen, allowing them to offer homage to a tooth, homage that is rightfully due only unto God. An assembly of the officers of the military and the church was convened, deciding in the end that the needs of the state to replenish its treasury were outweighed by the need to prevent the worship of false gods. The archbishop placed the tooth in a mortar and smashed it to powder. After burning the powder in a brazier, the ashes were cast into the river. Yet the tooth reappeared in Sri Lanka and was captured by the British in 1815. The tooth relic of the Buddha can be seen in Kandy today.

Stūpas and the relics they preserved were also pivotal in the social history of Buddhism: these monuments became magnets attracting monastery building and votive construction as well as local ritual traditions and regional pilgrimages that produced rewards both spiritual and material. Buddhist devotionalism at these centers generated income for local monks, artisans, and merchants, an alliance basic to Buddhism throughout its history. At these geographical centers arrayed around the monument, diverse devotional exertions, textual studies, and devotees' mercantile pursuits could all prosper. And new teachings were proclaimed in the shadow of the stūpa.

THE BODIES OF THE BUDDHA

Although what might be deemed a biography of the Buddha did not appear until some six centuries after his death, the story recounted above of the Buddha's life and death is generally accepted, albeit with both major and minor additions and elisions, throughout the Buddhist world. Where the various schools of Buddhism part company is not so much on the events of the Buddha's life as on what he taught, a question that has profound implications for their understanding of the identity of the Buddha. Some four centuries after the Buddha's death, we see the first textual references to something called the Mahāyāna, the "Great Vehicle." It may be an overstatement to refer to the Mahāyāna as a self-conscious movement, at least in its early centuries. It may be more accurate to speak of the appearance of new texts that called themselves Mahāyāna sūtras.

Regardless of its humble origins and, as we shall see, its ambiguous status in India, the Mahāyāna would go on to become of central importance for the Buddhisms of China, Tibet, Mongolia, Korea, and Japan.

The Mahāyāna seems to have begun with the production of texts, texts that purported to be the authentic word of the Buddha, despite the fact that they appeared centuries after his death. Their belatedness is variously explained: some of the Mahāyāna sūtras state that the Buddha knew that what he taught in these sūtras was so profound that it would be misconstrued if it was widely disseminated to the audience of his day. The sūtras, once spoken by the Buddha and recorded, therefore had to be spirited away, sometimes to a heaven, sometimes to a cave, sometimes to a bejeweled casket at the bottom of the sea guarded by dragons, to be held in safekeeping until the time was ripe for their revelation. Other texts were divinely inspired, miraculously heard, and committed to writing by a person endowed with the power of clairaudience. It is difficult to say what it was that spurred the explosion of writing that resulted in the Mahāyāna sūtras. Although the contents of the sūtras are too diverse to be regarded as in any way systematic, a number of apparently new conceptions are to be found among their pages.

Perhaps the most important is a new conception of the Buddha. No longer was the Buddha seen, if he had ever been after the first generation of followers, as a human being who, having achieved enlightenment, taught for forty-five years and passed into nirvāṇa upon his death. One of the most important Mahāyāna sūtras for the new conception of the Buddha, the *Lotus Sūtra* (*Saddharmapuṇḍarīka*), explains that the Buddha only feigned his death. Knowing that if he remained forever accessible to the world, his followers would feel no sense of urgency about the need to escape from rebirth themselves, the Buddha only pretended to pass into nirvāṇa. His life span is, in fact, immeasurable. Furthermore, in the *Lotus Sūtra* the Buddha explains that his six years of austerities, culminating in his achievement of enlightenment under the Bodhi tree, were merely a pretense. He had in fact become a buddha aeons before, only pretending to become disillusioned with his princely life, only pretending to give it all up, only pretending to strive diligently in the quest for enlightenment. This was all a performance designed to inspire the world.

It is not so much that the events of the Buddha's life are amended in the Mahāyāna sūtras but rather that they are reinterpreted. The accounts of the Buddha include a host of human concerns; monks fan the Buddha in the heat, wash his feet, rub his back, and bring him medicine when he is sick. Ānanda brings the Buddha water to wash his face and a stick to clean his teeth. Ānanda carries messages for the Buddha, assembles the monks at his request, and makes sure that monks who come to visit the Buddha do not accidentally leave any belongings behind. The Buddha begs for alms in a village and departs having received nothing. What we might regard as human moments are explained away in the Mahāyāna sūtras as instances of the Buddha's skillful means. The Buddha has no need for food because he does not have an ordinary body. Yet he pretends to go empty-handed on his alms round so that when a monk in the future is also unsuccessful, he might console himself with the thought that even the Buddha sometimes had to go hungry.

Indeed, the tradition seemed to have struggled with the identity of the Buddha, with the Buddha's true nature, from early on. Early scholastics speak of the Buddha having a physical body and what was called a "mind-made body" or an "emanation body," a second body that he used to perform miraculous feats such as visiting his mother in the Heaven of the Thirty-Three on top of Mount Meru after her death. The question was also raised as to whom precisely the Buddhist should pay homage when honoring the Buddha. Was it the physical body, which seems to have died of dysentery and then was cremated, or the ashes being distributed among the followers and entombed in stūpas? Or was it something less corruptible? A term was coined to describe a more metaphorical body, a body or collection of all of the Buddha's good qualities or dharmas: his wisdom, his compassion, his fortitude, his patience. This corpus of qualities was called the *dharmakāya* and was identified as the body of the Buddha to which one turned for refuge.

All of this would be recast in the Mahāyāna sūtras. The emanation body was no longer the body that the Buddha employed on special occasions to perform supernatural feats. The emanation body was the only body that appeared in the world, the only body that was visible to humans. It was the emanation body that was born as a prince, it was the emanation body that went forth from the city in the chariot. It was the emanation body that renounced the princely life, it was the emanation body that achieved enlightenment and taught the dharma to the world. That is, the Buddha that we know is a magical display. Furthermore, the Buddha was not restricted in his emanations to the resplendent form so familiar to us from Buddhist iconography. He could appear as inanimate objects such as an inspiring sentence or word, a cooling breeze, or a bridge across an impassable river. The Buddha could appear in human form, especially as a musician or an artist. The true buddha, the source of the emanations, was the dharmakāya, a term that still referred to the Buddha's transcendent qualities but, playing on the multivalence of the term *dharma,* came to mean something perhaps more cosmic, an eternal principle of enlightenment and ultimate truth, described in later Mahāyāna treatises as the Buddha's omniscient mind and its profound nature of emptiness.

The doctrine of the bodies of the Buddha was not simply a theological innovation; it was to be put to a wide range of other uses beyond Buddhist India, perhaps most famously in Tibet. With the decline of the Tibetan monarchy in the ninth century, both political and religious authority (although the strict distinction between the two should not be immediately assumed in many Buddhist societies) shifted gradually to Buddhist teachers. Since many of these teachers were Buddhist monks who had taken vows of celibacy, the problem of succession arose. In some cases, authority was passed from a monk to his nephew. However, by the fourteenth century (and perhaps even earlier), a form of succession developed in Tibet that, although supported by standard Buddhist doctrine, seems unique in the Buddhist world. It was asserted that great teachers could determine their next rebirth and that the new incarnations of past teachers could be identified as young children.

Tibetans chose the term for a body of a buddha to name this notion of incarnation. That is, the next incarnation of a former great teacher is called a tulku, (*sprul sku*), the Tibetan translation of *nirmāṇakāya,* "emanation body." The implication is that there is a profound difference in the processes whereby ordinary beings and incarnate lamas take birth in the world. For the former, rebirth is a harrowing process, a frightful journey into the unknown, a process over which one has no control. One is blown by the winds of karma into a new lifetime. The rebirth of an incarnate lama is a very different matter. As "emanation bodies," incarnate lamas are technically buddhas, free from the bonds of karma. Their rebirth is thus entirely voluntary. They need not be reborn at all, yet they decide to return to the world out of their compassion for others. Furthermore, they exercise full control over their rebirth. For ordinary beings, rebirth must take place within forty-nine days from the time of death. Incarnate lamas are under no such constraints. For ordinary beings, the circumstances of the rebirth—the place, the parents, the form of the body, and the capacity of the mind—are all determined by karma. For the incarnate lama, all of these are matters of choice and are said to have been decided in advance so that a dying incarnation will often leave instructions for his disciples as to where to find his next rebirth.

Since the fourteenth century, all sects of Tibetan Buddhism have adopted the practice of identifying the successive rebirths of a great teacher, the most famous instance being, of course, the Dalai Lamas. But there are some three thousand other lines of incarnation in Tibet (only a few of whom are female). The institution of the incarnate lama has proved to be a central component of Tibetan society, providing the means by which authority and charisma, in all of their symbolic and material forms, are passed from one generation to another. Indeed, the spread of Tibetan Buddhism can usefully be traced by the increasingly large geographical areas in which incarnate lamas are discovered, extending today to Europe and North America. It is important to note, however, that this system did not solve all of the more material problems of succession. Many of the more bloody events in the history of Tibetan Buddhism occurred in intrasectarian rivalry over the disposition of the power and property of a powerful lama, the point of contention often being whether that power and property should be passed to a family member or a chief disciple, or to the lama's next incarnation.

Along with additional bodies of the Buddha, the Mahāyāna sūtras also revealed the presence of multiple universes, each with its own buddha. These universes, sometimes called buddha fields, sometimes called pure lands, were described as abodes of extravagant splendor, luxuriant gardens where the trees bore a fruit of jewels, the birds sang verses of the dharma, and the inhabitants devoted themselves to its practice. These buddha fields, described in detail in certain sūtras, became preferred places for future rebirth, and the buddhas who presided there became objects of devotion, especially the buddha of infinite light, Amitābha, and his Land of Bliss called Sukhāvatī. Some pure lands were accessible only to those far advanced on the path, and there the buddhas appeared in yet a third form (in addition to the emanation body and the dharma body). This was the enjoyment body (*saṃbhogakāya*), the form of a youthful prince adorned with the thirty-two major marks and eighty minor marks of a superman.

HĪNAYĀNA AND MAHĀYĀNA

Why is it that the Buddha merely seemed to achieve enlightenment under the Bodhi tree, that he merely seemed to enter nirvāṇa, that he merely seemed to teach that nirvāṇa was the cessation of the mind and the body? The Mahāyāna sūtras were clearly seeking to recast the person of the Buddha and the structure of his path. But such a revision had also to take into account the earlier tradition, what the Buddha had already taught, the path of the arhat that culminated in nirvāṇa. In the *Lotus Sūtra,* the Buddha tells of a group of travelers who set out for a distant city, led by an experienced guide. At the end of a long journey they reach their destination, only to be told the next morning that they must go farther, that they have not yet reached their goal. The guide reveals, in fact, that the city in which they had spent the night was an illusion, a city he had conjured as a way station on their long path; if he had revealed to them from the outset that the road was so long and the goal so distant, the travelers never would have set out in the first place. The travelers are those who seek enlightenment, their guide is the Buddha. Knowing that the goal of highest enlightenment, buddhahood, is far away, too distant for some to seek, he fabricates an easier goal, called nirvāṇa, on which some can set their sights. But this nirvāṇa is an illusion, it does not exist, it is not the final goal.

By the time that sūtras like the *Lotus* were composed, three different paths seem to have been delineated and accepted by various schools of Indian Buddhism. The first and most common was the path of the *śrāvaka,* literally, "the listener," the disciples of the Buddha who listened to his teachings and put them into practice. The śrāvaka path passed through the stages of stream-enterer, once-returner, and never-returner, culminating in the stage of the arhat, who passed into nirvāṇa at death. The second path was that of the *pratyekabuddha,* the "solitary enlightened one." This term appears to apply to a distinct group among the early followers who preferred not to live communally with other monks but who practiced in solitude, often in silence. They achieved the same nirvāṇa and passed through the same stages as the śrāvaka but did not rely on the teachings of the Buddha (at least, according to some renditions, during their last lifetime). They were said to achieve enlightenment during the time when the teachings of a buddha were not present in the world. And having achieved enlightenment, they did not speak of the path to others.

The third of the three paths was the path of the *bodhisattva.* The term, variously interpreted, seems to mean one who aspires to enlightenment. The Buddha often uses the term to refer to himself in the period prior to his enlightenment, "when I was a bodhisattva." In the story of the Buddha's past lives, the bodhisattva is a person who encounters the teachings of a buddha and is fully capable of becoming an arhat in that very lifetime. But rather than becoming an arhat, the bodhisattva decides to delay his liberation in favor of a greater good. Recognizing that there will come a time when the teachings of Buddhism will have disappeared from the world, when the world will be bereft of a path to liberation, the bodhisattva vows to follow the long path to buddhahood so that he may uncover the path to nirvāṇa and show it to the world, after it has been long forgotten.

In the Theravāda tradition, this vision of the bodhisattva is found in the story of Sumedha. Four countless aeons and one hundred thousand aeons ago, there lived a brahmin named Sumedha who, realizing that beings are subject to birth, aging, sickness, and death, set out to find a state beyond death. He retired into the mountains, where he lived the life of a renunciate and gained yogic powers. Flying through the air one day, he looked down and saw a great crowd gathered around a teacher. Sumedha descended and asked who this teacher might be and was informed that he was the buddha Dīpaṃkara. When he heard the word *buddha* he was overcome with joy. As Dīpaṃkara approached, Sumedha loosened his long matted locks and lay down in the mud to make a bridge across the mud for the Buddha. As he lay there awaiting the arrival of the Buddha, Sumedha reflected that he had the capacity in that very lifetime to practice the teachings of Dīpaṃkara and become an arhat, thereby freeing himself from birth and death. But he concluded that rather than crossing the ocean of suffering alone, he would postpone his liberation by following the longer, nobler path to buddhahood; as a buddha he could lead many across the ocean to the further shore. Dīpaṃkara stopped before Sumedha's prone form and announced that many aeons hence this austere yogin with matted locks would become a buddha. Dīpaṃkara went on to prophesy the details of the lifetime in which Sumedha would become a buddha: who his parents would be and who his disciples. He foretold of the tree under which he would sit on the evening he achieved enlightenment. In his last lifetime, the Buddha predicted, his name would be Gautama.

The commentary to this story enumerates the qualifications Sumedha fulfilled to become a bodhisattva, qualifications that, by implication, anyone who wishes to become a bodhisattva must meet according to the Theravāda. In the lifetime in which the vow to become a buddha is first made, (1) he must be a human, (2) he must be a male, (3) he must be able to achieve liberation in that lifetime, (4) he must make the vow in the presence of a living buddha, (5) he must be a renunciate, (6) he must possess yogic powers, (7) he must be capable of sacrificing his life, and (8) he must have great zeal. This extraordinary person, having made the vow to achieve buddhahood for the sake of others and whose destiny has been confirmed by the prophecy of a buddha, sets out on a long and arduous path of thousands of lifetimes to become a buddha in a time when the teachings of the previous buddha have been long forgotten.

What distinguishes the bodhisattva from the śrāvaka in the early tradition and in the Theravāda of Sri Lanka and Southeast Asia, then, is not so much the goal of nirvāṇa but the path by which they find it. The śrāvaka relies on the teachings of the Buddha, but the bodhisattva must rely only on himself, for there is no buddha to teach him. The bodhisattva has, therefore, a much more difficult task, and his path is consequently much longer. In order to empower himself to find the city of nirvāṇa when the path to it has become overgrown, the bodhisattva perfects himself over millions of lifetimes through the practice of virtue, motivated always by compassion.

Because he had a full memory of the past, the Buddha would recount stories of his past lives. These Jātaka, or "birth stories," are among the most popular in all of Buddhist literature. In many of his past lives, the Buddha was an animal; as a rabbit, he throws himself into a fire to provide a meal for a starving sage. As an elephant, he encounters seven hundred men lost and starving in the desert. The elephant directs the men to a mountain in the distance, at the foot of which they will find the carcass of an elephant that they can eat. He then runs ahead to the mountain and jumps from its summit. As a prince, he commits suicide by throwing himself off a cliff so that a hungry tigress can feed her cubs. As a merchant, he and five companions are shipwrecked and doomed to drown, when he recalls that the ocean will not bear a dead body but will cast it upon the shore. Instructing his five companions to hold on to him, he slits his own throat. Finally, in his last life, Prince Siddhārtha completed the path, passing through the four stages during the night of his enlightenment, to become an arhat himself and to enter nirvāṇa at death. The bodhisattva and the śrāvaka differ, then, not in the goal that they reach but in the difficulty and length of their paths, the bodhisattva being the extraordinary person, unique in each age, to find the path to nirvāṇa through his own efforts and teach it to the world. So long as the teachings of this new buddha remain in the world, there is no need for another buddha, for the path to nirvāṇa is known. This appears to have been the view of the bodhisattva prior to the rise of the Mahāyāna. It remained the view of the dozens of non-Mahāyāna schools of Indian Buddhism, schools that some scholars refer to collectively as "mainstream Buddhism." And it remains the view of the bodhisattva in the Theravāda school of Sri Lanka and Southeast Asia.

And this is the story that many of the Mahāyāna sūtras seek to retell. In the *Lotus Sūtra,* the Buddha tells of a great mansion in a state of decay. Its walls are crumbling, its pillars are rotten, and it has become inhabited by all manner of vermin. Inside the house, three children are playing. Suddenly the house catches fire. The children's father calls to them to come out, but they are so absorbed in their games that they ignore him. Finally, in desperation, knowing what they most want, he tells them that he has three carts waiting outside, a goat-drawn cart for one, a deer-drawn cart for another, an ox-drawn cart for the third. Delighted, the children run from the house to safety, where they find not three carts but one, a magnificent chariot drawn by a great white ox, festooned with garlands of flowers. The burning house is, of course, saṃsāra. The children represent all beings, their father the Buddha. Absorbed in the transient pleasures of the world, beings are oblivious to the impending doom that surrounds them. The Buddha knows, however, that sentient beings have different interests and dispositions. He therefore tells them that there are three vehicles, the vehicle of the śrāvaka, the vehicle of the pratyekabuddha, and the vehicle of the bodhisattva. It is only when they have turned away from saṃsāra that he tells them there are not three vehicles, that there is, in fact, only one, the great vehicle, the vehicle of the Buddha. In the *Lotus Sūtra,* which according to historians was composed centuries after the Buddha's death, the Buddha declares that his earlier teaching of the nirvāṇa of the arhat and the path to it had been a pretense, an expedient measure taken to attract the attention of those initially incapable of aspiring to the only goal there is, the goal of buddhahood. Thus, the *Lotus* declares (although not all Mahāyāna sūtras would agree, as discussed in chapter 3) that there is only one final vehicle that everyone, even those who have already followed the other path to become arhats, will eventually mount, the great vehicle, which will take them along the bodhisattva path to buddhahood. After telling the parable of the burning house, the Buddha makes a prophecy that the wisest of the śrāvakas, Śāriputra, will become a buddha, and soon all the arhats in the audience are clamoring for prophecies of their own future enlightenment.

The Buddha's skillful methods are such that he does not always teach what is ultimately true but what is most useful at the moment. Indeed, in other texts it is said that when an audience gathers to hear a discourse of the Buddha, each person hears what is most appropriate for him or her, spoken in their own language, and each person in the vast audience thinks that they are receiving private instruction from the Buddha.

But the Buddha's skillful means serve not only as a means of inclusion. It is also a means of accounting for and incorporating what had come before. The earlier tradition—at least those elements within it at odds with a particular Mahāyāna sūtra and those who may not accept a particular Mahāyāna sūtra as authentic—is thus dismissed and sometimes referred to (although not in the *Lotus Sūtra*) as the Hīnayāna, a word often daintily rendered in English as the "Lesser Vehicle." But *hīna* is a pejorative term in Sanskrit, meaning base, discarded, mean, and low. And *Hīnayāna* came to be used as a term of derision; it did not refer to any historically identifiable school or sect, even by another name. It is therefore most definitely not some kind of equivalent for the modern Theravāda school of Sri Lanka and Southeast Asia, nor does it function adequately as a general term for as many as thirty-four defunct Indian Buddhist schools. It was an insult available to be hurled at any number of apparent opponents, a term particularly vitriolic perhaps because it arose within rather than between communities.

What conditions could account for such rancor? The historical record is scant, but one might imagine that in the centuries after the Buddha's death, the legacy of the Buddha, both doctrinal and social, came under the control of powerful monasteries and their patrons. What came to be called the Mahāyāna might have begun as a number of local reactions against the monastic establishment, reactions in which certain monks and nuns joined with the laity to produce new texts that offered a different vision, a different ideal, a different aspiration. The Mahāyāna, if it was a movement at all, was certainly not anticlerical. There is some evidence to suggest that some of its texts were associated with stūpas. As discussed above, these monuments that held the sanctified remnants of the teacher became important pilgrimage sites as well as sites for the burial and enshrinement of the pious. One might imagine that the stūpas would provide a place where new teachers could teach, where new texts could be recited. Telling tales of the compassionate deeds of the bodhisattva, the new teachers might predict that members of the audience would also, if they only accepted this or that new sūtra as the word of the Buddha, become bodhisattvas and even buddhas themselves. One might imagine that such prophecies had a special potency, transforming, as they would, an ordinary life into the past life of a future buddha. In order for these new sūtras to gain authority—and it is often appropriate to think of each new sūtra as its own Mahāyāna with its own community of people who had vowed to undertake the more arduous bodhisattva path—they would have to defend themselves against charges of fraud and fabrication brought against them by the monastic establishment.

These charges must have been widespread, for they even make their way into the Mahāyāna sūtras themselves. A sūtra will often begin with someone rising from the assembly to reverently ask a question, sometimes a question as simple as why the Buddha is smiling. The Buddha will often give a short answer and then will be asked to elaborate, with his answer forming the body of the sūtra. In certain Mahāyāna sūtras, there is a strange interlude in which a group of monks rises and leaves before the Buddha begins his discourse. The most famous case occurs in the *Lotus Sūtra,* when a group of five thousand monks, nuns, laymen, and laywomen exit as the Buddha is about to deliver the true dharma. This literary device is generally interpreted to represent those members of the contemporary community who rejected the teachings of the *Lotus.* In another sūtra, various members of the audience attain various levels of progress on the path after the Buddha's teaching, but five hundred monks, accomplished in meditation, rise and leave because they have not comprehended what the Buddha had taught. The Buddha explains to Ānanda that in a past life they had been followers of a non-Buddhist teacher and had listened to a discourse of a previous buddha with contempt.

Indeed, we find Mahāyāna texts for the next millennium defending the Mahāyāna as the authentic word of the Buddha. A sixth-century text, the *Blaze of Reasoning* (*Tarkajvālā*) by Bhāvaviveka, listed the charges brought by the śrāvakas, including that the Mahāyāna sūtras were not to be found in the compilations of the word of the Buddha; that the Mahāyāna contradicts the teaching that all conditioned phenomena are impermanent by claiming that the Buddha is permanent; that because the Mahāyāna teaches that the Buddha did not pass into nirvāṇa, it implies that nirvāṇa is not the final state of peace; that the Mahāyāna belittles the arhats; that it praises bodhisattvas above the Buddha; that the Mahāyāna perverts the entire teaching by claiming the Buddha was an emanation.

The defenses of the authenticity of the Mahāyāna as the word of the Buddha are many. They center often on the function of the sūtras, claiming, for example, that the Mahāyāna is an effective antidote to the afflictions of desire, hatred, and ignorance and therefore must have been taught by the Buddha. It is also claimed that the Mahāyāna sūtras most effectively set forth the path to buddhahood for all beings, a goal, it should be noted, set forth only in the Mahāyāna sūtras. That this defense, or perhaps better, defensiveness, of the Mahāyāna, persists into some of the last treatises preserved from Indian Buddhism suggests that when we step back from the rhetoric of the Mahāyāna and turn instead to its practice in India, two things seem clear. First, the Mahāyāna was never a self-conscious "school" of Indian Buddhism, in the sense of an institution of individuals committed to a set of doctrinal principles. Rather than a wholesale substitution for forms of earlier Buddhist practices, the Mahāyāna appears to be a rather vague supplement to them. For example, there was no separate monastic code for Mahāyāna monks. This makes the term *Mahāyāna* very difficult to define with any precision. One can perhaps do no better than the rather tautological description of the Chinese pilgrim Yijing, who wrote in his 691 *Record of Buddhist Practices,* "Those who worship the bodhisattvas and read the Mahāyāna sūtras are called the Mahāyāna, while those who do not perform these are called the Hīnayāna."

The second point to be suggested is that the Mahāyāna may have remained a minority movement throughout its history in India. As we know from histories of various Christian sects, the mere bulk of literary output is not a reliable measure of popularity; it may indeed suggest the opposite. Chinese pilgrims report that the populations of the great monasteries were mixed, with the devotees of the Mahāyāna in the minority. We know, of course, of the subsequent ascendancy of the Mahāyāna outside India, in China, Japan, Korea, and Tibet. But the Mahāyāna may have been better established abroad even in the last centuries of Indian Buddhism. The great Bengali master Atiśa undertook a perilous sea voyage to Sumatra in order to receive Mahāyāna teachings unavailable in India. Atiśa would eventually leave India permanently in order to teach the dharma in Tibet, arriving there in 1042. Yet one wonders why the monk regarded as the greatest Buddhist scholar in India (at least as described by the Tibetans, who had a certain self-interest in such a description) would have left a prominent post at the monastery of Vikramaśīla in order to go and teach in what his abbot described as "the yak pen" of Tibet. As one scholar has described it, the situation would be somewhat akin to Einstein leaving his post at Princeton to accept a professorship at the University of the Andaman Islands. It is not to demean in the least Atiśa's storied compassion to say his decision makes greater sense if one considers the possibility that the condition of Mahāyāna Buddhism in India in the eleventh century was not strong enough to induce him to stay.

THE BODHISATTVA

In order to become a bodhisattva, one must develop *bodhicitta,* literally, "the aspiration to enlightenment." It is glossed to mean the commitment to achieve buddhahood in order to liberate all sentient beings from suffering, a commitment made in the form of a vow. The most famous version of the bodhisattva vow in East Asia was articulated by the Chinese monk Zhiyi: "Sentient beings are numberless. I vow to ferry them across [the ocean of saṃsāra]. Delusion is inexhaustible. I vow to uproot it completely. The gates of the dharma are endless. I vow to enter them all. The way of the Buddha is unsurpassed. I vow to actualize it." In such a formulation, the goal is the liberation of all beings from suffering; buddhahood is simply seen as the best means for its achievement. As Nāgārjuna wrote, "Thus far, other than the aspiration to enlightenment, the buddhas have perceived no other way in the world to achieve one's own and others' welfare." Three routes are described. The vow of the bodhisattva is construed according to the simile of the king, who assumes the powers of a buddha and then leads all beings to enlightenment; or the simile of the ferryman, who arrives simultaneously with his passengers at the further shore of buddhahood; or the simile of the shepherd, who follows his flock into the shelter of the pen and closes the gate behind him. The bodhisattva leads all beings to buddhahood before becoming a buddha himself.

Bodhicitta is not, then, simply a feeling of pity or compassion, although these are its prerequisites; it is the active wish to free all beings from suffering. Buddhist texts do not seem to regard this wish as somehow natural or spontaneous. It is represented instead as something that must be cultivated, and various techniques are set forth to this end.

One technique derives from the doctrine of rebirth. Based on the belief that the cycle of rebirth is beginningless and that the number of beings in the universe is vast yet finite, it is possible to conclude that, over the long course of saṃsāra, one has been in every possible relationship with every other being in the universe. Each human, animal, insect, hell being, god, and ghost has been one's friend and foe, ally and adversary, protector and assailant, savior and murderer. The story is often told of the monk Śāriputra encountering a woman with a baby on her lap, eating a piece of pork. When a dog approaches, she kicks it away. Śāriputra weeps at the sight, explaining that through his knowledge of the past he sees that the woman is eating the flesh of a pig that had been her father in its past life. The dog had been her mother. Her parents had been murdered by an enemy who had died and been reborn as the woman's child, now coddled on her lap.

In the technique for developing bodhicitta, one relationship among all others is singled out: that of mother and child. Every being in the universe has been one's human mother in a past life.

This relationship is presumably chosen because it is universal. Although everyone in the universe has also been one's child, not everyone has been a parent in this lifetime. But everyone has been a child, and everyone has had a mother. One is instructed to see every being that one encounters as having been one's mother in a past life, to the point that this is the first thought that one has when meeting someone. All of the sacrifices that the mother makes for the child are described in poignant detail, noting that, after all of the pain and discomfort the child causes for the mother during the months of pregnancy, it is surprising that the mother does not simply discard the child when it ultimately emerges from the womb. Instead, she treats the child with great love, sacrificing her own health for its welfare, patiently teaching it to walk and to talk, such that every step one takes and every word one speaks for the rest of one's life is the direct result of the mother's kindness.

The meditator is then instructed to imagine his or her own mother, grown old and blind, gone mad, carrying a great burden on her back, and staggering toward an abyss. What kind of child, they ask, would not run to rescue its mother? Perhaps a mother's ability to create guilt in her child is as universal as the experience of childhood. The mother is old because she has been reborn endlessly over the long course of saṃsāra, the cycle of birth and death. She is blinded by ignorance and crazed by desire and hatred. She carries on her back the burden of all of her past actions and staggers toward rebirth as an animal, ghost, or hell being. It is assumed that any child would rush to its mother's aid in such a situation, seeking to relieve her of her present suffering and preventing her from undergoing further suffering in the future. According to the prescription, it is at this point that the meditator develops not only the wish that all beings will be freed from suffering but also the conviction to effect that liberation oneself. Having surveyed all of the possible means to benefit others, one should conclude that buddhahood affords the ultimate opportunity for benefit to others, both because of a buddha's extraordinary powers and because of a buddha's unique pedagogical skills. As a sūtra states, "Buddhas neither wash sins away with water, nor remove the sufferings of beings with their hands. They do not transfer their realizations to others.

Beings are freed through the teaching of the truth." When this wish to become a buddha in order to free all beings from suffering becomes spontaneous, such that it is equally strong whether one is standing, sitting, walking, or lying down, one has become a bodhisattva.

Another argument for compassion is offered by the eighth-century Indian poet Śāntideva, who begins by declaring that all the suffering in the universe is caused by what he calls the self-cherishing attitude, that all pain, from the most trivial to the most tortuous, from the most private to the most global, can be traced back ultimately to the wish to promote one's own welfare over that of others. This self-cherishing derives from the false belief in self, the ignorance that motivates desire and hatred, which in turn motivate the nonvirtuous deeds that bring about suffering, both now and in the future. All happiness, on the other hand, is the result of cherishing others, putting the welfare of others before one's own. Therefore, paradoxically, it is in one's own best interests to abandon concern for one's own welfare. Śāntideva thus counsels what he calls the exchange of self and other, in which the neglectful attitude with which one has so long regarded others is now directed to the self, and the sense of care and protection with which one has regarded oneself is now transferred to others. He argues that "self" is simply an arbitrary designation and that the sense of identification with a body that has arisen from the physical constituents of others—one's parents—is simply a matter of habit. If one can regard this impersonal body as "I," why can't one come to regard the bodies of others as "I" and protect them as one now protects this body?

He compares the situation of the beings in saṃsāra to that of the Buddha. The former have been maniacally seeking their own happiness over countless lifetimes, yet they still encounter only suffering. The Buddha, on the other hand, at some point in the past decided to abandon his own welfare and seek the happiness of others. "Look at the difference between them," says Śāntideva. By abandoning his own welfare, the Buddha has found perfect freedom and happiness. By seeking their own welfare, others have found only pain. This would suggest that the great emphasis on compassion that one finds in Buddhist texts does not imply the existence of a purely altruistic act in which the actor derives no benefit; Śāntideva's argument seems to rest at times on the conclusion that unless he is compassionate, he will burn in hell. Instead, dedication to the welfare of others is promoted as the most effective means of gaining true happiness for oneself. The current Dalai Lama sometimes calls this "wise selfishness."

Śāntideva distinguishes between two forms of bodhicitta, the aspirational and the practical, which he likens to the decision to make a journey and actually embarking on the path. This second type, practical bodhicitta, is generally set forth in terms of what are known as the six perfections, the bodhisattva deeds. Both in the mainstream schools and in the Mahāyāna, the bodhisattva was regarded as a person of extraordinary dedication, someone who could follow the much shorter path of the arhat and escape from saṃsāra but who eschewed this lesser goal in order to seek the far more difficult and lofty goal of buddhahood out of compassion for the world. In the ancient mainstream schools and the modern Theravāda, this involved vowing to become a buddha when there was no buddha in the world to teach the dharma; the bodhisattva would thus have to find the path to nirvāṇa on his own.

In the Mahāyāna delineations of the path, it was said that there were two obstacles to overcome on the path to enlightenment. The first were called the obstructions to liberation. These were the afflictions of desire, hatred, and ignorance, and anyone who sought liberation from rebirth by either the Hīnayāna or Mahāyāna path must destroy them with wisdom. More subtle and difficult to overcome were the obstructions to omniscience, subtle and deeply ingrained forms of ignorance that caused objects to appear falsely and that prevented the simultaneous knowledge of all phenomena in the universe. Bodhisattvas sought to destroy not only obstructions to liberation, as the arhat did, but the obstructions to omniscience as well. To achieve this more difficult task, the bodhisattva would require great stores of virtue as sustenance over the billions of lifetimes of practice that compose the path to buddhahood. These virtues were called the perfections. Ten (and sometimes thirty) are listed in some Theravāda texts, but the classic formulation is of six: giving, ethics, patience, effort, concentration, and wisdom.

Giving is the ability to give sentient beings whatever they require, and there are numerous tales of bodhisattvas giving away their bodies to those who request them. For example, a wise and virtuous king was approached by five brahmins who asked him for a meal. When the king agreed to provide it, the brahmins assumed their true form as cannibal-vampires, informing the king that they only ate human flesh and blood. The king kept his promise to feed them, over the protests of his ministers. The king was the Buddha in a previous life. The five vampires were his first five disciples, receiving here the gift of his flesh, receiving later the gift of the dharma.

Ethics in Buddhism generally refers to the keeping of vows. Although those who aspired to the bodhisattva path were often monks, ordination as a monk or a nun was not deemed a requirement. The most important of all vows for the bodhisattva is the commitment to achieve buddhahood for the sake of all beings in the universe. But beyond this central vow, a separate set of vows was formulated for bodhisattvas (described in chapter 4).

Patience is the ability both to withstand the difficulties encountered on the path and to forbear mistreatment by others. Numerous tales are told of the bodhisattva's extraordinary patience. A drunken king awoke to find his female attendants seated at the feet of a sage. The king demanded to know what doctrine he preached, and the sage replied that he preached patience. The king asked him to define patience, and the sage replied that patience is not becoming angry when struck or abused. Determined to test the sage's commitment to his teaching, the king had him lashed with thorns and then, in turn, had his executioner cut off the sage's hands, then his feet, then his nose, and then his ears. Each time he asked the sage what he preached, and the sage replied that he taught patience, and patience was not to be found in his amputated extremities. Before he died, the sage wished the king a long life. The Buddha had been that sage in a previous life. Indeed, it is said that if the Buddha were flanked by two people, one of whom was massaging his right arm with fragrant oils and another who was stabbing his left arm with a knife, he would regard the two equally.

Śāntideva offers an interesting argument for patience and against anger. When someone strikes us with a stick, do we become angry at the stick or the person wielding the stick? Both are necessary for pain to be inflicted, but we feel anger only for the agent of our pain, not the instrument. But the person who moves the stick is himself moved by anger; he serves as its instrument. If we are directing our anger against the root cause of the pain, we should therefore direct our anger against anger. He also notes that, according to the law of karma, everything unpleasant that happens to us is the result of our own past deeds. Therefore, the person who harms us is in fact only the unwitting conduit of our own past nonvirtue, returning in the form of feelings of pain. And as a result of harming us, the other person will himself or herself incur negative karma for which he or she will have to suffer in the future. If we respond with anger, we are both planting the seeds for our own future suffering and causing further pain for the person who already will have to suffer for the harm they have done us. Anger is thus self-destructive; a moment of anger can destroy stores of virtue accumulated over many lifetimes. Śāntideva describes a world covered with sharp stones. In order to walk without cutting one's feet, there are two solutions. One can either cover the entire surface of the earth with leather, or one can cover the soles of one's feet with leather. The world is filled with enemies, those who find fault with us in varying degrees. In order to avoid the harm caused, to oneself and others, by responding in anger, there are two solutions. One can destroy all the enemies, or one can practice patience.

The fourth perfection, effort, is the ability to take delight in virtue in all situations and never to be daunted by obstacles along the path to buddhahood. The perfection of concentration entails mastering a vast number of states of deep concentration, called *samādhi,* many of which provide the bodhisattva with magical powers. The minimal requirement, however, is the state called serenity, which provides the mental strength needed to penetrate beyond deceptive appearances and discern reality. The perfection of wisdom is the knowledge of emptiness, understanding the absence of self, or any intrinsic nature, in all persons and things.

The Mahāyāna sūtras repeatedly declare that the practice of the bodhisattva is to amass the two collections, the collection of merit and the collection of wisdom. Merit (or method) and wisdom are called the two wings of the bird flying to enlightenment. The six perfections are divided into the categories of merit and wisdom in various ways. For example, giving, ethics, and patience are classed as merit, wisdom as wisdom, with effort and concentration necessary for both. Bodhisattvas are enjoined, indeed, to practice each of the thirty-six combinations of the six perfections: the giving of giving, the giving of ethics, the effort of patience, the concentration of wisdom. Indeed, according to some, these six virtues are perfected only when they are informed by the knowledge of emptiness. To give a gift with the bodhisattva's motivation is the virtue of giving. To give a gift knowing that the giver, the gift, and the act of giving are empty of any intrinsic nature is the perfection of giving. This is the interpretation given to the statement from the *Diamond Sūtra,* mentioned earlier, where the bodhisattva is said to vow to lead all beings into the final nirvāṇa, knowing that there are no beings to be led to the final nirvāṇa.

The bodhisattva thus embarks on a path that is said to require three periods of countless aeons, calculated by one scholar at 384×10^{58} years. With the bodhisattva's initial yogic vision of emptiness, he embarks on what are called the ten stages (*bhūmi*), with names like Joyous, Radiant, Difficult to Overcome, Gone Afar, Immovable, and Cloud of Doctrine. Over their course he acquires greater and greater power, moving from the position of an ordinary being who turns to the buddhas and bodhisattvas for aid to the position of an advanced bodhisattva to whom ordinary beings now turn. In order to gain the ability, possessed only by a buddha, to be in a state of direct realization of emptiness while at the same time being fully cognizant of all the phenomena of the world, the bodhisattva practices entering into and rising from the vision of emptiness over and over again, more and more rapidly, alternating between the two states many times in an instant. Over the course of the ten levels, a bodhisattva achieves extraordinary powers, powers that only multiply on the slow ascent toward buddhahood. On the first level, for example, a bodhisattva can see one hundred buddhas in an instant, can live for one hundred aeons, can see for one hundred aeons into the past and the future, can go to one hundred buddha lands, can illuminate one hundred worlds, and can bring one hundred beings to spiritual maturity in an instant.

With these great powers, advanced bodhisattvas are not only models to emulate but saviors to beseech. In the Mahāyāna Buddhist cultures of East Asia and Tibet, such bodhisattvas have become objects of particular devotion, called upon to intervene in all manner of crises, deemed more approachable than the distant Buddha. The most famous of these bodhisattvas is Avalokiteśvara, the "lord who looks down." Indeed, much of the *Lotus Sūtra*'s fame in East Asia derives from one brief chapter, the twenty-fifth chapter devoted to the bodhisattva Avalokiteśvara or, as he was known in China, Guanyin, "he who discerns the sounds of the world." In the chapter, the Buddha explains that if suffering beings single-mindedly call his name, this bodhisattva will rescue them from all forms of harm, including fire, flood, shipwreck, murderers, demons, prison, bandits, and wild animals. This chapter was so popular that it often circulated as an independent text, and it was considered a great act of piety to copy the sūtra; some even wrote it in their own blood. In the centuries after the sūtra was translated into Chinese, miracle stories began to circulate about the bodhisattva's wondrous powers, how those who called upon him in times of dire need would find that the shackles had fallen from their ankles and the prison door stood open, that their names had been erased from execution lists, that they could walk through hordes of bandits unnoticed, that their houses remained undamaged in the midst of a great fire, that they had been cured of leprosy.

Guanyin, precisely as the sūtra promised, was known to be especially adept at rescuing the drowning. In the midst of a river battle, a fat man meditated on the bodhisattva and abandoned ship. The water was deep and the river was raging, yet the water came up only to his waist, as if he were standing in shallow water. Eventually, a boat came to rescue him, but the man's weight was so great that he could not be lifted aboard. The man looked down and saw four men pushing him up. Once he was on the ship he looked back, but no one was there.

A Japanese story tells of a monk who was making the perilous voyage from Japan to China when a great storm forced him and a hundred fellow travelers to abandon ship into a smaller boat. The boat drifted for ten days, the passengers having no food to eat or fresh water to drink. A monk on board suggested that they should all recite the Guanyin chapter of the *Lotus Sūtra* thirty-three times (the chapter enumerates thirty-three forms that Guanyin assumes in order to rescue suffering beings). The monk himself wrapped a wick around the little finger of his left hand, soaked it in oil, and set it on fire, and he began to recite the chapter. At the end of the thirty-third recitation, a wave of foam could be seen approaching from the south. When it reached the boat, one of the passengers dipped a ladle into the foam and tasted it. It was fresh water. The passengers all drank the water, which sustained them until a ship appeared and rescued them.

The sūtra also promised that Guanyin would provide sons to the childless. This power was particularly associated with the White-Robed Guanyin, who begins to be represented in Chinese art and literature in the tenth century. Although the Indian bodhisattva Avalokiteśvara and his early Chinese counterparts were male, the White-Robed Guanyin, dressed in long flowing hooded robe and often carrying a child, is female. Her special power is to grant sons and to protect women during pregnancy and childbirth. A white placenta is the sign of her intercession.

Avalokiteśvara also took human form. In Tibet, it was the Dalai Lama. In China, it was the princess Miaoshan ("Wondrous Goodness"), whose story is told in a twelfth-century text called the *Precious Scroll of Fragrant Mountain* (*Xiangshan baojuan*). Princess Miaoshan was the third daughter of the king. From the time of her childhood she refused to eat meat. When it came time for her to marry, she refused the husband her father had selected for her. The king punished her first by restricting her to the royal gardens, but when she did not relent he became increasingly enraged and his punishments became increasingly severe. He sent her next to work as a laborer in a nearby nunnery. When she still refused to marry, he burned down the nunnery, killing five hundred nuns. Princess Miaoshan survived the blaze, and the king ordered her to be executed by strangulation. Her body was carried by a deity to the Forest of Corpses. The bodhisattva Kṣitigarbha (known as Dizang in Chinese, Jizō in Japanese) gave her spirit a tour of the regions of hell. Along the way, the princess preached the dharma to the hell beings, as a result of which they were reborn in Amitābha's pure land. The Lord of Death heard of her work, and, fearing that his realm would soon be depopulated, he asked the princess to return to the world of the living. Restored to life, she went to Fragrant Mountain and practiced the dharma for nine years. Meanwhile, the king began to suffer the effects of murdering five hundred nuns, contracting an incurable disease. Hearing of her father's illness, Princess Miaoshan disguised herself as a monk and returned to the court, declaring that the king could be cured with a medicine made from the eyes and hands of a person without hate. She said that such a person lived on Fragrant Mountain. The king sent his servants to the mountain, where they found the princess, who cut off her hands and gouged out her eyes and presented them to the servants. As she had predicted, the king was cured, and he went to Fragrant Mountain to offer thanks to the great sage who had made such a sacrifice. When he arrived, he recognized the eyeless and handless person as his own daughter. He repented his misdeeds and took refuge in the three jewels (the Buddha, the dharma, and the saṅgha), praying that his daughter's eyes and hands be restored. The princess then explained that she was, in fact, the bodhisattva Guanyin and appeared with one thousand golden arms and eyes of diamonds. Fragrant Mountain in Henan province has remained a popular center of pilgrimage, especially for women, until the present day.

The most famous female bodhisattva in Tibetan Buddhism is Tārā, born from a lotus blossom that sprang from a tear shed by Avalokiteśvara as he surveyed the suffering universe. She is thus said to be the physical manifestation of the compassion of Avalokiteśvara, himself said to be the quintessence of all the compassion of all the buddhas. Because buddhas are produced from wisdom and compassion, Tārā, like the goddess Prajñāpāramitā ("Perfection of Wisdom"), is hailed as "the mother of all buddhas" despite the fact that she is most commonly represented as a beautiful sixteen-year-old maiden.

But like Avalokiteśvara, Tārā is best known for her salvific powers, appearing in the instant her devotee recites her mantra, *oṃ tāre tuttāre ture svāhā*. She is especially renowned for her ability to deliver those who call upon her from eight fears—lions, elephants, fire, snakes, bandits, prison, water, and demons—and many tales are told recounting her miraculous interventions. She can appear in peaceful or wrathful forms, depending on the circumstances, her powers extending beyond the subjugation of these worldly frights into the heavens and into the hells.

She is often depicted as one of two female bodhisattvas flanking Avalokiteśvara: Tārā, the personification of his compassion, and Bhṛkutī, the personification of his wisdom. But Tārā is the subject of much devotion in her own right, serving as the subject of many stories, prayers, and tantric rituals. Like Avalokiteśvara, she has played a crucial role in Tibet's history, in both divine and human forms. In the seventh century she took human form as the Chinese princess who married King Songtsen Gampo (Srong btsan sgam po), the first Buddhist king of Tibet, bringing with her the buddha image that would become the most revered in Tibet. In the next century, she appeared as Yeshe Tsogyal (Ye shes mtsho rgyal), the wife of King Tisong Detsen (Khri srong lde btsan) and the consort of the Indian tantric master, Padmasambhava. In addition to becoming a great tantric master herself, she served as scribe as Padmasambhava dictated the texts that he would hide throughout Tibet, ready to be discovered centuries later. Tārā was also the protective deity of the Indian scholar Atiśa, appearing to him at crucial points in his life, advising him to make his fateful journey to Tibet, despite the fact that his life span would be shortened as a result. Later Tārā is said to have appeared as the great female practitioner of the chö (*gcod*) tradition, Machig Lapdön (Ma gcig lab sgron, 1055–1152?), described in chapter 6. Indeed, aeons ago, when she first vowed to achieve buddhahood and free all beings from suffering, Tārā also vowed to always appear in the female form.

OTHER BUDDHAS, OTHER WORLDS

In order that the dharma be preserved in the long period between buddhas, Śākyamuni (the "sage of the Śākya clan," as our buddha is commonly called) requested a number of arhats to prolong their lives and remain in the world, not passing into nirvāṇa, until the advent of Maitreya, the next buddha, asking them to preserve the dharma and to serve as worthy objects of the charity of the laity. There are various traditions as to the number of these arhats, some listing four, some eight, some sixteen or eighteen. It is this latter number that became established in China, where the arhats (*lohans* in Chinese) were objects of particular devotion and lore, depicted widely in painting and sculpture as often austere Indian figures of wizened body and serious mien. One of these arhats was the Buddha's own son, Rāhula. Various locations throughout the Buddhist world have been identified as the abode of one or another of these arhats, who are known to appear as mendicants from time to time, unrecognized by all but a few.

Maitreya, presently a bodhisattva, will appear in the world when the human life span is once again eighty thousand years. He will replicate the deeds of Gautama, with certain variations. For example, he will live the life of a householder for eight thousand years, but, having seen the four sights and renounced the world, he will practice asceticism for only one week before achieving buddhahood. As the Buddha, he will visit the mountain where the great arhat Mahākāśyapa has been entombed, in a state of deep samādhi, awaiting the advent of Maitreya. Mahākāśyapa keeps the robe of Śākyamuni, which the previous buddha had entrusted to him to pass on to his successor. When Maitreya accepts the robe, it will cover only two fingers of his hands, causing people to comment at how diminutive the past buddha must have been.

But for those who know how to contact him, Maitreya is present even today. The fourth-century Indian monk Asaṅga was known as the greatest scholar of his time, so great, in fact, that there was no one to whom he could turn with his questions. He determined, therefore, to put his questions to the future buddha, Maitreya. It would be millennia before Maitreya took human rebirth to become the next buddha, but Asaṅga knew that Maitreya was residing in Tuṣita, the Joyous heaven. Asaṅga concluded that, by cultivating a state of deep concentration, he would be able to communicate with the coming buddha. He retired to a cave and meditated for three years, without result. When he emerged, he noticed that water dripping from the roof of the cave had created a slight depression in the rock floor. Inspired by the fact that the steady effort of weak water had eroded hard stone, Asaṅga determined to return to his meditation. He emerged from the cave three years later, again without having been able to communicate with Maitreya. As he prepared to leave, he noticed that the spindly wings of the bats that flew out of the cave at dusk and into the cave at dawn had smoothed the rough stone surface of the ceiling of the cave. Again inspired, Asaṅga returned to his meditation for another three years, emerging yet again, after a total of nine years. As he gathered his few possessions and prepared to leave, he noticed a man walking down the road, rubbing a large metal spike with a cotton cloth. Puzzled, Asaṅga asked the man what he was doing and the man explained that he was a tailor and that he was making a needle. He showed Asaṅga a small box containing several other needles he had made using the same technique. Impressed by the tailor's industry, Asaṅga returned to his cave.

Three years later he emerged, now having devoted twelve years to the futile attempt to communicate with Maitreya. A dog lay outside the mouth of the cave. It had been injured somehow and carried a deep gash on its thigh. The wound had become infested with maggots. Moved by pity for the dog, Asaṅga wanted to clean and dress the wound. But to do so would be to deprive the maggots of their sustenance, and as a Buddhist monk he had vowed not to kill any living being. He needed to provide the maggots with another meal. Not knowing what else to do, he stopped a passer-by and traded his begging bowl for a knife, with which he cut a piece of flesh from his own thigh. He placed the flesh next to the dog and determined to transfer the maggots, one by one, from the dog to the piece of flesh. He thought first that he would use a stick, but that would injure the maggots. He would use his fingers, but the maggots were so delicate that some would certainly be injured in the process. He concluded that he had no other recourse but to transfer the maggots with his tongue. At this thought, even Asaṅga felt a wave of revulsion and so closed his eyes, extended his tongue, and lowered his head toward the dog's wound in order to transfer the first maggot. But to his surprise his tongue touched the cold stone of the cave floor.

He opened his eyes to see the bodhisattva Maitreya standing before him, resplendent in silk robes. Asaṅga recognized him immediately and could not resist asking where Maitreya had been for the past twelve years. Maitreya responded that he had been with Asaṅga all the time; he had been so close to Asaṅga in fact that the front of Maitreya's robe was soiled by the crumbs from Asaṅga's noon meal. It was just that the obstacles in Asaṅga's mind blinded him to Maitreya's presence, obstacles that could not be removed by twelve years of diligent meditation but that evaporated in the face of Asaṅga's moment of compassion for the dog. Asaṅga was skeptical at this explanation and so lifted the bodhisattva onto his shoulder and carried him into town. No one saw Maitreya; most people saw only Asaṅga walking alone. An old woman saw Asaṅga carrying a dog on his shoulder. Maitreya then magically transported Asaṅga to the Joyous Pure Land, where he answered all of his questions. Asaṅga returned to transcribe these teachings into what are known as the Five Books of Maitreya. But Asaṅga was unusual in his abilities to communicate with the coming Buddha. Many Buddhists, especially in Southeast Asia, do not consider it possible to achieve nirvāṇa during the current times of degeneration. They therefore direct their merit making toward a rebirth in the far future when they can meet Maitreya when he is the next buddha and thereby benefit from his dharma.

The origins of the notion of the "pure land" (a Chinese term that does not appear in Indian literature) remain somewhat unclear. In Buddhist cosmology there are billions of universes like our own, with a similar structure including a central mountain surrounded by four island continents, with heavenly realms above the peak of the mountain and infernal realms located below the surface. The worlds (and regions within the world) differ largely in terms of the degree of happiness and suffering to be found there. This is, in turn, dependent on two factors: the karma of the inhabitants and whether or not the world is considered "fortunate," that is, whether or not a buddha is present in the world during a given aeon. In such a fortunate time and fortunate place, the world becomes a "buddha field," a site for the deeds of a buddha. The purpose of the buddha is to purify the world, both by teaching the dharma and through miraculous deeds. Worlds exist in various degrees of purification, with the most pure having no realms of hell beings, ghosts, or animals, or even a central mountain; in an agricultural society such as ancient India, the absence of topographical variation was considered a sign of fortune and purity.

How pure is our own world, and what is the capacity of our buddha, Śākyamuni, to purify it? This question is raised in the opening scene of the *Vimalakīrti Sūtra*. After the Buddha reveals the marvels of the buddha fields to his audience, someone asks why it is that the fields of other buddhas are so splendid, filled with jeweled lotuses, while the field of Śākyamuni Buddha, that is to say, our own world, is so ordinary, even impoverished, filled with dust and squalor and (apparently worst of all) an uneven topography. In response, the Buddha simply touches the earth with his big toe, and the world is miraculously transformed into a bejeweled paradise. The Buddha then explains that what he has revealed is the true nature of his land, that he uses his miraculous powers to make it appear squalid in order that his disciples will develop a sense of renunciation and practice the path. This is an extraordinary statement, that the impermanence and suffering so central to the basic doctrines of Buddhism, which are set forth as the reasons why saṃsāra must be abandoned, are presented here simply as instantiations of the Buddha's powers, of his skillful methods to bring others to enlightenment.

Numerous buddha fields are described, sometimes in passing, sometimes in detail, in the Mahāyāna sūtras. But no pure land is more famous than the Land of Bliss. The *Sūtra of the Land of Bliss* begins with Ānanda noticing that the Buddha is looking especially serene one day, and he asks him the reason. The Buddha responds that he was thinking back many millions of aeons in the past to the time of the buddha Lokeśvararāja. The Buddha tells a story, in the form of a flashback.

In the audience of this buddha was a monk named Dharmākara who approached Lokeśvararāja and proclaimed his aspiration to become a buddha. Dharmākara then requested the Buddha to describe all of the qualities of a pure land. Lokeśvararāja compassionately complied, providing a discourse that lasted one million years, in which he described each of the qualities of the lands of eight hundred thousand million trillion buddhas. Having listened attentively, Dharmākara then retired to meditate for five aeons. In his meditation, he tried to concentrate all the marvelous qualities of the millions of pure lands that had been described to him into a single pure land, a pure land, that is, that would be the quintessence of all pure lands. When he completed his meditation, he returned to describe this imagined land to Lokeśvararāja. But he did not simply describe the land, he promised to make real the pure land he had so precisely visualized, creating a place of birth for fortunate beings, vowing that he himself would follow the long bodhisattva path and become the buddha of this new buddha field. He described the land he would create in a curious way, in a series of promises, stating that if this or that marvel was not present in his pure land, may he not become a buddha. For example, he said, "If in my pure land there are animals, ghosts, or hell beings, may I not become a buddha." He made forty-eight such promises. These included that all of the beings in the pure land will be the color of gold; that beings in the pure land will have no conception of private property; that no bodhisattva will have to wash, dry, or sew his own robes; that bodhisattvas in his pure land will be able to hear the dharma in whatever form they wish to hear it and whenever they wish to hear it; that any woman who hears his name, creates the aspiration to enlightenment in her mind, and feels disgust at the female form will not be reborn as a woman again. Two vows have been the focus of particular attention. In the eighteenth vow (seventeenth in the East Asian version), Dharmākara promised that when he is a buddha, he will appear at the moment of death to anyone who creates the aspiration to enlightenment, hears his name, and remembers him with faith. In the nineteenth vow (eighteenth in the East Asian version), he promises that anyone who hears his name, wishes to be reborn in his pure land, and dedicates their merit to that end will be reborn there, even if they make such a resolution as few as ten times during the course of their life. Only those who have committed one of the five deeds of immediate retribution (killing one's father, killing one's mother, killing an arhat, wounding a buddha, causing dissension in the saṅgha) are excluded.

The scene then returns to the present. Ānanda asks the Buddha whether Dharmākara was successful, whether he did indeed traverse the long path of the bodhisattva to become a buddha. The Buddha replies that he did in fact succeed and that he became the buddha Amitābha, the buddha of Infinite Light. The pure land that he created is called Sukhāvatī, the Land of Bliss. Because Dharmākara became a buddha, all of the things that he promised to create in his pure land are now manifest, and the Buddha proceeds to describe Sukhāvatī in great detail. It is carpeted with lotuses made of seven precious substances, some of which reach ten leagues in diameter. Each lotus emits millions of rays of light, and from each ray of light there emerge millions of buddhas who travel to world systems in all directions to teach the dharma. The pure land is level, like the palm of a hand, without mountains or oceans. It has great rivers, the waters of which will rise as high or sink as low as one pleases, from the shoulders to the ankles, and will vary in temperature as one pleases. The sound of the river will take the form of whatever auspicious words one wishes to hear, such as *buddha, emptiness, cessation,* and *great compassion*. The words *hindrance, misfortune,* and *pain* are never heard, nor are the words *day* and *night* used, except as metaphors. The beings in the pure land do not need to consume food. When they are hungry, they simply visualize whatever food they wish, and their hunger is satisfied without needing to eat. They dwell in bejeweled palaces of their own design. Yet there is a hierarchy even in the pure land. Some of the inhabitants sit cross-legged on lotus blossoms while others are enclosed within the calyx of a lotus. The latter do not feel imprisoned, because the calyx of the lotus is quite large, containing within it a palace similar to that inhabited by the gods. Those who dedicate their merit toward rebirth in the pure land yet who harbor doubts are reborn inside lotuses where they must remain for five hundred years, enjoying visions of the pure land but deprived of the opportunity to hear the dharma. Those who are free from doubt are reborn immediately on open lotuses, with unlimited access to the dharma.

The structure of the sūtra provides its narrative potency. What begins as a story about a bodhisattva long ago and in a universe far away ends with the description of a pure land that is present here and now to all who would seek it. Further, the fact that

Dharmākara describes his pure land in a series of vows, saying, "If this not be the case in my pure land, may I not achieve buddhahood," means that all of the things he promised to create there are now a reality because he did achieve buddhahood. The dedication of roots of virtue and the cultivation of the aspiration to enlightenment are classic practices of the Mahāyāna. But in the sūtra it is revealed that these can now be directed toward a goal far more immediate than distant buddhahood, that one can be reborn in a pure land in the very next lifetime through the power of Dharmākara's vow. Such rebirth would become a common goal of Buddhist practice, for monks and laity alike, throughout East Asia (see chapter 6).

There are yet other buddhas who are neither predicted to appear in this world nor who preside over a famous pure land. One such buddha, important in tantric Buddhism (discussed in chapter 6), is Vajrasattva, the "diamond hero." Although it is said that buddhas do not wash away sins with water, Vajrasattva seems to do precisely that. The visualization of Vajrasattva is an important form of purification, deemed a prerequisite for more advanced tantric meditation in Tibet. One begins the Vajrasattva meditation by sitting in the meditative posture and visualizing above one's head a lotus flower with one hundred thousand petals. The stalk of the flower actually extends inside one's head to a depth of the breadth of four fingers. Lying at the top of the lotus blossom are the discs of the sun and the moon, upon which sits the buddha Vajrasattva. He is brilliant white in color and appears as a youthful prince, wearing a crown. He is adorned with jewelry, a necklace, armlets, and earrings and is dressed in robes of the finest silk. He holds a vajra in his right hand and a bell in his left. He sits in sexual union with his consort, the beautiful Vajratopa, dressed in similar finery. They face each other in sexual embrace, his arms, holding vajra and bell, wrapped behind her back. In the space between their hearts there floats a moon disc, around the edge of which are written the letters of Vajrasattva's hundred-syllable mantra. Unlike many mantras that seem to have no semantic meaning, Vajrasattva's mantra can be translated. It means, "Oṃ Vajrasattva, keep your pledge. Vajrasattva, reside in me. Make me firm. Make me satisfied. Fulfill me. Make me compassionate. Grant me all powers. Make my mind virtuous in all deeds.

Hūṃ ha ha ha ha hoh. All the blessed tathāgatas, do not abandon me, make me indivisible. Great pledge being. Āh hūṃ."

While visualizing Vajrasattva and his consort, the meditator begins to recite the mantra silently, imagining that as each syllable is recited, the letters begin to slowly melt, producing camphor. The liquid drips down from the moon disc, passing over the place where the deities are joined, and down through the stem of the lotus blossom into the crown of the meditator's head. The liquid begins to fill the body from above. At the same time, all of the karmic impurities accumulated over countless lifetimes begin to be expelled from the anus and the soles of the feet. At this point, all the while reciting the mantra and imagining the pure camphor entering from above, the meditator imagines that the earth opens up below to a depth of ten stories. At the bottom of this great pit stand all the beings to whom one owes some karmic debt: the person one cheated in a past lifetime, one's parents whose kindness was never repaid, as well as all of the animals whose flesh one has consumed—the cattle, chickens, pigs, and sheep—over one's many lifetimes as a carnivore. The motley host stands below, staring up with open mouths, waiting to be fed. As the torrent of liquid and solid filth emerging from one's nether parts descends toward them, it is magically transformed into whatever they desire—gold for some, food for others—and each is satisfied, its debt repaid.

Now the meditator's body has entirely filled with camphor, all impurities dispelled. At this point, Vajrasattva, his consort, and the one-hundred-thousand-petaled lotus disappear, and the meditator is transformed into Vajrasattva himself. In the center of his chest is a flat moon disc, around the edge of which stand the letters of the mantra, *oṃ vajrasattva hūṃ*. As one recites the mantra silently, rays of light begin to emanate from Vajrasattva's body in all directions, eventually extending to the limits of the space and striking the body of every being in the universe. As each being is touched by the ray of light, each is transformed into Vajrasattva and begins reciting the mantra, until all beings in the universe are the buddha Vajrasattva and all sounds are the sound of his mantra.

Now the entire universe begins to melt into light, beginning at the outer reaches and moving slowly toward the center until the meditator as Vajrasattva is left alone. His body then begins to dissolve into light until all that remains is the moon disc and the letters of the mantra. Then the moon disc fades and *oṃ* dissolves into *vajra, vajra* dissolves into *sattva,* and *sattva* dissolves into *hūṃ*. The letter *hūṃ* then begins to melt from below until all that is left is a flaming dot, which itself dissolves into light, leaving only emptiness.

As we have seen, in the early tradition the Buddha was perceived as that most rare hero, occurring once in each age, who was willing to traverse the aeons-long bodhisattva path in order to find the truth and teach it to the world at a time in history when that truth had been forgotten. In the Mahāyānā, buddhahood became a universal goal; according to some formulations, all beings will follow the long bodhisattva path to buddhahood. Here, in the Vajrasattva meditation, considered a preliminary practice, the goal becomes the path. That is, in order to begin the path to buddhahood, one imagines oneself to be a buddha now, who emanates rays of light from a mantra in his heart, magically transforming all beings in the universe into buddhas.

BUDDHA IMAGES

It is difficult to overstate the importance of images in Buddhism. In the first centuries of its introduction into China, Buddhism was known as "the religion of images." In societies where only a tiny portion of the population was literate, other modes of communication played a far larger role than the texts that have so often provided the primary focus for our understanding of Buddhism. The preaching that the Buddha sent his monks out to do "for the benefit of gods and humans," and that must have played such an important role in the propagation of the dharma, took the form of words that disappeared into the air as they were spoken. The incense lit in a ceremony went up in smoke, and the flowers presented in an offering wilted. The stories that captivated the minds and imaginations of so many became memories. The rituals performed for purposes both personal and universal, mundane and exalted, were completed before they could be preserved on film, the intonation of the chant, the subtlety of the gesture often impossible to reproduce from a manual. What remains are those things that bear a sufficient material weight to allow them to persist through time, the weight of ink on paper, the weight of lacquer on wood.

There is no historical evidence that images of the Buddha were made until centuries after his death. Yet there are a number of images whose sanctity derives from the belief that the Buddha posed for them. The most famous of these is the image made for King Udayana, the ruler of the kingdom of Vatsa and a patron of the Buddha. The Buddha's mother, Queen Māyā, had died shortly after his birth and was therefore unable to receive the benefit of her son's enlightenment. He therefore magically traveled to the place where his mother had been reborn, the Heaven of the Thirty-Three on the summit of Mount Meru, and spent the summer rain retreat teaching the dharma to his mother and the assembled gods. The Buddha taught her and the assembled gods the Abhidharma, over the course of three months. The Buddha returned to earth briefly each day to collect alms, pausing to give Śāriputra a summary of what he had been teaching the gods, which Śāriputra would then pass on to the saṅgha. Śāriputra is thus renowned as the master of the Abhidharma. King Udayana was devastated when he learned that he would be unable to behold the Buddha for so long and approached Maudgalyāyana, the arhat who surpassed all others in his supernormal powers. He asked him to magically transport a piece of sandalwood and thirty-two artists to the Heaven of the Thirty-Three, where together they would carve a statue of the Buddha, with each artist responsible for depicting one of the thirty-two marks of a superman that adorned the Buddha's body. When they had completed their work, the sandalwood statue was brought back to earth. At the end of the rain retreat, the Buddha descended from heaven. When he approached, the statue rose to meet him (and it is thus a standing image of the Buddha). The Buddha blessed the image and predicted that it would play an important role in the propagation of the dharma.

As one might imagine, a number of statues of the Buddha were subsequently identified as the Udayana image. According to one account, the image was brought to China in the first century. But the famous Chinese scholar and pilgrim Xuanzang (596–664) reported seeing the image during his visit to India six centuries later. In the tenth century, the Japanese pilgrim Chōnen (938–1016) traveled to China and had a copy of the Udayana image made to take with him back to Japan. According to one story, the original image magically traded places with the copy en route so that the image Chōnen brought to Japan was the image made for King Udayana. It has since been worshiped at the Seiryōji temple in Kyoto. A panel on the back of the image was opened in 1954 to reveal a miniature set of organs made from silk, along with coins, crystals, scriptures, and historical documents related to the history of the statue.

A Buddhist image, whether painted or sculpted, is not considered finished until it has been animated in a consecration ceremony. In the case of a Tibetan sculpture, the interior must be filled with rolls of mantras wrapped around a wooden dowel, called the "life stick," that runs from the crown of the head to the base of the image. Often incense or the soil from a sacred place is added as well, before the bottom of the image is sealed shut and marked with the sign of a crossed vajra. Paintings are marked with mantras, often the letters *oṃ āḥ hūṃ* on the reverse of the scroll, aligned with the head, throat, and heart of the figure on the front. A consecration ceremony, sometimes brief, sometimes quite elaborate, is then performed, the purpose of which is to cause the deity represented in the image (most commonly, a buddha) to enter into and thus animate the image. According to the Mahāyāna, a buddha is said to be in what is called the unlocated nirvāṇa, because he abides in neither the maelstrom of saṃsāra nor the solitude of the arhats' nirvāṇa. The consecration rite thus causes the buddha to move from the unlocated nirvāṇa to become located in the physical image. The image has to be transformed into a buddha in order for it to become localized as a site of merit making. In the ceremony, the unconsecrated image is (in the visualization of the person performing the consecration) made to dissolve into emptiness (which is its true nature) and then reappear as the deity itself, often through the use of a mirror, which reflects the ultimate nature of the deity into the conventional form of the image.

A standard component of the ceremony is the recitation of the verse, "As all the buddhas from [their] abodes in Tusita heaven, entered the womb of Queen Māyā, likewise may you enter this reflected image." In consecration ceremonies in northern Thailand, monks recite the biography of the Buddha to the image of the Buddha being consecrated, focusing on his path to enlightenment, his achievement of enlightenment, and the extraordinary states of knowledge he attained. The consecrated image of the Buddha is thus not a symbol of the Buddha but, effectively, is the Buddha, and there are numerous stories of images speaking to their devotees. The emanation body of the Buddha includes not only the form of the Buddha that appears on earth, once in each age, in the guise of a monk, adorned with the thirty-two major marks and eighty minor marks of a superman; the Buddha can also appear in the guise of ordinary beings, as well as (apparently) inanimate objects. Indeed, epigraphic evidence indicates that Indian monasteries had as a standard component of their design, beginning at least in the fourth or fifth century, a room called the "perfumed chamber" that housed an image of the Buddha. The chamber was regarded as the Buddha's active residence, with its own contingent of monks assigned to it.

The substance from which an image is made is often of great power. A Vietnamese story tells of a devout girl working as a cook at a monastery who was impregnated by a monk while she was sleeping. She left in shame and gave birth to a daughter, whom she entrusted to the monk's care. The monk went out during the night and placed the baby in the hole of a hibiscus tree, promising that both the tree and the child would attain buddhahood. Fifty years later the tree, now grown tall, fell into the river and drifted to the monastery. Three hundred men were unable to bring it ashore, but the child's mother pulled it from the river single-handedly. Four buddha images were made from the tree and installed in the monastery. Called Dharma Cloud, Dharma Rain, Dharma Thunder, and Dharma Lightning, they were renowned for responding to the prayers of the faithful.

There are countless stories about the origins and power of particular images of buddhas and bodhisattvas. The most famous buddha image in Burma is known as the Mahāmuni, the great sage. According to its creation myth, the Buddha and five hundred arhats flew from India to Selagiri Hill in Burma in response to the wish of the king to pay homage to the Buddha. The Buddha was invited to the capital, where he taught the dharma for seven days. Upon his departure, the king requested that the Buddha leave behind his likeness. A divine sculptor spent seven days casting an image that was a precise duplicate of the Buddha's form. The Buddha breathed upon the image to animate it, at which point the two were indistinguishable to those who beheld them. The Buddha predicted that although he would pass into nirvāṇa in his eightieth year, the statue would remain for five thousand years. The twelve-foot bronze statue has remained an object of veneration, surviving fire and seizure by rival kings. Its face is bathed by a monk in an elaborate ceremony each morning at dawn. To merely observe the ceremony is said to be a source of great merit.

But images were not limited to distant figures, like the Buddha. In China, it was commonly reported that eminent monks would remain seated in the meditation posture after their deaths and that their bodies would not decay, emitting instead a divine fragrance. The bodies of some of these monks were eventually mummified and became objects of veneration, installed in places of honor in the temple. In some cases, these mummies were further preserved through a lacquering process that effectively transformed them into living statues. Often the statues would be painted gold, the earlobes would be lengthened, and a dot would be placed between the eyebrows; golden skin, long earlobes, and a circle of hair between the eyebrows are three of the thirty-two marks of a buddha. One scholar has speculated that the art of lacquered statuary in China derives from this process of preserving mummies. Even when a master's body was not preserved and was cremated, it was common to make a statue of him in which the relics resulting from his cremation were deposited.

Numerous Buddhist texts extol the virtues of producing images of the Buddha. One of the earliest texts translated into Chinese, the *Scripture on the Production of Buddha Images* (*Zuo fo xingxiang jing*), promises, "One who produces an image of the Buddha will most certainly be born to a wealthy family, with money and precious jewels beyond reckoning. He will always be loved by his parents, siblings, and relatives. Such is the fortune obtained by one who produces an image of the Buddha." The text goes on to say that anyone who sees an image of the Buddha and piously takes refuge in the Buddha's stūpa or his relics will not be reborn as a hell being, ghost, or animal for one hundred aeons.

But images sometimes offer more immediate aid. An old couple in Japan was so poor that they did not have reeds to thatch their roof. The wife gave her husband a piece of cloth she had woven and told him to take it to the market and sell it. But no one would buy it, and he turned for home as snow began to fall. It was New Year's Eve. He met a weaver of straw hats who had also been unable to sell anything. The old man traded the piece of cloth for five straw hats. On his way home, he passed six statues of the bodhisattva Jizō, covered with snow. He brushed off the snow and placed a straw hat on the first five statues. Since he had only five hats, he took off his own hat and put it on the sixth statue. He returned home and, with nothing to eat, fell asleep with his wife. They were awakened during the night by the sound of men pushing something up the mountain path toward their house. When they opened the door they found a bundle of food and money, enough to sustain them for many days. In the distance, they could make out the form of six small figures walking single file down the mountain.

BUDDHA NATURE

The word *tathāgatagarbha* has been widely translated. *Tathāgata* is an epithet of the Buddha, meaning either "one who has thus come" or "one who has thus gone." *Garbha* has a wide range of meanings in Sanskrit, including "element," "inner chamber" (and by extension "treasure room"), "husk," and the "calyx of a flower." It was translated into Chinese as *zang,* meaning "storehouse." It refers to the potential for buddhahood that (according to only some Mahāyāna thinkers) resides naturally and eternally in all beings.

This buddha nature is proclaimed in a number of Mahāyāna sūtras, employing similes of something of great value hidden from view and therefore remaining unrecognized until its presence is revealed by a person with the eyes to see it. Thus, the tathāgatagarbha is like pure honey in a cave, entirely covered by bees, which prevent one from seeing it. In the same way, this pure buddha nature is covered by the afflictions of desire, hatred, and ignorance but can be seen by the Buddha, who expounds the dharma and discloses the presence of the tathāgatagarbha in order that beings may destroy the afflictions and make manifest their buddha nature. The tathāgatagarbha is like a kernel of wheat that is covered by a husk so coarse that an unknowing person might discard it, yet when cleaned it is food fit for a king. The tathāgatagarbha is like a piece of gold that has lain at the bottom of a cesspool for many years. Yet the gold does not decay and when retrieved and cleaned is of great value. The tathāgatagarbha is like a treasure hidden beneath the house of a poor family. The treasure is silent and so cannot announce its presence, yet when it is discovered poverty is dispelled. In the same way, the buddha nature abides silently within the bodies of all beings, untainted by their afflictions, as they take rebirth in saṃsāra again and again. Buddhas appear in the world in order to announce to all beings the intimate presence of this great treasure in their bodies. The tathāgatagarbha is like the seed of a mango fruit. It does not decay and can be planted in the ground and grow into a great tree.

In one allegory about the tathāgatagarbha, a man had a gold statue of great value that he needed to transport on a long journey. Fearing that he would be robbed en route, he wrapped the statue in old rags so that it would not be noticed. The man died along the way, and the statue lay in an open field, where it was kicked and trodden upon by other travelers until it was filthy. A person with supernormal sight saw through the rags, uncovered the statue, and worshiped it. In another, a master craftsman cast a golden statue in an earthen mold and then buried the mold and the statue upside down within it so that the statue would cool. When it was unearthed, it looked like a scorched and dirty piece of pottery. Then the mold was removed to reveal a statue of pure gold. In the same way, the Buddha instructs beings to use wisdom to break the mold of the afflictions to reveal their buddha nature.

With the development of the Mahāyāna philosophical schools,

the doctrine of the tathāgatagarbha, a pure buddha nature eternally present in all sentient beings, became subject to exegesis and controversy. For example, some Yogācāra scholars argued that the tathāgatagarbha was not a universal quality. They held that all seeds for future experience reside in something called the foundation consciousness. Present there was a seed that would determine one's ultimate destiny, an enlightenment gene, so to speak. There were four kinds of such seeds. Some beings had the śrāvaka seed and would eventually enter the Hīnayāna, follow the śrāvaka path, and become an arhat entering the nirvāṇa without remainder. Others had the pratyekabuddha seed and would enter the Hīnayāna, follow the pratyekabuddha path, and become an arhat, entering the nirvāṇa without remainder. Still others were endowed with the bodhisattva seed and would enter the Mahāyāna and follow the bodhisattva path to buddhahood. Finally, there were those who had an indeterminate seed and, depending upon the teachings they encountered over the course of their births, would enter either the Hīnayāna or the Mahāyāna. Most controversially, these same exegetes also held that there were certain beings who had no enlightenment seed. They were called *icchantikas,* beings of great desire, and were considered constitutionally doomed to wander forever in saṃsāra. In fifth-century China, the question of whether such benighted beings also had the buddha nature became a subject of great controversy until a new edition of the *Mahānirvāṇa Sūtra* made its way to China. This sūtra, said to be the record of the Buddha's last words, proclaimed that even the icchantikas have the buddha nature.

Yet another controversy derives from the fact that the tathāgatagarbha is often described in such a way that it sounds like the self, something that Buddhism is supposed to deny. This is explicitly the case in the *Lion's Roar of Queen Śrīmālā Sūtra,* where the list of the four inverted views is reiterated. Ignorant beings see conditioned phenomena as being endowed with permanence, pleasure, self, and purity, when in fact they are impermanent, miserable, selfless, and impure. The sūtra goes on from this traditional point to claim that, when referring to the tathāgatagarbha, these four correct views of impermanence, misery, no-self, and impurity are themselves inverted and wrong. They must be inverted once again to become the four perfect qualities of the tathāgatagarbha: permanence, pleasure, self, and purity. In a commentary on one of the texts Asaṅga is said to have received from Maitreya, he explains that the four perfect qualities describe the dharmakāya of the Buddha. It is pure because the Buddha has turned away from the impurity of saṃsāra. It is blissful because the Buddha has attained all states of bliss and has no fear of the sufferings of saṃsāra. It is permanent because the Buddha compassionately works for the benefit of all beings as long as the world exists. It is self because the Buddha turns away from the self that the non-Buddhists mistakenly believe to exist in the five aggregates. It is the reality of no-self, which the Buddha has understood, that is held to be the true self.

Such explanations were unsatisfying to Madhyamaka exegetes, who explained the tathāgatagarbha as a provisional teaching, that is, something that the Buddha taught for a given audience and for a given purpose but that was not a statement of his final position. For these authors, it is unthinkable that a fully enlightened buddha could remain hidden in the heart of each sentient being. The magnificence of buddhahood could not be obscured by the afflictions, no matter how thick. Instead, the tathāgatagarbha, the buddha nature, was in fact the emptiness of the mind, with which all beings were indeed endowed. It was this emptiness that allowed for all transformation and that would eventually become the omniscient mind, the dharmakāya of a buddha. Knowing that if he had spoken of emptiness directly, many in his audience would have been frightened, mistaking it for nihilism, the Buddha compassionately chose to speak, in more positive and substantialist terms, of the tathāgatagarbha instead.

Despite, or perhaps because of, the many philosophical problems that attended it, the doctrine of the tathāgatagarbha remained an animating source of both controversy and inspiration. In tenth-century Tibet, it was declared that the tathāgatagarbha, when properly cultivated, flowed out through the eyes to transform all that was seen into a buddha field. In seventh-century China, the members of the Three Levels school believed that in the degenerate age it was inappropriate to take refuge in a particular buddha because humans were no longer capable of accurately discriminating between the enlightened and the unenlightened, much less between buddhas. For them, the Buddha encompassed all living beings because all beings were equally endowed with the buddha nature. They were renowned in Tang China for bowing down to stray dogs (regarded in China with particular disgust) as complete embodiments of the enlightenment of the Buddha. The Buddha, it seemed, was everywhere.

Suggested Reading

Cowell, E. B. *The Jātaka or Stories of the Buddha's Former Births.* London: Pali Text Society, 1957.

Gómez, Luis O. *Land of Bliss: The Paradise of the Buddha of Measureless Light: Sanskrit and Chinese Versions of the Sukhāvatīvyūha Sūtras.* Honolulu: University of Hawaii Press, 1996.

Hurvitz, Leon. *Scripture of the Lotus Blossom of the Fine Dharma (The Lotus Sūtra).* New York: Columbia University Press, 1976.

Jayawickrama, N. A., trans. *The Story of Gotama Buddha: The Nidāna-kathā of the Jātakaṭṭhakathā.* Oxford: Pali Text Society, 1990.

Lamotte, Étienne, trans. *The Teaching of Vimalakirti (Vimalakīrtinirdeśa).* London: Pali Text Society, 1976.

Lopez, Donald S., Jr., ed. *Buddhism in Practice.* Princeton: Princeton University Press, 1995.

———. *Religions of China in Practice.* Princeton: Princeton University Press, 1996.

———. *Religions of Tibet in Practice.* Princeton: Princeton University Press, 1997.

Narada Maha Thera. *The Buddha and His Teachings.* Colombo, Sri Lanka: Lever Brothers Cultural Conservation Trust, 1987.

Ngyuen, Cuong Tu. *Zen in Medieval Vietnam.* Honolulu: University of Hawaii Press, 1997.

Nyanaponika Thera and Hellmuth Hecker. *Great Disciples of the Buddha: Their Lives, Their Works, Their Legacy.* Boston: Wisdom Publications, 1997.

Patrul Rinpoche. *The Words of My Perfect Teacher.* San Francisco: HarperSanFrancisco, 1994.

Śāntideva. *The Bodhicaryāvatāra.* Translated by Kate Crosby and Andrew Stilton. Oxford: Oxford University Press, 1998.

Schober, Juliane, ed. *Sacred Biography and Buddhist Traditions of South and Southeast Asia.* Honolulu: University of Hawaii Press, 1997.

Voice of the Buddha, The Beauty of Compassion: The Lalitavistara Sūtra. Berkeley: Dharma Publishing, 1983.

Warren, Henry Clarke. *Buddhism in Translations.* Cambridge: Harvard University Press, 1953.

3

THE DHARMA

The first of the three jewels is the Buddha, who shows the world where to find a place of refuge from the sufferings of birth, aging, sickness, and death. Variously translated as "teaching," "doctrine," or "law," the *dharma* is said to be that refuge. The dharma is traditionally said to be of two types, the verbal doctrine and the realized doctrine, that is, the words of the Buddha's teachings and the realization of those teachings through the practice of the path. In this chapter, we will be concerned primarily with the verbal doctrine but will turn to the realized doctrine in chapter 6.

One might assume that the verbal doctrine is more accessible than the realized doctrine because it is more public; it exists in physical form in all manner of texts, in many languages. Yet because these texts were written down so long after the death of the Buddha, the question of authorship and hence authority remains a vexed one, not only in the case of the more fantastic Mahāyāna sūtras, but even in the case of the Pali suttas, regarded by contemporary Theravāda Buddhists as the most accurate record of what the Buddha actually taught. The term *Buddhist apocrypha* has sometimes been used to describe those texts composed outside of India (in China or Tibet, for example) that represent themselves as being of Indian origin. Sometimes, the Mahāyāna sūtras composed in India have been called apocryphal. Yet strictly speaking all Buddhist sūtras, even those composed in Indian languages, are apocryphal because none can be identified with complete certainty as a record of the teaching of the historical Buddha. And even when Buddhists of a particular school or historical period or region accept a given set of texts as the authentic word of the Buddha, they are inevitably faced with the problem of interpretation, a problem that appears to have been present from the time of the Buddha's death.

THE WORD OF THE BUDDHA

As the Buddha was about to pass into nirvāṇa, he told Ānanda, "It may be, Ānanda, that some of you will think, 'The word of the teacher is a thing of the past; we now have no teacher.' But that, Ānanda, is not the correct view. The dharma and the vinaya, Ānanda, that I have taught and made known to you is to be your teacher when I am gone." The Buddha appointed no successor. Furthermore, he had taught the dharma over an extended geographical area to a wide range of audiences over the course of forty-five years. And nothing that he had taught had been written down during his lifetime. It was, therefore, inevitable that when groups of disciples assembled to discuss what the teacher had taught, which teaching, indeed, would be the teacher in his absence, disagreements arose about authenticity. How was one to determine what was the authentic word of the Buddha?

The first attempt to collect the teachings of the Buddha is said to have occurred shortly after the Buddha's death. Mahākāśyapa was alarmed to hear that one monk had rejoiced at the death of the Buddha because it meant that he would no longer be bound by the rules of monastic discipline and could do whatever he pleased. Fearing that this view might become widespread and that the teachings of the master would pass away with him, Mahākāśyapa proposed that a council of arhats convene to gather the words of the Buddha. However, upon the death of the Buddha many arhats had decided also to pass into nirvāṇa, and Mahākāśyapa had difficulty persuading five hundred arhats to remain in the world long enough to aid in the compilation of the Buddha's word. As the personal attendant of the Buddha who had heard more than any other, Ānanda was invited, even though he was not an arhat; he was given the ultimatum to become one before the meeting began. He was able to do so the night before, just as his head was about to touch his pillow, thus becoming enlightened in none of the four traditional positions: sitting, standing, walking, or lying down.

The code of monastic discipline was recited by its leading expert, Upāli, and Ānanda recited the teachings that would become the five collections of sūtras. Because of his extraordinary powers of mindfulness, Ānanda was said to be able to repeat sixty thousand words of the Buddha without omitting a syllable and could recite fifteen thousand stanzas of the Buddha. Ānanda also mentioned that, shortly before he passed into nirvāṇa, the Buddha had said that the monks could abolish the minor rules of monastic discipline after his death. But because Ānanda had failed to ask the Buddha which rules he was referring to, the assembly decided not to revise the monastic code.

The question also arose as to what should be counted as the word of the Buddha. Even the earliest formulations do not suggest that the dharma is limited to what was spoken by the Buddha himself. Some schools included both what the Buddha himself said as well as discourses delivered by a disciple of the Buddha and certified by him as being true. Another school held that the dharma is what is proclaimed by the Buddha, by his disciples, by sages, and by gods such as Indra. A second set of criteria considered not the speaker but what was said. A monk might report that he had heard the teaching of the Buddha from the Buddha himself, from a community of elder monks, from a group of monks who were specialists in a particular teaching, or from a single monk who was such a specialist. However, what the monk had heard was not to be accepted as the word of the Buddha, even if he claimed to have heard it from the Buddha himself, unless the monastic community determined that the teaching conformed with accepted discourses of the Buddha and conformed with the code of monastic discipline. Such criteria effectively sanctioned only those doctrines and practices that were already accepted. It appears to be the product of a community simultaneously lamenting the loss of teachings already forgotten and hence seeking to discover and preserve whatever still remained while at the same time wary of the introduction of innovation.

The Buddha is said to have described his teaching as the *dharma vinaya,* the doctrine and the discipline, and the early organization of the Buddha's teaching reflected this twofold structure, thereby trying to provide a common body of doctrine and a common code of conduct for the community. The discourses of the Buddha, called sūtras, comprised one category and were organized not according to subject matter but according to length: there was the collection of long sūtras, the collection of medium-length sūtras, the collection of grouped sūtras, and the collection of enumerated sūtras (that is, sūtras that spoke of things that occur in pairs, in sets of three, sets of four, and so forth up to eleven). The second major category was of the vinaya, the rules of monastic discipline. It contained not only a listing of the rules but an account of the circumstances that led to their institution. A third category of texts was later added, called the *abhidharma,* concerned with scholastic elaboration and analysis of the many lists of physical and mental constituents mentioned in the sūtras. These three categories of texts would be known as the *tripiṭaka,* the three baskets. But this was only one of a number of structures under which the teachings of the Buddha would be collected.

The first reference to the *tripiṭaka* and its commentary being committed to writing occurs in a Sinhalese chronicle in which it is stated that during the reign of Vaṭṭagāmani Abhaya (29–17 B.C.E.) the monks who remembered the canon wrote it down, apparently fearing that otherwise it might be lost as a result of war, famine, or infighting among monasteries. Scholars speculate that prior to this time the Buddha's words had been crafted into oral texts designed with the aim of mnemonic preservation, employing techniques such as redundancy, versification, and the arrangement of works according to length, all methods that had been used in India for centuries for the oral preservation of the Vedas. It seems that no single monk was expected to have the legendary memory of Ānanda, able to recall all that the Buddha taught. The saṅgha was therefore organized toward the task of preservation; there is reference, for example, to the "reciters of the long discourses" and to the "reciters of the medium-length discourses."

This process of identifying and regulating the word of the departed Buddha entailed many decisions, and according to traditional accounts, those decisions were made by the arhats, those disciples of the Buddha who were believed to have destroyed all the afflictions, who themselves would pass into nirvāṇa at death. But if we follow the traditional accounts of the early community, the authority of these liberated beings was soon called into question at the second (or third) council with the proclamation of the five theses of a monk called Mahādeva, the first and most important of which was the shocking claim that arhats were subject to nocturnal seminal emissions, seduced by goddesses in their dreams. In the rules of monastic discipline, the Buddha had forbidden masturbation but had declared that nocturnal emission was not an offense since it was unintentional. But an arhat was believed to have attained two knowledges: the knowledge that all of the passions had been destroyed and the knowledge that the passions would never occur again. Thus, Mahādeva's claim raises the question of whether the enlightenment of the arhat, specifically, his transcendence of passion, extends to acts that are unintentional, what might be referred to today as unconscious acts.

This claim has been widely interpreted by both ancient and modern exegetes. Some saw it simply as Mahādeva's attempt to maintain his own status as an arhat, despite the fact that he himself on occasion presumably succumbed to dream-state temptation. By this time, the followers of the Buddha had become divided into schools, or factions, and some scholars have seen Mahādeva's claim as an indication of the laxity of the group with whom he is associated (called the Mahāsāṃghika), making the highest attainment more accessible to themselves. But it is also possible to see his claim as a challenge to an authority beyond sectarian rivalry, as an attempt to humanize and thereby problematize the enlightenment of the arhat. The Mahāsāṃghikas and their subsects are reported to have held a view of the Buddha that came to be accepted by the Mahāyāna—that the Buddha was transcendent and undefiled from birth, never experiencing a moment of desire, hatred, or ignorance, even prior to his enlightenment under the Bodhi tree. By claiming both the corporeality of the arhat and the transcendence of the Buddha, the Mahāsāṃghikas effectively wrest enlightenment, and hence authority, away from the surviving arhats and restore it solely to the Buddha. This was just one of the controversies of the early community, left to preserve and protect the word of the Buddha after his passage into nirvāṇa.

The rise of the Mahāyāna some four centuries after the Buddha's death was marked by a proliferation of new sūtras (although the original meaning of *sūtra,* "aphorism," was lost as the new sūtras came to encompass hundreds of pages), each claiming to be the word of the Buddha, each beginning with the phrase, "Thus did I hear." Often the "I" was said to refer, as it had in earlier works, to Ānanda. But often the "I" referred to a bodhisattva, such as Mañjuśrī or Vajrapāṇi. And sometimes the person who heard the sūtra was not identified. To say that the hearer (and hence reporter) of the words of the Buddha was Mañjuśrī or Vajrapāṇi was to imply that the Mahāyāna sūtras were secret teachings not intended for the Hīnayāna disciples of the Buddha and thus purposefully delivered in their absence; Ānanda could not report these words of the Buddha because he was not there to hear the sūtra. To say that it was Ānanda who heard the words was to attempt incorporation, that just as the "early" sūtras were heard and reported by the Buddha's attendant, so also were the Mahāyāna sūtras. To say that the hearer was Ānanda, but that he was empowered by the Buddha to perform the task and that, even then, he merely heard but did not understand what he would later report, was to attempt both to preserve the Mahāyāna as the most profound of teachings, beyond the ken of Hīnayāna disciples, but still to count it among the discourses heard in the physical presence of the Buddha himself. Finally, to leave the hearer unnamed was to allow sūtras to be heard by anyone with the qualifications of faith, and several Mahāyāna sūtras set forth techniques for coming into the presence of buddhas in other buddha fields and receiving their teachings.

The question of who heard the Mahāyāna sūtras immediately raises the question of their authenticity and hence their authority. And, as discussed in chapter 2, their authenticity and authority were questioned by their opponents and defended by their proponents. In pursuing the question of the authenticity of the Mahāyāna further, we may move away from the texts for the moment, to consider recent theories of the origins of the Mahāyāna, by postulating two admittedly rather amorphous periods of the Mahāyāna in India, the period of the sūtras and the period of the treatises (*śāstra*). The first would have begun around the beginning of the common era, with the rise of a disparate collection of cults centered around newly composed texts and their charismatic expositors. Some of these texts, like the *Lotus,* in addition to proclaiming their own unique potency as the means to salvation, would also praise the veneration of stūpas. Others, like much of the early perfection of wisdom corpus, would proclaim their superiority to stūpas, declaring themselves to be substitutes for the body and speech of the Buddha, equally worthy of veneration and equally efficacious as objects of devotion. These early sūtras seem to have functioned in mutual independence, with each sūtra deemed by its devotees to be complete unto itself, representing its own world. It was here that the problem of interpretation had to be most explicitly confronted.

THE INTERPRETATION OF THE WORD

The latter phase of Indian Mahāyāna, the period of the treatises, is the period in which there seems to have been, rather than a relatively disconnected collection of cults of the book, a self-conscious, although not internally consistent, scholastic entity that thought of itself as the Mahāyāna. The scholars who described themselves as proponents of the Mahāyāna devoted a good deal of energy to surveying what was by then a very large corpus of sūtras and then attempting, through a variety of interpretative strategies, to craft the myriad doctrines contained there into a coherent system of philosophy and practice. In order to accomplish this, the self-contained worlds presented in individual sūtras were fragmented into repositories from which commentators could extract citations in support of their systems; indeed, treatises were composed that were essentially anthologies of statements from sūtras, thematically arranged. In short, it is in this latter period that the sūtras, which seem at first to have been recited and worshiped, became, in addition, objects of scholastic reflection and analysis.

All Buddhist exegetes, regardless of scholastic or vehicular affiliation, were also faced with the problem of the interpretation of the sūtras. It is a common tenet of all schools of Buddhism that, just as a physician does not prescribe the same medicine to cure all maladies, so the Buddha did not teach the same thing to everyone. Therefore, two teachings could be the authentic word of the Buddha yet be at odds with each other. The Buddha is said to have taught different things to different people based on his extraordinary knowledge of their interests, capacities, dispositions, intelligence, and past lives. Yet as an enlightened being, the Buddha, and hence his teachings, must be free of all error and contradiction. How was one to harmonize the Buddha's statements in one context that "the self is one's protector" with his numerous declarations that "there is no self"? The Buddha may also appear to say something quite contrary to the tenor of the doctrine, unconstruable as even provisionally true. A commonly cited example of such a statement is the declaration in the *Dhammapada* that one becomes pure through killing one's parents, which the commentators must bring into doctrinal consistency by explaining that parents are to be understood here to mean negative mental states such as desire.

Such problems were only exacerbated by the Mahāyāna, where the Buddha's admonition in his first sermon that suffering is to be identified, its origin abandoned, its cessation attained, and the path to that cessation followed, had to somehow be made compatible with the statement that "there is no suffering, no origin, no cessation, no path." What did it mean to read in one sūtra that from the night of his enlightenment to the night that he passed into nirvāṇa the Buddha never stopped teaching the dharma and to read in another that from the night of his enlightenment to the night that he passed into nirvāṇa the Buddha did not utter a single word?

To answer such questions, one had to be able to claim knowledge of the Buddha's own intention, to know what the Buddha's final position on a given point of doctrine might have been, to know what the Buddha really meant. The major schools of Buddhist thought in Asia set forth their own position on the Buddha's final view. But they faced the larger problem of accounting for those statements that seemed to contradict what they understood the Buddha's final position to be on some point of doctrine.

One strategy adopted in the Theravāda was to classify the teachings of the Buddha in terms of the audience to whom he spoke and then rearrange them into a single progression to nirvāṇa, beginning with the most preliminary teachings and ending with the most advanced. Works such as the *Instructions on the Piṭaka* (*Peṭakopadesa*) explain that the teachings of the Buddha have been broken up according to meaning and phrasing, and they provide guidelines by which the interpreter can restore their original coherence. In order to achieve this, elaborate sets of interlocking categories are introduced, such as the three kinds of disciple to whom teachings are directed (the ordinary person, the learner, and the arhat); the three personality types (desirous, hateful, and deluded); the four basic topics dealt with in the sūtras (the afflictions, morality, insight, and the arhat). For example, sūtras on the afflictions set forth the effects of deeds motivated by desire, hatred, and delusion. Sūtras on morality set forth the benefits of deeds such as giving; a man who gave a garland of flowers to the Buddha was reborn in heaven for eighty-four thousand aeons. The teachings on the afflictions and on morality are directed to ordinary people. Sūtras on insight are intended for monks and set forth the path to nirvāṇa. Sūtras on arhats describe those who have destroyed desire, hatred, and ignorance and have no need to accumulate merit for rebirth in heaven, for they will enter nirvāṇa upon their death. Thus, the four kinds of sūtras are presented in a progression with the sūtras on morality superseding the sūtras on the afflictions, the sūtras on insight superseding the sūtras on morality, and the sūtras on the arhat superseding the sūtras on insight.

Another set of criteria, found in many texts, both "mainstream" (that is, non-Mahāyāna schools) and the Mahāyāna schools, is the so-called four reliances: (1) Rely on the dharma, not on the person. (2) Rely on the meaning, not on the letter. (3) Rely on the definitive meaning, not on the provisional meaning. (4) Rely on knowledge, not on (ordinary) consciousness. In themselves, these do not provide a great deal of clarity on the issue. They do, however, introduce two key terms that would themselves be subjected to wide interpretation: *provisional* and *definitive*.

In their most straightforward sense, *provisional* and *definitive* refer to individual statements and by extension to the sūtras in which those statements are contained. Those that cannot be taken literally are regarded as provisional or subject to interpretation. Those that can be taken literally are regarded as definitive. An example of a definitive statement is that giving gifts in the present results in wealth in the future, a simple articulation of the law of karma. The Buddha may also make a provisional statement, that is, something not to be taken literally, for any number of reasons. He may, for example, assure lazy persons who are incapable of any virtuous practice whatsoever that they will be reborn in Sukhāvatī, the paradise of Amitābha, if they will simply pray. He does this in order to cause them to accumulate a modest amount of merit, although he knows that they will not be reborn in the pure land immediately or even in their next lifetime but at some point in the distant future. In another case, when the Buddha encountered those who did not believe in rebirth and saw no existence beyond death, he taught the immortality of the soul and rebirth in different universes, although he knew in fact that there is no immortal soul.

Adapting his teachings to the needs of his audiences, the Buddha taught specific antidotes to various faults. Thus, as an antidote to hatred, he taught the cultivation of love; as an antidote to desire, he taught meditation on the foul, such as a decomposing corpse; as an antidote to pride, he taught meditation on dependent origination; as an antidote to a wandering mind, he taught meditation on the breath. He indicated that these faults can be completely destroyed by these antidotes, calling each of them a supreme vehicle. In fact, he knew that these faults can be completely destroyed only with full insight into the absence of self. Thus, the Buddha had overstated their potency. Elsewhere, he would criticize a virtue in an advanced disciple and praise it in a beginner, again seeking to inspire both to progress further on the path.

But the categories of the provisional and definitive do not solve the problem of the conflict of interpretation; they simply bring it into relief, as two famous sūtras demonstrate, sūtras in which the Buddha himself acknowledges the difficulty and provides criteria for adjudicating conflicts. Indeed, the Buddha does so in a number of texts, resulting in interpretative guidelines that themselves come into conflict yet must be regarded as the word of the Buddha.

The Buddha's first teaching of the four truths to the five ascetics in the deer park at Sarnath is known as the turning of the wheel of dharma. In a famous Mahāyāna text, the *Perfection of Wisdom in Eight Thousand Stanzas* (*Aṣṭasāhasrikāprajñāpāramitā*), the gods declare that when the Buddha taught the perfection of wisdom, he turned the wheel of the dharma a second time, superseding the first turning of the wheel. Yet another important Mahāyāna sūtra, called, interestingly, the *Sūtra Untying the Intention* (*Saṃdhinirmocana*), goes one step further, setting forth yet a third wheel. A bodhisattva explains that the first turning of the wheel had occurred in the deer park at Sarnath, where the Buddha had taught the four noble truths to those of the śrāvaka vehicle. Yet, he says, "This wheel of dharma turned by the Buddha is surpassable, an occasion [for refutation], provisional, and subject to dispute." Referring presumably to the perfection of wisdom sūtras, the bodhisattva goes on to explain that the Buddha then turned the wheel of dharma a second time for those who had entered the Mahāyāna, teaching them the doctrine of emptiness, that phenomena are "unproduced, unceased, originally quiescent, and naturally beyond sorrow." But this wheel also is provisional. The Buddha turned the wheel of doctrine a third time for those of all vehicles, clearly differentiating how things exist. "This wheel of doctrine turned by the Bhagavan is unsurpassed, not an occasion [for refutation], of definitive meaning; it is indisputable." The sūtra thus takes something of a historical perspective on the Buddha's teaching, declaring that both his first sermon on the four truths to śrāvakas and his teaching of the perfection of wisdom to bodhisattvas were not his final and most clearly delineated view. That view is found in the third turning of the wheel of dharma, a wheel that includes, minimally, the *Sūtra Untying the Intention* itself.

The *Sūtra Untying the Intention* is closely associated with the Yogācāra, one of the two major Mahāyāna schools in India, who accepted its chronology in order to support their superiority over the Madhyamaka (the other major school), whom they associated with the second wheel. As one might predict, the Madhyamakas, who regarded the teachings of the perfection of wisdom sūtras to be the Buddha's highest and final teaching, did not accept such a typology, declaring the *Sūtra Untying the Intention* itself to be provisional, intended for those lesser bodhisattvas who could not yet understand the profound emptiness. The opinion of the many non-Mahāyāna schools, whose teachings were consigned to the first wheel, are not known. They would presumably have dismissed the entire story as a concoction of the Mahāyāna, denying that it is the word of the Buddha.

At the same time, the Madhyamakas looked to a different sūtra for their understanding of what was provisional and what was definitive, an understanding that did not depend on the claim of insight into the Buddha's intention. The *Sūtra Taught to Akṣayamati* (*Akṣayamatinirdeśa*) declares, "Sūtras that teach the establishment of the conventional are called sūtras of provisional meaning. Those sūtras that teach the establishment of the ultimate are called sūtras of definitive meaning. Sūtras that teach with various words and letters are called sūtras of provisional meaning. Those sūtras that teach the profound—difficult to see and difficult to understand—are called sūtras of definitive meaning." That is, because emptiness is the definitive, final nature of reality, sūtras that set forth this final nature are definitive; all others require interpretation. This method of categorizing scripture focuses interpretation on the ontological question of the true nature of things, excluding from consideration questions of the Buddha's intention, the circumstances of his teaching, his audience, his skillful methods, and the literal acceptability of his words. It makes matters rather simple. Sūtras that speak about emptiness are definitive. Sūtras that discuss other topics are provisional. Thus, although it is certainly the case that the practice of giving brings about the karmic effect of wealth in the future, this is a provisional teaching because it does not set forth the true nature of giving; that is, it does not set forth the emptiness of giving. Such a scheme does not solve the question of what is literally acceptable, but it turns the question of interpretation away from intention. But the question of what was definitive and what was provisional was not solved by this sūtra or by any other and continued to pose problems for generations of thinkers throughout the Buddhist world.

In China, the problem of authenticity and interpretation was complicated by the fact that Buddhist texts arrived in a haphazard fashion over several centuries, and the Chinese were rightfully bewildered by the conflicting claims to authority made by various texts and teachers. They responded by devising a number of classification systems that attempted to order the various sūtras according to when they were taught during the Buddha's life and according to the audience to whom he taught them. As was the case in India, there was a divergence of opinion over chronology and over what constituted the Buddha's highest teaching: Was it the first thing he taught after his enlightenment or the last thing he taught before he passed into nirvāṇa? The Tientai school placed the *Lotus Sūtra* at the top of its hierarchy, for example, while the Huayan school reserved this position for the *Flower Garland Sūtra* (*Avataṃsaka*), which they claim was taught by the Buddha in the second week after his enlightenment, while he still sat beneath the Bodhi tree. It therefore represents his most immediate and direct expression of the content of his enlightenment, prior to the time that he rose from his seat to set out to teach a dharma modified in order that it be comprehended by a diverse audience of the unenlightened. Seeking to surpass the claim of a particular text as representing the Buddha's highest teaching (and thus proclaim its own legitimacy), Chan described itself as "a special transmission outside the teachings."

In Japan, one of the most comprehensive attempts to categorize the teachings of the Buddha (and establish the supremacy of his own school) was made by Kūkai (774–835), who outlined ten stages of spiritual development, beginning with a person of the most base concerns, whom he called the "goatlike," and moving gradually upward to those best served by Confucian teachings and then Daoist teachings. Moving then upward to Buddhism, he identified those best served by the teachings for śrāvakas, then pratyekabuddhas. Ascending to the Mahāyāna, he set forth the characteristics of those who would benefit from the Yogācāra, the Madhyamaka, the *Lotus Sūtra,* and the *Flower Garland Sūtra*. The most advanced disciples of all were worthy of the teachings of his own new school, the Shingon (True Word). It is noteworthy that in this scheme, all of the contemporary schools competing for royal favor in Japan are identified (although we have no evidence for a Goat School, its adherents were surely numerous) and are ranked, all below Kūkai's school.

Problems of interpretation were not limited to the Mahāyāna, with its seemingly endless array of sūtras to draw from. Nor were such problems confined to questions of authority, where one text was judged definitive while another was dismissed as provisional. Even among the mainstream schools of Indian Buddhism, schools whose canons of sūtras varied little, one finds a host of controversies over a host of options, some seemingly pedantic, others dealing with the question of how to interpret the most fundamental points of Buddhist doctrine.

Buddhism is famous for its doctrine of impermanence, which describes how all conditioned things are produced, abide for an instant, age, and then disintegrate. But precisely how does this process work? Is there an instant of production, an instant of abiding, an instant of aging, and an instant of disintegration? If so, it would seem that things do not last for an instant, as the sūtras declare, but for four instants, unless production, abiding, aging, and disintegration somehow occur simultaneously. And what precisely are production, abiding, aging, and disintegration? Are they inherent in all things, or are they separate and discrete entities, external forces that act upon things to cause them to be produced, abide, age, and disintegrate?

These were the kinds of problems that concerned the Abhidharma scholar-monks of schools like the Sarvāstivāda ("Proponents of Everything that Exists") and the Sautrāntika ("Followers of Sūtras") in India. The former held that production, abiding, aging, and disintegration (known as the "four characteristics") are conditions that all impermanent things possess and that perform the function of causing those things to be produced, abide, age, and disintegrate. (Permanent entities, such as space and nirvāṇa, are not susceptible to the four characteristics and are thus referred to as "unconditioned.") For example, production draws an entity out of the future and causes it to enter into the present. Yet even within the Sarvāstivāda, there was debate over whether there are four characteristics or three: to include "abiding" seems to some to run counter to the doctrine of impermanence. The Sarvāstivāda position was opposed by the Sautrāntika scholar Vasubandhu, who argued that the four characteristics are not separate entities but are instead descriptions or designations for processes that occur naturally to impermanent things without anything else acting upon them. Thus, when the necessary causes and conditions come together, something is produced. And once produced, nothing further is required for it to abide, age, and disintegrate. It is the nature of conditioned things to arise and pass away. He supported his argument by asserting that no statement by the Buddha can be found to support the separate existence of the four characteristics. The Sarvāstivāda opponent responded by providing such scriptural support. And so the debate continued. Such scholastic controversies were not limited to India but traveled with Buddhism across Asia.

HOW MANY VEHICLES TO ENLIGHTENMENT?

As discussed in chapter 2, the Mahāyāna sūtras proclaimed a bodhisattva path that was not reserved for a single individual in each age but was open to all who would develop the aspiration to buddhahood. This proclamation carried with it a reevaluation of the path that had previously been regarded as the ideal, the path of the arhat, culminating in a nirvāṇa that was the cessation of all suffering, and hence of mind and body. The nirvāṇa of the arhat was presented as a lesser attainment. But what precisely did this mean? What was the ultimate fate of the arhat? This question brings us again to the question of scriptural interpretation, for the Mahāyāna sūtras present two conflicting answers. The question is traditionally posed in terms of vehicles. Some sūtras said that there are three: the vehicle of the śrāvaka, the vehicle of the pratyekabuddha, and the vehicle of the bodhisattva. Some sūtras said that there is but one, the vehicle of the bodhisattva.

For those who championed one final vehicle, there was the prophecy in the *Lotus Sūtra* that the wisest of the śrāvakas, Śāriputra, would enter the bodhisattva path to eventually become the buddha named Padmaprabha. It must be possible, therefore, for the arhats not to pass into the nirvāṇa without remainder but to follow the long path to buddhahood. Those who argued for one vehicle, called the Mahāyāna, the "Great Vehicle," the *buddhayāna*, the

"Buddha Vehicle," or the *ekayāna,* "the Single Vehicle," proclaimed that the compassionate Buddha would not lead sentient beings to a lesser liberation than he himself had attained. For this reason, all beings in the universe will eventually become buddhas, regardless of which path they initially follow. Thus, the nirvāṇa of the śrāvaka is like an illusory city conjured by a skillful guide, a way station for weary travelers to keep them from turning back on their long journey to a distant goal. Such statements suggest that the nirvāṇa of the Hīnayāna is a penultimate achievement. Those who upheld this position argued that the presence of the buddha nature in all beings provides further proof of one final vehicle, that all beings are endowed with the buddha nature and, consequently, all are of the buddha lineage.

Yet the proponents of one vehicle were also confronted with a historical dilemma: the fate of great arhats of the past who achieved liberation and passed into nirvāṇa without recourse to the Mahāyāna. If all beings are destined to enter the Mahāyāna and become buddhas, what is to be done about the arhats who have already entered the nirvāṇa without remainder? The proponents of one vehicle, if they wished to uphold their position, have to redefine nirvāṇa, not as a state of the utter cessation of mind and body, but as a state in which mind and body persist in a purified form. That is, in order to bring the arhats of the past on to the Great Vehicle, it was necessary to deny the existence of a nirvāṇa without remainder, the state that, according to the earlier tradition (and competing traditions) the arhat entered, never to emerge. The proponents of one vehicle therefore accepted that arhats sever the continuum of a birth and death that are the products of the afflictions and the actions they induce, but they held that this does not entail the final annihilation of mind and body. Indeed, they argued that it is simply unseemly to think that the buddhas, knowing the supremacy of the Mahāyāna, would, in the final analysis, teach anything else. And so they claimed that there is but one vehicle because it is unthinkable that there be three. But even if the nirvāṇa of the arhats is merely a contrivance of the compassionate Buddha, the Mahāyāna must provide some explanation of their attainment and give some account of their whereabouts. Thus, arhats abandon the afflictions of the realms of rebirth and, consequently, are not born there. Instead, they take birth in a pure land in a meditation body seated inside a closed lotus blossom, and they abide in this uncontaminated realm for many aeons until the time when they are roused from their deep meditation by buddhas, who exhort them to enter the Mahāyāna. They then return to saṃsāra by their own wish and undertake the long path of the bodhisattva.

The opposing view was held by the proponents of three vehicles. They turned for scriptural support to the *Sūtra Untying the Intention,* which explained that śrāvakas are incapable of entering the Mahāyāna and achieving buddhahood, "because their compassion is meager and they are horrified by suffering and because they are naturally of an inferior lineage." The possibility of transferring to the Great Vehicle was held out for some, but they must do so before entering the nirvāṇa without remainder; those arhats who have entered the nirvāṇa in which the mind and body no longer remain cannot return to saṃsāra to undertake the bodhisattva path. But arhats who have achieved the nirvāṇa with remainder, that is, those who have destroyed the afflictions but continue to experience the effects of the karma that caused their present lifetime, are able to lengthen that lifetime magically to enable themselves to begin the bodhisattva path. Thus, the proponents of three vehicles were in a sense more traditional, retaining the category of the nirvāṇa without remainder as it was understood by the non-Mahāyāna schools but reserving it only for those who fail to undertake the bodhisattva path.

Those who argued for three vehicles pointed out that sentient beings differ in their personalities. Some delight in the sufferings of others, some are pained by them. These various dispositions are neither the result of social conditioning nor the products of past karma. Instead they are, in effect, genetically determined by a seed, a potency, possessed by each sentient being, present from the beginningless beginning of saṃsāra. The proponents of three vehicles postulate a kind of spiritual determinism in the form of three lineages: the śrāvaka lineage, the pratyekabuddha lineage, and the bodhisattva lineage. From the presence of these three lineages, a corresponding set of ultimate destinations is inferred. Those with the śrāvaka seed attain the nirvāṇa of the śrāvaka, those with the pratyekabuddha seed attain the nirvāṇa of a pratyekabuddha, those with the bodhisattva seed attain the unsurpassed enlightenment of the buddha. Because arhats who have entered the remainderless nirvāṇa of the śrāvaka and pratyekabuddha have abandoned all the causes for rebirth in saṃsāra, it is impossible for them ever to achieve buddhahood, which requires many more lifetimes of practice. This is their fate, determined by their seed. Thus, for the proponents of three vehicles, not all beings have the buddha nature. Some have the śrāvaka seed and they will become arhats, some have the pratyekabuddha seed and they will also become arhats, some have the bodhisattva seed and they will become buddhas. Unwilling to deny the possibility that some śrāvakas become bodhisattvas, the proponents of three vehicles also said that some possess an undetermined seed, which means that they may begin one path and then move to another.

As with the case of other clashes of scriptural interpretation, the problem is not so much finding support for one's own position as accounting for the fact that the Buddha seems also to support the opposing position. As one might expect by now, both parties ascribed the opponent's position to the Buddha's skillful methods in compassionately teaching what is not ultimately the truth to those who are not prepared for it. Thus, the proponents of one vehicle would claim that the Buddha taught that there are three vehicles to those who are unable to comprehend the grandeur of the single vehicle. The proponents of three vehicles are somewhat more specific. A text called the *Ornament for the Mahāyāna Sūtras* (*Mahāyānasūtrālaṃkāra*) explains, "In order to lead some, in order to hold others, the perfect buddhas teach one vehicle to the uncertain." Those to be led are śrāvakas and pratyekabuddhas of indefinite lineage, that is, those who have entered the Hīnayāna path but are not predestined to complete it. They are told by the Buddha that there is but one vehicle, which begins with the practices of śrāvakas and then proceeds to the practices of bodhisattvas. The others, those to be held, are bodhisattvas of indefinite lineage, who are in danger of forsaking the Mahāyāna because they have become discouraged about saṃsāra when they see that sentient beings irrationally do one another harm. To keep them from despondently turning to the śrāvaka vehicle and seeking liberation for themselves alone, the Buddha tells them that there is but one vehicle, the Mahāyāna, that there is no other alternative.

The apparent inclusivism of one vehicle and the exclusivism of three vehicles should not obscure the fact that each of these Mahāyāna doctrines also performs a certain polemical role in its treatment of the prior tradition, which they name the Hīnayāna. By claiming that there are three vehicles, the presence of the prior path and its goal of the nirvāṇa without remainder is conceded but deposed to a lesser rank. By claiming that there is but one vehicle, the prior tradition is subsumed entirely as an expedient teaching, offered to those of lesser capacity until they are prepared to receive the true dharma.

THE POWER OF THE WORD

The interpretation of an individual sūtra and the attempt to make sense of conflicting claims of multiple sūtras remained constant concerns of scholar-monks across the Buddhist world. But these sūtras were not simply the purview of the scholastics, and they were not simply read as repositories of arcane doctrine. As the word of the Buddha—whether provisional or definitive mattered little—the same sūtras that were mined for doctrinal positions held other treasures for those who could read them, recite them, or simply pronounce their names.

Buddhism shared with other Indian traditions an abiding belief in the power of sound. The dharma is called the word of the Buddha, and sūtras begin with the testimony, "Thus did I hear." Even with the great proliferation of writing that resulted in a massive corpus of sūtras, and the continued composition of texts throughout the Buddhist world, there is almost always some attempt to preserve the pretense of speech. In the case of the Mahāyāna sūtras, the anonymous author served merely as a scribe, writing down what has been heard from a buddha, a bodhisattva, or a deity in a vision or in a dream or recording what has been passed down from long ago. The trope of dictation pertained in realms both human and divine. Certain tantric texts were said to have been spoken by the bodhisattva Vajrapāṇi on a mountain in a mythic Sri Lanka (considered a place of mystery and danger in much Indian literature) to five sages, one of whom, a kind of demon known as a *rākṣasa,* inscribed them in malachite ink on pages of gold. The texts were then placed into a treasure chest, which was hidden in the sky and watched over by goddesses.

The words of sūtras and tantras, whether inscribed on pages of gold, etched on to palm leaves, written on scrolls of paper, or carved into wooden blocks, retained a power that was released when the words were read aloud, and recitation has been regarded as an efficacious practice throughout the Buddhist world. In Sri Lanka, sūtras or portions of sūtras called *pirit* ("protection") are chanted by Buddhist monks as a means of averting danger. In the ceremony a long thread is twisted around the neck of a clay pot filled with water. One end of the thread is held by the chanting monks, the other end by those assembled to receive the blessings. The power of the recitation is thus channeled through the thread from the monks to the audience. After the ceremony, the water in the pot is sprinkled on the audience and the thread is broken into pieces and distributed, to be worn around the wrist or neck as a kind of talisman.

In a Japanese tale, a monk had memorized the entire *Lotus Sūtra* and chanted it regularly but was consistently unable to remember two words in the second chapter, *pure heart.* He went to the Hasedera temple and prayed to the famous statue of the bodhisattva of compassion. After seven days, a man appeared to him in a dream and explained that in his past life he had been reading the *Lotus Sūtra* near a fire, when an ember jumped from the flame and landed on the scroll, burning those two characters. He did not repair the text before he died. As a result, he would not be able to remember those words in his next life unless he made amends. The man repented his misdeed, whereupon he was able to recite the sūtra without difficulty. He traveled to the town where the man in the dream had told him he had lived in his last life. He found his former parents, who showed him the damaged copy of the sūtra, which he repaired. He served his parents of this life and his last life and practiced the teachings of the *Lotus Sūtra*.

But the sūtras seem also to have taken cognizance of their own prolixity and often offered, again within the sūtra itself, alternatives to the memorization and mastery of the contents of an entire text. Among these were *dhāraṇīs*, essentially long mantras, that were said to contain, in a highly condensed form, the essence of the sūtra. Hence, the recitation of the dhāraṇī functioned as the retention of the sūtra. Some scholars of Buddhism have regarded the proliferation of mantras and dhāraṇīs in Buddhist texts as late accretions, signs of the degeneration of the original rationalistic creed of the Buddha into popular superstition. However, even in the Pali suttas, once considered by some to be the closest approximation of what the Buddha taught, one finds short recitations that are prescribed to protect against certain maladies and dangers, such as snakebites. Nor should the presence of such spells be regarded as a concession to the unlettered; stories abound of great scholar-monks also being adept at the recitation of mantra. Instead, these mantras, which have been transliterated into the vernaculars of the Buddhist world in order to preserve their sound, offer testimony to the enduring power of speech.

And the power of mantra is great. The wrathful bodhisattva Vajrapāṇi was able to subdue all the deities in the universe simply by intoning the mantra *hūṃ*, causing them, on threat of death, to take refuge in the Buddha, dharma, and saṅgha. Only the chief of gods, Śiva, remained unwilling to submit, even after Vajrapāṇi revived him from death. Vajrapāṇi had Śiva and his consort dragged upside down into his presence, as all the world laughed at them. He then placed his left foot on the prone Śiva and his right foot on his consort and intoned a mantra that caused Śiva to strike his one thousand heads with his one thousand arms, inflicting great pain upon himself. Vajrapāṇi then recited the mantra of love, *oṃ buddha maitri vajra rakṣa hūṃ*, whereby the soles of his feet transmitted not misery but deliverance, and Śiva experienced the bliss of the liberation of all the buddhas and was instantly born as a buddha in a distant universe.

Mantras thus have power even over gods. They seem also to have power over something more powerful than the gods, the inexorable law of karma. A criminal sentenced to death wore a bracelet inscribed with the mantra of a goddess known as one of the five protectors. He chanted the mantra as the executioners raised their swords to behead him, and the swords were smashed to pieces. Next he was thrown into a cave of monsters, but his body blazed with flame and the monsters were afraid to eat him. Next he was bound and thrown into a river, but the river dried up. The king commuted his sentence. (Should the reader be interested, the mantra is *oṃ namo bhagavatyai āryamahāratisarāyai.*)

This mantra is so powerful that it could even counteract the karma of other beings. A particularly greedy monk who stole offerings left at the foot of a stūpa was afflicted with a terrible disease as the result of his misdeeds. A kind man placed an amulet with the mantra around the monk's neck. The monk regained consciousness long enough to regret his misdeeds but died that same night and was reborn in the most torturous hell. Immediately the fires of hell became extinguished and could not be rekindled and the sufferings of the denizens of hell were relieved. The demons of the Lord of Death were unable to slice the bodies of the damned, denizens cast into the Grove of Swords emerged unscathed, their beds of needles felt like velvet, the cauldrons of molten lead had become mysteriously cool. When they complained to the Lord of Death, he explained to them that a bodhisattva had died in the city of Puṣkarāvatī and that his body, bearing an amulet with the dhāraṇī, was being protected and honored by gods. The demons went to the city and saw that this was true; when they returned to hell, the spirit of the monk had already departed, to be reborn in the Heaven of the Thirty-Three.

The perfection of wisdom sūtras are renowned for their declaration of the emptiness of all things, identifying the insight into emptiness as the perfect wisdom that bestows buddhahood. If the perfection of wisdom has the power to destroy the most pernicious ignorance, it is reasonable to assume that it should also be a potent weapon against less formidable foes. This is confirmed by the sūtras themselves. In the *Perfection of Wisdom in Eight Thousand Stanzas,* the deity Māra assembles an army of demons to attack the Buddha. Discerning their approach, the king of gods, Indra, calls to mind and then recites the perfection of wisdom, and the demons are repulsed. The perfection of wisdom sūtras have retained this talismanic power throughout the Mahāyāna world. Among the many perfection of wisdom sūtras, none is considered more efficacious than the *Heart Sūtra,* praised as their essence. The *Heart Sūtra* need not be recited; its very inscription offers protection, and today in Japan one can purchase fans, neckties, credit cards, and tea mugs decorated with the characters of the *Heart Sūtra.* A Japanese story illustrates its magical powers.

A blind boy named Hōichi had the rare ability to recite the epic *Tale of Heike* in a beautiful voice, accompanying himself on a stringed instrument called a *biwa.* He lived in the temple of Amidaji, near the town of Shimonoseki on the coast of southern Honshu, near the site of the decisive battle in which the ships of the Heike clan met their doom. Late one summer evening, Hōichi was sitting outside playing the biwa when he heard someone call his name. From the sound of the footsteps, he knew that the mysterious visitor was a samurai warrior in full armor. He told Hōichi that his lord was passing through the area and wished to have the epic performed, especially the part that told of the final sea battle. Hōichi was led to what must have been an opulent villa where the women spoke in the refined language of the court. He was given a kneeling cushion and began to sing the mournful song of the battle. His performance was so poignant that the whispered expressions of admiration of his voice soon changed to sobs and wails. The lord himself was so moved that he invited Hōichi to return for six more nights. The soldier then led the blind boy back to the temple before daybreak.

The next night the soldier arrived at the appointed hour and brought Hōichi back to the villa. This time, however, some servants of the monastery followed. They lost Hōichi in the evening fog but eventually heard his song in the distance and followed it to the cemetery of Amidaji, where Hōichi sat alone. They led him back to the monastery, where one of the monks determined what had happened. Hōichi was in grave danger, for he had not been taken to a villa each night but to a cemetery, where he performed not for a noble family and its retainers, but for the ghosts of the Heike clan, who listened rapt to the story of their own demise. On the night that he completed his song, he would surely be killed.

That night, the abbot devised a plan to save his life. The monks took calligraphy brushes and ink and wrote the words of the *Heart Sūtra* over every inch of Hōichi's body. This would render him invisible to the ghosts. If Hōichi sat silent and did not betray his presence with his voice when the soldier came to fetch him that night, the ghost would not find him. The next morning the monks discovered Hōichi sitting in the monastery's garden, alive. But blood was flowing from holes on either side of his head, holes where his ears had been. The monks had forgotten to write the sūtra on his ears, which alone had remained visible to the puzzled ghost, who tore them off and took them with him to present to his lord. From then on, the famous singer of the *Tale of Heike* was known as Miminashi Hōichi, "Hōichi the Earless."

As this story illustrates, written records of the words of the Buddha were themselves potent objects of devotion. It is typical for a Mahāyāna sūtra to contain a detailed description of the benefits that accrue from its copying. The *Lotus* states that anyone who copies the *Lotus Sūtra* will, without even reading or reciting it, be reborn in their next life as a god in the Heaven of the Thirty-Three. And texts were indeed copied; scrolls have been preserved in Chinese of numerous texts, often the Guanyin chapter of the *Lotus,* written in the scribe's blood. Colophons identify all manner of motivations, seeking that the merit resulting from the act of copying go to assist a deceased family member in finding a good rebirth, that the merit be retained for future use to provide a happy rebirth for the scribe, or that it relieve the sickness of a loved one.

In a Theravāda text, the *Chronicle of Discourses on the Scriptures* (*Sangītīyavaṃsa*), the Buddha explains the eighty-four thousand units of the dharma. Those eighty-four thousand units are like eighty-four thousand buddhas who will teach after he is gone. Thus anyone who preserves the dharma by copying the tripiṭaka will accrue the merit of preserving eighty-four thousand buddhas; each letter is an image of the Buddha. The same text explains that anyone who builds a library for the dharma will be reborn as the lord of four continents, surrounded by two thousand islands, with eighty-four thousand palaces made of various precious stones. Those who give cloth for the wrapping of books will receive eighty-four thousand treasuries; those who give string for tying books will receive inexhaustible wealth; those who give wicker cabinets for books will receive eighty-four thousand palaces made of gems.

The *Lotus* recommends five practices for preachers of the dharma: receiving and maintaining the sūtra, reading it, reciting it, copying it, and explaining it to others. It is noteworthy that reading and reciting are listed separately, suggesting that these were regarded as different acts. Reciting, especially from memory, was considered to be particularly potent. But each of these five practices was performed in China, and miraculous tales are told about them. During the reign of the Emperor Wu-cheng of the Northern Qi, a man was once digging on the slope of a mountain when he unearthed what appeared to be a pair of human lips, with a tongue protruding from between them. He reported his discovery to the emperor, who asked various scholars what the significance might be. A learned monk explained that the sense faculties of anyone who recites the *Lotus Sūtra* more than one thousand times are not subject to decay, even after death. The emperor dispatched some monks to the site, where they placed the lips and tongue on an altar, circumambulated it, and offered incense. In response to their request that it manifest its marvelous powers, the tongue and lips began to move, as if chanting.

Certainly the most extreme form of devotion to the *Lotus* derived from the twenty-third chapter in which a bodhisattva named Bhaiṣajyarāja ("Medicine King") in a previous life decided to express his dedication to a buddha by transforming himself into a flame. In order to do this, he ingested all manner of oils and fragrances for twelve hundred years. He then coated his body with oil, donned a jeweled cloak soaked in oil, and set himself ablaze, creating a light that illumined the universe for twelve hundred years. Reborn in the presence of the buddha he had so honored, he was entrusted with the task of cremating the buddha upon his death, collecting his relics, and erecting stūpas. Having completed this task, he immolated his forearm in offering. His deed was praised by the Buddha, who remarked that burning even a finger or a toe as an offering to a stūpa accrues greater merit than offering all that is precious in the universe. Although there is little evidence to suggest that such a practice was emulated in India, it was in China, where cases of self-immolation have been documented into the twentieth century. Stories are told of monks and nuns who wrap themselves in waxed cloth and then set themselves alight, chanting the twenty-third chapter of the *Lotus Sūtra* until their voices fall silent. A less extreme and far more common practice was the burning of fingers or the joints of fingers. The finger (or joint) would be anaesthetized by tying a string very tightly below the portion to be burned, in order to cut off the circulation. The finger would next be wrapped in pine resin and sandalwood and then set ablaze, as the monk (and those who attended him) chanted. Here, the *Lotus Sūtra,* which elsewhere explains that the Buddha does not always mean what he says, seems to have been taken quite literally.

Suggested Reading

Buswell, Robert E., Jr., and Robert Gimello, eds. *Paths to Liberation: The Mārga and Its Transformations in Buddhist Thought.* Honolulu: University of Hawaii Press, 1992.

Cox, Collett. *Disputed Dharmas: Early Buddhist Theories of Existence.* Tokyo: International Institute for Buddhist Studies, 1995.

Hakeda, Yoshito S. *Kūkai: Major Works.* New York: Columbia University Press, 1972.

Lamotte, Étienne. *History of Indian Buddhism.* Louvain, Belgium: Peeters Press, 1988.

Lopez, Donald S., Jr. *Elaborations on Emptiness: Uses of the Heart Sūtra.* Princeton: Princeton University Press, 1996.

———, ed. *Buddhism in Practice.* Princeton: Princeton University Press, 1995.

———. *Buddhist Hermeneutics*. Honolulu: University of Hawaii Press, 1988.

Mizuno, Kōgen. *Buddhist Sūtras: Origin, Development, Transmission*. Tokyo: Kōsei Publishing Company, 1982.

Wisdom of the Buddha: The Saṁdhinirmocana Mahāyāna Sūtra. Translated by John Powers. Berkeley: Wisdom Publications, 1995.

4

MONASTIC LIFE

It is difficult to overstate the centrality of the saṅgha for the practice of Buddhism. Buddhist nations tend to tell their histories around the founding of monasteries. After the death of the Buddha the decline of the dharma is measured in degrees of deviation of monks from their vows. Buddhist history and Buddhist texts agree that without monks there can be no Buddhism, a view supported by Buddhist views of the end time. In the final stages of disappearance of the dharma, it is said that when all Buddhist texts disappear, the last to go will be the codes of monastic discipline, at which point the saffron robes of the monks will turn white, the color of the robes of the laymen.

The Buddha and his followers probably began as a group of wandering ascetics, who required only four things: a tree to sleep beneath, alms food to eat, rag robes to wear, and fermented cow's urine for medicine. The traditional possessions of a monk (greatly expanded in practice in many places throughout the Buddhist world) were a set of three robes, a begging bowl, a belt, a razor for shaving the head, a needle for sewing the robes, a water strainer to prevent the unintentional consumption of insects, a walking staff, and a toothpick. Sandals for feet, a sitting pad for the ground, an umbrella for the sun, and a fan for heat were also permitted. Although in the early years the Buddha and his monks are said to have wandered during all seasons, they soon adopted the practice of other ascetic groups of remaining in one place during the months of the rainy season that occurs in northern India from the middle of July to the middle of October. Wealthy patrons had shelters built for their use, with the end of the rainy season marking a special occasion for making offerings of food and provisions (especially cloth for robes) to monks. These shelters eventually evolved into monasteries that were inhabited throughout the year. It seems that early on in the tradition, the saṅgha became largely sedentary, although the tradition of the wandering monk continued. Whether they wandered without a fixed abode or lived in monasteries, monks and nuns who lived in a designated region were expected to gather twice a month, at the full moon and new moon, to confess and affirm their vows communally. This practice was strictly followed in some parts of the Buddhist world, virtually ignored in others.

One indication that the domestication of the saṅgha must have occurred early in the tradition is the fact that a range of activities classically associated with the Buddhist monk came to be regarded as ascetic practices followed only by the most devoted of renunciates. Thirteen such practices are enumerated: wearing robes made from discarded cloth rather than from cloth donated by laypeople (there were apparently laypeople who had their servants guard piles of old rags so that they could be taken only by Buddhist monks); wearing only three robes; eating only food acquired through begging rather than meals presented to the saṅgha; begging for food from house to house rather than begging only at those houses known to provide good food; eating only what can be eaten in one sitting; eating only what can be placed in one bowl; refusing more food once one has indicated that one has eaten enough; dwelling in the forest; dwelling at the foot of a tree; dwelling in the open air, using only a tent made from one's robes as shelter; dwelling in a charnel ground; sleeping in any bed that is offered, without concern for its quality; and never lying down. Indeed, one of the schisms that occurred in the saṅgha during the Buddha's life involved a dispute over the degree of asceticism required of monks. The Buddha's cousin, Devadatta, led a faction that favored a more extreme discipline than that counseled by the Buddha, requiring, for example, that monks live only in the forest and never eat meat. When Devadatta failed in winning control of the order, he tried to assassinate the Buddha by sending a wild elephant to trample him and later by rolling a boulder down upon him. But the elephant stopped in his charge and bowed at the Buddha's feet, and a piece of the rock only grazed the Buddha's toe. Nonetheless, Chinese pilgrims to India many centuries later encountered monks that followed the discipline of Devadatta. Another schism arose between monks of a monastery over a minor infraction of lavatory etiquette. Unable to settle the dispute, the Buddha retired to the forest to live among the elephants for an entire rainy season.

The saṅgha was by no means a homogeneous community. The vinaya texts describe monks from a wide variety of social backgrounds. Mention is made of monks from all four of India's social castes. There was also a wide variety of monastic specialties. The texts describe monks who are skilled in speech, those who memorize and recite the sūtras, those who memorize and recite the vinaya, and those who memorize and recite lists of technical terms. There were also monks who specialized in meditation, monks who served as advisers to kings, and monks responsible for the administration of the monastery and its property. This last responsibility required all manner of specific skills, including the keeping of keys, the regulation of bathrooms, the acquisition of land, the administration of sharecropping, and the supervision of labor (including that of lay servants who had been donated to the monastery, who may or may not be regarded as "slaves"). One of the tasks of the monastery administration was to ensure that the wandering monks were not given mundane work, that meditating monks not be disturbed by noise, and that monks who begged for alms received good food. The famous sixth-century Chinese text, the *Lives of Eminent Monks* (*Gaoseng zhuan*), categorizes its subjects under ten categories: translators, exegetes, theurgists, meditators, disciplinarians, self-immolators, cantors, promoters of good works, hymnodists, and sermonizers, and these categories only comprise the eminent.

As the defining sign of a monk or nun, robes are discussed at great length in Buddhist literature. Although the robes differ greatly in color and design across the Buddhist world, each tradition regards its style of robes to have been sanctioned by the Buddha and to be replete with Buddhist symbolism. Tibetan monks wear a vest under their upper robe that is said to signify the gaping mouth of the Lord of Death, thereby serving as a constant reminder of impermanence. Although sandals were sometimes disdained as a luxury during the time of the Buddha (and remain so in parts of Southeast

Asia), Tibetan monks wear high boots with features resembling a rooster, a snake, and a pig, the standard symbols of desire, hatred, and ignorance, which the monk tramples with every step.

As the symbol of monkhood, the robes are to be regarded by the laity as they would a stūpa, regardless of the purity of the one who wears them; the beauty of the jasmine flower is not diminished by the fact that some of the blossoms are eaten by insects. At the same time, there are vivid cautions against shaming the robes. In one sūtra the Buddha says that it would be preferable for someone to wrap his body in burning sheets of iron than for a monk who has broken the precepts to accept a gift of robes from a faithful layman; the man who wears the iron sheets must suffer only until his quick death, but the monk who accepts the robes will burn in hell for aeons. Indeed, the improper comportment of monks, from the way they wear their robes to their disposition of offerings to their relations with women, is often decried in Buddhist texts, sometimes in the form of prophecies, in which the Buddha predicts the sad state of affairs that will pertain in the future. These descriptions are thought to derive from contemporary sources, placed in the mouth of the Buddha as a social commentary on the state of the saṅgha and what must be done to correct it. A nineteenth-century Cambodian text describes a time of warfare and chaos in which the seasons are reversed and monks break the monastic code. The period ends in a seven-year battle in which blood flows as high as the belly of an elephant and only four monks are left alive. This text has been used in recent years to explain the reign of the Khmer Rouge, during which almost a quarter of the Cambodian people lost their lives and Buddhism was nearly destroyed.

The practice of begging for alms, going silently with lowered eyes from door to door, seems to have become less common as Buddhist monks became more sedentary, and it was irregularly practiced in the Buddhist world. The practice has largely disappeared in Sri Lanka yet is important in Thailand, especially after reforms in the late nineteenth century. Monks did not beg in Tibet; the monastic population was too large and the distances too great. Monks seem also not to have gone on begging rounds in China, although some large monasteries would have an annual procession, complete with chanting, drums, and gongs, in which the local populace would turn out to make offerings of money, rice, incense, and medicine. Begging for alms may have been rare even in India, resorted to only under unusual circumstances of need. Indeed, monks and nuns in India seem to have maintained their private property upon entering the saṅgha, sometimes building their own monasteries, and to have inherited property on the death of their parents; the names of monks and nuns figure prominently in the lists of donors of stūpas and statues, with inscriptions dedicating the merit of the gift to the welfare of their parents and of all beings or to the health of a family member or friend.

The saṅgha was also a community where disputes arose and had to be settled. Here we find not a romantic scene of monks living apart from the world, devoting every waking moment to the practice of meditation, but a perhaps more human world where monks and nuns, far from being dead to the world, are much a part of it. They are just as concerned, for example, with the funeral rites of their parents as any layperson might be. And they are concerned that their own funerals be properly performed. A vinaya text tells of a deceased monk who haunts the monastery because his possessions have been divided among the community without a proper funeral ceremony being performed for him. Indeed, there seem to have been rather strict property lines in the Indian monastery, with some goods belonging to the stūpa, some goods belonging to the saṅgha in a general sense, and some belonging to individual monks. It was important that these divisions be respected and that goods belonging to the stūpa, for example, not be used for the saṅgha, unless the goods were borrowed and a proper accounting was made, including a notation of when the goods would be returned.

Upon the death of an ordinary monk in a Chinese Buddhist monastery (as opposed to an abbot, who received a more elaborate funeral), the local authorities were notified and permission to perform the funeral requested. The corpse was then washed and the head shaved. Dressed in clean robes, the corpse was placed in a round coffin, seated in the meditation posture. The coffin remained in the monastery's infirmary, adorned with flowers and banners inscribed with Buddhist teachings. Monks assembled before the coffin to chant the name of Amitābha and to recite the monastic vows. The next day, incense was offered at the coffin and the name of Amitābha chanted, and the coffin was carried by monastery workers to the cremation site, followed by a procession of monks. Upon arrival, the monks burned incense and recited scriptures on behalf of the deceased monk. The abbot of the monastery then delivered a brief sermon before he lit the funeral pyre. After more chanting of sūtras and of Amitābha's name, the monks returned to the monastery. The next day, a monk returned to the cremation site to gather the ashes, either to be cast into a river or installed in a stone pagoda.

It is a common misconception that Buddhist monks and nuns do not eat meat. In the early tradition, monks and nuns were enjoined to eat whatever was placed in their begging bowls, and the Buddha himself is said to have died from eating bad pork. In later Indian Buddhism, injunctions against meat eating occur in some Mahāyāna sūtras, including the *Mahānirvāṇa Sūtra,* regarded as the Buddha's final instructions. These statements came to be regarded as definitive in China, where monks and nuns abstained from meat as well as from what were known as the five strong flavors: leeks, garlic, onions, ginger, and scallions. The prohibition against eating meat in China led to something that the Buddha perhaps had not intended: the development of a tradition of opulent vegetarian cuisine, complete with tofu creations that looked and tasted exactly like chicken and pork. Such dishes can still be found on the menus of Chinese restaurants with such names as "Arhat's Delight." This sumptuous tradition continued in Japan, where the monastery and nunnery became fashionable sites for noblemen and women to retire from the world after a shift in the winds of power.

Throughout the Buddhist world, monks and laypeople have lived in a symbiotic relationship: the laity provide material support for monks while monks provide a locus for the layperson's accumulation of the merit that results from supporting monks who maintain their vows. This merit was often very specifically directed, with donors providing donations in exchange for which the monks performed recitations of sūtras, the resulting merit being assigned to the donor or the donor's deceased relative. Monks were often constrained not only to accept gifts from the laity but to use them, whether or not they had any need for them, in order that the donor's merit could be obtained. Even for a monk to accept a gift from a layperson and then offer it elsewhere was frowned upon. The merit of the gift resulted from the gift being used, and gifts of a more permanent nature, such as a monk's cell, would continue to accrue merit for the donor after the donor's death. Thus, although there are certainly exceptions, one does not often find in the Buddhist world monasteries sponsoring charitable activities or founding orphanages and hospitals, especially in the premodern period. There are many stories of the compassionate deeds of Buddhist monks, and many monks have effectively encouraged the laity in such activities, but for the most part Buddhist monasteries have been understood as factories for the making of merit; more tangible forms of value have therefore generally flowed into the monastery rather than out of it.

The distinction between monk and layperson is thus generally sharply drawn, even in Japan, where, since the Meiji era, monks have married. The distinction is not so much about celibacy, although outside Japan the pretense of celibacy and its attendant misogyny have remained important. The distinction is, instead, one of a division of labor. The role of the monk is to maintain a certain purity, largely through keeping an elaborate set of vows. Such purity renders the monk as a suitable "field of merit" to whom laypeople can make offerings, thereby accumulating the favorable karma that will result in a happy rebirth in the next life. This view persists in modern Japan. The so-called training monasteries of the Sōtō Zen sect are special centers where young monks train for two or three years to receive instruction in meditation (often the only sustained period of meditation practice of a Zen priest) and engage in various rituals of austerity. Because of the potency and purity of these monks, the training monasteries are considered particularly auspicious sites for the offering of prayers for the concerns of everyday life, called "this-worldly benefits" (*genze riyaku*) in Japanese.

By adopting a certain lifestyle, in which the transient pleasures of married life are renounced, monks provide the opportunity for the layperson to amass a certain karmic capital. In return, monks receive the fruits of labor of the laity—labor that they themselves have eschewed—in the form of their physical support. More specifically, monks do what laypeople cannot do because they generally do not know how: recite texts, remain celibate, perform rituals, and sometimes meditate. Laypeople do those things that monks are forbidden to do: till the soil, engage in business, raise families. (In Southeast Asia, monks should not touch money. In China and Tibet, where lay and state support for monks was often less generous than in some Theravāda countries, monks commonly engaged in commerce, either individually or on behalf of the monastery.) The rules and regulations in the vinaya texts were meant to govern the lives of Buddhist monks and to structure their relations with the laity. Monks in the vinaya literature are caught in a web of social and ritual obligations; they participate in a wide range of domestic rituals, from those at a child's birth to those at a patron's death. In Buddhist traditions across Asia, ritual maintenance of these monastic codes has served as the mark of orthodoxy, much more than adherence to a particular belief or doctrine. Indeed, it is said that the teaching of the Buddha will endure only as long as the vinaya endures.

Buddhist monks have traditionally been consulted by laypeople on all manner of personal affairs, such as the best date for starting the construction of a house or having a wedding. Some monks have been valued for their knowledge of astrology and hence their ability to predict the future. Other monks have gained reputations as healers with the power to cure illnesses and make amulets. In many Buddhist countries, the largest communal interactions between monks and laypeople occur at festivals. One such festival is the annual celebration of the Buddha's birthday in Korean monasteries. Much of the monastery remains off limits to laypeople during the year, but this rule is relaxed for the festival to celebrate the Buddha's birth. On the morning before the main ceremony, many monasteries hold a ceremony of bathing the Buddha. In a small building draped with flowers is placed a statue of the baby Buddha at the moment of his birth, standing upright, with his right arm raised, proclaiming that he is foremost among gods and humans. Laypeople line up to make offerings to the Buddha and receive from the monks a small cup of water, which they pour over the head of the statue, bathing the Buddha. They then receive a cup of medicinal water to drink.

This simple ceremony is a source of great income for the monastery. On the Buddha's birthday itself, the monks string hundreds of paper lanterns on cords that connect every building in the monastery compound. The most elaborate lanterns are shaped like lotus flowers. Laypeople line up at the main gate of the monastery and make offerings to the monastery, in return for which the monks write the names of the family, including the deceased members, on a merit certificate. Each of these certificates is next attached to a lantern. If any lanterns are left without certificates, the monks will write the names of their own relatives on a certificate and paste it to a lamp. In the evening, the laypeople go out in search of the lamp with their certificate, place a candle inside, and light it. The monks light the unlit lamps. The monks and laypeople stroll around the monastery to enjoy the sight of the lamps in the spring evening, sometimes climbing a hill for a more panoramic view. Throughout the evening, the monks take turns going to the main hall to join in the chant of "Sokkamuni-pul," Śākyamuni Buddha.

Many motives, in addition to the desire for liberation from rebirth, have moved men to become monks. Buddhist texts themselves concede that monkhood provides a livelihood that is free from tyrannical rulers, safe from thieves, and protected from creditors. Secular works throughout Asia often take a somewhat more cynical view, seeing the Buddhist monk as someone unfit, either by disposition or choice, for respectable society. Indeed, the caricature (and perhaps fantasy) of many popular portrayals of the Buddhist monk is that of a scoundrel who escapes from his responsibility to the family and to the state in order to live a life devoted to the pursuit of food, drink, and equally immoral nuns. Buddhist monks thus often appear as comic characters in novels, dramas, and stories throughout Asia. In *Drunken Games* (*Mattavilāsa*), a South Indian play composed around 600 C.E., a Buddhist monk explains that the Buddha instructed monks to live in mansions, to sleep on good beds, to eat good food in the morning, to drink delicious beverages in the afternoon, to chew perfumed leaves, and to wear comfortable clothes. He is puzzled that he has found no instructions from the Buddha requiring that monks marry and drink liquor. He suspects that the Buddha did indeed instruct monks to do so but that old monks, jealous of young monks, had removed these rules from the monastic code. The monk goes out in search of the complete and unedited text. The sixteenth-century Chinese epic novel *Journey to the West* (better known in English in Arthur Waley's abridged translation *Monkey*), tells the story of the heroic pilgrimage of the monk Tripiṭaka, who sets out on foot for India in search of Buddhist scriptures. Tripiṭaka is portrayed as a pious and learned young man but utterly inept in all worldly situations, dissolving in tears at the slightest difficulty. Fortunately, the bodhisattva Avalokiteśvara sends along a monkey with magical powers, who rescues the monk from all manner of natural and supernatural enemies.

A story from the Theravāda tradition plays on the notion of the "act of truth," a kind of oath that is said to have efficacious power. For example, when Prince Siddhārtha cut off his royal locks as a sign of his renunciation of the world, he threw his hair into the sky and said, "If I am to become a buddha, let them stay in the sky. If not, let them fall to the ground." (The hair did not descend.) In this story, a young boy is bitten by a poisonous snake. The distraught parents stop a passing monk and ask him to use his medical knowledge to save the child. The monk replies that the situation is so grave that the only possible cure is an act of truth. The father says, "If I have never seen a monk that I did not think was a scoundrel, may the boy live." The poison leaves the boy's leg. The mother says, "If I have never loved my husband, may the boy live." The poison retreats to the boy's waist. The monk says, "If I have never believed a word of the dharma but found it utter nonsense, may the boy live." The boy rises, completely cured.

Men and women entered the order with a wide range of motivations. Some certainly saw saṃsāra as a prison and sought to escape from rebirth with the zeal, as the texts say, with which a man whose hair is on fire puts out the blaze. Some became monks as orphans, and some were promised to the monkhood as a result of recovery from illness (whether that of a family member or their own). There was a saying in China that when a son became a monk his ancestors for nine generations went to heaven. In certain regions of Tibet there was a policy according to which farmers employed by monastic estates were required to have one of their three sons become a monk of the monastery. Some men sought refuge from conscription into the army or wanted to escape from financial troubles. It would be inappropriate to assume that one's initial motivation provided any indication of one's future success, however that might be measured. One of the most prominent Tibetan monks of the modern period explained that he decided to enter the order because he liked the look of the monks' robes.

THE RULES OF DISCIPLINE

According to the traditional account, during the early years of the Buddha's teaching there were no rules for monks. When Śāriputra requested that the Buddha announce regulations, the Buddha replied that he would do so at the appropriate time; at the time of Śāriputra's request there was no need for rules because all the members of the saṅgha were destined for nirvāṇa and their behavior was therefore naturally correct: all stream-enterers have given up any belief in mistaken rules and rituals. As the true dharma began to vanish, there would be more rules and fewer arhats. The rules of monastic discipline were not offered by the Buddha in toto but evolved over time, being formulated one by one in response to given situations. A rule prescribed in the vinaya therefore carries with it a story describing the circumstances of its formulation, and these stories, whether they are considered as originating from the Buddha himself or from the later community (although according to the tradition, all rules were formulated by the Buddha himself), offer fascinating insights into the concerns of monastic life. The rule against allowing criminals to enter the order was formulated when people complained that the Buddha had admitted Aṅgulimāla, a murderer who wore a necklace made of the little fingers of the right hands of 999 people; the Buddha was to be the thousandth, but he converted Aṅgulimāla instead. In each case, the monk whose actions occasioned the formulation of the rule was not punished because the rule to be broken had not existed at the time. Aṅgulimāla remained a monk and became an arhat.

The rule forbidding sexual intercourse was established not after a monk surrendered to lust but when a monk who had left his parents and his wife to join the saṅgha honored his mother's request to produce an heir to inherit the family's wealth. The monk's brief but successful return to the ways of a householder was condemned by the Buddha, who told him it would have been better for him to have inserted his penis into the mouth of a poisonous snake than to have placed it in the vagina of a woman. Buddhist ethical treatises discuss sexual relations in the context of karma; "sexual misconduct" is the third of ten deeds that produce negative karma, which in turn creates suffering in the future. The great fourth-century compendium of Buddhist doctrine, Vasubandhu's *Treasury of Knowledge* (*Abhidharmakośa*), explains that sexual misconduct is censured in the world because "it is the corruption of another man's wife and because it leads to retribution in a painful rebirth." He goes on to describe four kinds of sexual misconduct. The first is sexual intercourse with an improper partner, such as another man's wife, one's mother, one's daughter, a nun, or a female relative up to seven times removed. In keeping with the misogyny so prevalent in Buddhism, it is noteworthy that sexual misconduct is defined from the male perspective, prohibiting intercourse with women who are somehow off limits, protected by a husband, a family, the saṅgha, or the incest taboo.

The other types of sexual misconduct involve a man's intercourse with his own wife but in ways that are somehow improper. Thus, to use "a path other than the vagina" is to commit sexual misconduct. The sex act also becomes a misdeed if it is performed in an unsuitable location, such as a public place, near a stūpa, in a forest retreat, or in the presence of images of the three jewels. Finally, there are unsuitable times for sex, such as when one's wife is pregnant, nursing, ill, or menstruating, or during the daytime.

For monks, the penetration of any orifice—of a male, female, animal, or spirit—with the penis even to the depth of a mustard seed, whether one is the active or passive party, entails expulsion from the order. A monk may also not penetrate any of his own orifices. This rule was made to discourage two remarkable monks, one of whom was capable of auto-fellatio and another who performed auto-sodomy. The monastic texts dwell, as one might expect, on the various permutations of the sexual act at some length, proscribing all manner of bestiality and necrophilia and dwelling especially on the question of intention. A monk who fell asleep with an erection was taken advantage of by a group of passing women, without the monk being disturbed from his slumber. The Buddha ruled that no offense had been committed but henceforth allowed monks to close their doors while napping. Masturbation, in a wide variety of forms, was deemed a lesser offense, resulting in probation. The story associated with its formulation tells of a monk who was thin and jaundiced from the practice of austerities. On the advice of another, he began to eat and sleep more regularly and to masturbate. Contrary to Western stereotypes of the ill effects of masturbation, the monk soon became robust and healthy, causing his fellows to ask what medicine he had been taking. When he explained his miracle cure, the monks were disgusted that he used the same hand with which he ate his alms for other purposes as well and reported him to the Buddha, who made a rule forbidding the practice.

Upon ordination, novice monks and nuns took five vows (not to kill any living being, not to steal, not to engage in sexual activity, not to lie about spiritual attainments, and not to use intoxicants), plus vows not to eat after the noon meal (a rule widely transgressed in some Buddhist cultures through recourse to the evening "medicinal meal"), not to handle gold or silver, not to adorn their bodies, not to sleep in high beds, and not to attend musical performances. With full ordination, monks took an additional set of vows, for a total of 227 in the Theravāda tradition followed in Sri Lanka and Southeast Asia, 253 in the Mūlasarvāstivādin tradition followed in Tibet, and 250 in the Dharmaguptaka code followed in China. The vows covered the entire range of personal and public decorum and regulated physical movements, social intercourse, and property. It is these vows that have defined a Buddhist monk across the centuries, much more than adherence to a particular doctrinal position. Indeed, all Buddhist monks, even those who profess the Mahāyāna, follow one of these codes, all of which derive from the so-called Hīnayāna schools of India. The dozens of schools (*nikāyas*) of Indian Buddhism seem in fact to have been differentiated not by the goal to which they aspired or the doctrine they professed but by the ordination lineage and the particular version of the monastic code followed in their region of India. The second council, said to have occurred a century after the Buddha's death, was called to resolve disputes concerning monastic discipline.

The vows were organized according to the weight of their infractions. Four infractions—murder, sexual intercourse, stealing, and lying about spiritual attainments—warranted expulsion from the order. Consumption of alcohol was categorized as an offense to be confessed rather than one entailing expulsion. The Buddha was said to have formulated the rule after a monk renowned for his supernormal powers accepted a gift of liquor from some laymen and was subsequently discovered insensible at the city gate as the Buddha passed by. The monks carried him to the monastery and laid him down to sleep, with his head pointed respectfully toward the Buddha. The drunken monk immediately got up and lay down again, with his feet pointing toward the Buddha, a sign of disrespect. The Buddha noted that this once proper and deferential monk was now behaving improperly as a result of drinking alcohol. He therefore prohibited monks from drinking. Commentaries later defined the amount of alcohol that needed to be consumed to constitute an infraction as the amount on the tip of a blade of grass. Texts on Buddhist ethics note that the use of intoxicants differs from the other misdeeds because it does not in itself harm others. However, its dangers are illustrated by a story. A monk encountered a disturbed woman who was carrying a bottle of wine and leading a goat. The woman told the monk that if he did not either (a) kill the goat, (b) make love to her, or (c) drink the wine, she would kill herself. This presented the monk with an ethical dilemma: each of these deeds was prohibited by his vows, yet if he did not break one of them, he would be responsible for the death of a human being, a far graver misdeed. Knowing that killing and sexual intercourse entailed expulsion from the order but drinking did not, he drank the bottle of wine and ended up choosing the other two options as well.

Lesser infractions were atoned for through a temporary expulsion, the temporary loss of certain rights, some kind of penance, penalty, or probation, or simply by confession in the fortnightly communal recitation of the rules or by acknowledgment to another member of the saṅgha. During the period of probation, the monk had to announce his offense daily, had to use the worst bed and the lowest seat, and had to go to the end of the line when food was distributed. A monk on probation was also not allowed to leave the monastery unaccompanied. Infractions that entailed confession included digging in the earth (and hence tilling the soil), staying more than two or three nights with an army, and informing a layperson of spiritual attainments that one does indeed possess; to falsely claim attainments resulted in expulsion from the order. An entire section of the code prescribed rules of simple decorum, the violation of which was not deemed an infraction. These included the rules for eating and using the toilet. It also prevented monks from teaching the dharma to persons who showed disrespect by not removing their shoes, doffing their turbans, or setting down their parasols. Many rules in this category reflected the mores of an Indian society that sometimes proved baffling when the monastic code was translated into other languages in other lands.

Like all codes of conduct, the Buddhist monastic codes evidence a certain gap between theory and practice. And as in all codes, the individual prohibitions, said to have been pronounced by the Buddha himself after a particular infraction had been committed, provide some insight into the kinds of things that monks were doing. Rules are made to prohibit real or anticipated conduct. That these rules seem to have been transgressed, not only in India but throughout Buddhist Asia, should come as no surprise. It is therefore perhaps more accurate to regard the monastic rules as an ideal to aspire to rather than as a code of conduct. In 1235, the Japanese monk Shūshō vowed that during the weeks of his stay at a certain temple he would refrain from drinking liquor, engaging in sexual relations (apparently with males), and playing games of chance. From one perspective, such a statement appears shocking, that a monk would promise for a short period to refrain from doing things that should result in his permanent expulsion from the order. At the same time, Shūshō acknowledges by his promise a certain commitment to the practice of restraint and an aspiration to a lofty ideal.

ORDINATION

The formal ordination ceremony for a monk, still followed in many parts of the Buddhist world, seems to have developed after the death of the Buddha. During his lifetime, one became a monk simply by accepting the Buddha's call, "Come, monk." It later evolved into a two-step process, "going forth," or becoming a novice, and full ordination as a monk. In order to become a novice, a boy had to be old enough to scare away a crow, generally interpreted to be eight years of age. He was given a preceptor with whom he would reside and a teacher from whom he would learn the dharma. His head would be shaved, and he would don the robes of a monk. He would then prostrate himself before the preceptor and declare three times that he sought refuge in the Buddha, the dharma, and the saṅgha. He would then be instructed in the ten vows of a novice.

Ordination as a monk was a more formal ceremony, requiring the presence of ten monks (or five in remote areas). The novice had to be at least twenty years of age and free from various physical defects. He would thus be asked whether he was free (and not a slave), human (and not a demon), and male (and not a hermaphrodite), free from debt, exempt from the military, free from various diseases such as leprosy and asthma, had his parents' permission, and was at least twenty years of age. The novice would formally request ordination three times, after which the presiding monk would ask him a series of questions to determine his eligibility. The presiding monk would then ask the assembly three times to accept the novice into the order. The assembled monks would assent with their silence. Upon approval, the precise time of the ordination would be duly noted, for this would forever determine the new monk's seniority; seniority in the saṅgha is measured not by chronological age but by length of membership in the saṅgha, measured from the moment of ordination. The new monk would then be told that he would be expelled from the order if he killed a human, stole, engaged in sexual misconduct, or lied about his spiritual attainments.

Ordination as a monk or nun was considered a lifelong commitment, and in some Buddhist societies a certain stigma attached to those who returned to lay life. Yet in a Mahāyāna sūtra the Buddha explained that the gifts of the laity are to be received only by monks who practice purity; those who do not maintain the precepts rigorously amass great negative karma by accepting alms. Upon hearing this, five hundred monks rose and returned to lay life, feeling they were inadequate to the demands of monkhood. The Buddha praised them for their realistic assessment of themselves and predicted that they would be among the first disciples of Maitreya. In some Buddhist societies, it is indeed customary to return to lay life; ordination as a novice functions as a traditional rite of passage. In Thailand, for example, it is common for unmarried young men to be ordained and spend the three months of the rains retreat as a monk; in addition to serving as a rite of passage into manhood, the time spent as a monk is said to accrue great merit for the young man's parents. In China, the status of the monk was considered so potent that sickly children were sometimes ordained as novices at a very young age (which required nothing more than the shaving of the head). When the child reached adolescence in good health, a ceremony would be held in which the child was symbolically expelled from the order for some apparent offense, at which point he would again allow his hair to grow long. The status of monkhood was considered sufficiently auspicious for there to develop in Japan a tradition of posthumous ordination. As in the standard ordination ceremony, each precept was recited and the person was asked three times whether he or she intended to keep it. The fact that the deceased remained silent was interpreted in the Zen sect (which administered most funerals) as a sign of Zen insight. After the precepts had been administered, the deceased was presented with the possessions of a Buddhist monk or nun: a robe and a bowl. In addition, a *kechimyaku* (lineage certificate) was prepared, listing the deceased at the end of a long line of disciples, traced back over the generations to the Buddha himself. The name of the deceased, however, was a new Buddhist name. The degree of esteem of the monastic name so bestowed—an esteem measured by the number of characters and the number of strokes required to write each character—was (and continues to be) often related to the amount of money offered by the family. In modern funerals, more than half of the funeral fee paid to the temple can be for the Buddhist name. With the deceased now a monk or nun, a monastic funeral would be performed, with the deceased dressed in robes with head shaved. The kechimyaku would be placed inside the coffin with the body.

In China, it was common for men to enroll first at a local temple, where they would have their heads shaved and begin to observe the ten vows of a novice, although such vows had not been formally administered. The novice might remain at the local temple for one or two years of training before receiving ordination, which often took place at a large public monastery. Over much of the course of Chinese history, ordination was controlled by the government, with specific monasteries receiving permission to ordain a certain number of monks at given intervals. Monks would be exempted from military conscription and taxation, and thus the size of the saṅgha was a state concern; when the economy suffered, the government would sell ordination certificates to raise capital. The law code of the Ming Dynasty prohibited the building or rebuilding of any monastery without official authorization. Anyone who violated this law would receive one hundred blows with the long stick, and the monks of such a monastery would be returned to lay life and banished to the far frontiers of the empire.

In the large Chinese public monasteries, the ordination period traditionally lasted for fifty-three days. During the first two weeks, the monks were instructed in the daily schedule and rules of comportment and memorized the various verses that accompanied their every activity. They were instructed by senior monks, often stern disciplinarians who wielded a club to beat those who transgressed. In answer to any statement by this monk, the novices could only reply, "Amitābha." At the end of two weeks, the novices would kneel in assembly to recite the refuge formula and receive the ten vows of a novice. At the conclusion of the ceremony, they would receive the robes and begging bowl of a monk. The next portion of the ordination period was devoted to learning the 250 vows of a fully ordained monk, which would be again administered to the group. The final portion of the period was devoted to receiving the fifty-eight bodhisattva vows from the *Brahmā's Net Sūtra* (*Fan wang jing*). At least for the past century, it has been common for

Chinese monks and nuns to have a set of small round scars (from three to eighteen) on the top of their shaved heads, resulting from being burned with a stick of incense at the time of their ordination.

BODHISATTVA VOWS

Monks who followed the Mahāyāna also took another set of vows, the bodhisattva vows. Although those who aspired to the bodhisattva path were often monks, ordination as a monk or a nun was not deemed a requirement for the bodhisattva ordination. In India, China, and Tibet, the bodhisattva vows were generally seen as a supplement to the monk's vows. In Japan, they became a substitute. The most important of all vows for the bodhisattva is the commitment to achieve buddhahood for the sake of all beings in the universe. But beyond this central vow, separate sets of vows were formulated for bodhisattvas. In an Indian version, a bodhisattva promised eighteen things: (1) not to praise oneself and slander others out of attachment to profit or fame; (2) not to fail to give one's wealth or the doctrine, out of miserliness, to those who suffer without protection; (3) not to become enraged and condemn another, without listening to his or her apology; (4) not to abandon the Mahāyāna and teach a facsimile of the excellent doctrine; (5) not to steal the wealth of the three jewels; (6) not to abandon the excellent doctrine; (7) not to steal the saffron robes and beat, imprison, or expel a monk from the life of renunciation, even if he has broken the ethical code; (8) not to commit the five deeds of immediate retribution (killing one's father, killing one's mother, killing an arhat, wounding the Buddha, causing a schism in the saṅgha); (9) not to hold wrong views; (10) not to destroy cities; (11) not to discuss emptiness with those whose minds have not been trained; (12) not to turn someone away from buddhahood and complete enlightenment; (13) not to cause someone to abandon completely the monastic vow in order to practice the Mahāyāna; (14) not to believe that desire cannot be abandoned by the vehicle of śrāvakas or to cause others to believe it; (15) not to claim falsely, "I have accepted the profound emptiness"; (16) not to impose fines on renunciates or take donors and gifts away from the three jewels; (17) not to cause meditators to give up (the practice of) serenity (*śamatha*) or take the resources of those in retreat and give them to reciters of texts; (18) not to abandon the aspirational and practical commitment to achieve buddhahood. This list collects a wide range of concerns, some of which (like the vow not to commit any of the deeds of immediate retribution) are encompassed by the vows of monks and nuns; some of which (like the vow not to give up the commitment to achieve buddhahood) are central to the conception of the Mahāyāna; some of which (like the promise not to turn someone away from their monastic vows) demonstrate the compatibility of monastic and bodhisattva practice; and some of which (like the promise not to destroy cities) simply strike the modern reader as odd.

The tension between the demands of the monk and the demands of the bodhisattva are illustrated in some of the secondary infractions of the bodhisattva vows. For example, it is an infraction for a bodhisattva not to be willing to commit one of the nonvirtuous deeds of body and speech (killing, stealing, sexual misconduct, lying, divisive speech, harsh speech, senseless speech) out of compassion for others. Stories are told to illustrate the bodhisattva's compassion in this regard. An ascetic who had maintained celibacy for four billion years was approached by a woman. When he refused her advances she threatened to commit suicide. Moved by compassion, the ascetic consented and lived with her for twelve years before returning to the forest. As a result of his deed, the ascetic did not accrue the negative karma of sexual misconduct but instead shortened his path to enlightenment by one million aeons. A more extreme case is that of five hundred traders who embarked on a sea voyage in search of treasure. They were successful, but during the voyage home a thief aboard the ship concocted a plan to murder the five hundred and take their treasure. The leader of the five hundred learned of the plan in a dream and decided that the only way to save the lives of the five hundred was to murder the thief. He thereby not only saved their lives but prevented the thief from accruing the negative karma of five hundred murders. Indeed, the thief was reborn in heaven. And the murderer, rather than amassing the negative karma of murder himself, was able to reduce his own path to enlightenment by one hundred thousand aeons by means of his compassionate act. The murderer was none other than the future Buddha.

The bodhisattva vows used in China derived from the *Brahmā's Net Sūtra,* a Chinese apocryphon compiled in the fifth century. They consisted of ten major and forty-eight minor precepts. The ten major precepts included vowing not to cause the loss of life, not to steal, not to engage in sexual misconduct, not to lie, not to sell liquor, not to report the misdeeds of others, not to engage in praise of oneself or the criticism of others, not to be miserly, not to be resentful, and not to slander the dharma. These bodhisattva precepts could be received by either monks or laypeople who had not committed one of the heinous crimes (the standard list of five, augmented with killing a senior monk and killing a master of a Buddhist community). For monks in China (as was the case in India and Tibet), the bodhisattva vows were considered a supplement to the 250 monastic vows of the vinaya.

The bodhisattva vows took on a different role in Japan. As in China, they were derived from the *Brahmā's Net Sūtra.* However, the Tendai and Zen sects regarded these vows as a substitute for, rather than a supplement to, the monastic vows set forth in the vinaya. This interpretation developed, in part, for political reasons. During the Nara period, monks received both the vinaya and bodhisattva precepts. Indeed, an entire sect, the Ritsu, was dedicated to the practice and interpretation of the vinaya. The ordination of monks was controlled by the Nara sects, and it was required that they be administered in the city of Nara. The monk Saichō (767–822) traveled to China, where he studied the works of the Tientai sect and returned to Japan intent on spreading its teachings in Japan. Basing himself at Mount Hiei near Kyoto, he wished to establish a sect independent of the administration of the Nara sects, but in order to do so he had to be able to ordain monks, something prohibited outside of Nara. Saichō thus declared the standard monastic vows to be a Hīnayāna practice and established a form of monastic ordination derived solely from the bodhisattva precepts of the *Brahmā's Net Sūtra.* As might be expected, this innovation was not accepted by the Nara sects, who declared the monks of Mount

Hiei to be simply laymen in monks' robes. But Saichō's Tendai sect became, after his death, the most powerful Buddhist sect in Japan, and his innovation in ordination became the norm, with Mount Hiei becoming the training ground for leading figures of the Pure Land and Zen sects, who would develop their own interpretation of the role of precepts in the path to enlightenment.

For Shinran of the True Pure Land sect (Jōdo Shinshū), the precepts derived from an earlier age, when the followers of the Buddha were able to attain enlightenment through their own efforts. In the present degenerate age, to attempt to maintain precepts, even bodhisattva precepts, is a futile exercise; it is even an act of hubris, suggesting that one has the power to effect one's own enlightenment. Thus Shinran abandoned all precepts and ordinations. For him the only vow that mattered was the eighteenth vow of Amitābha, who had promised in the *Sukhāvatīvyūha* to deliver into the Pure Land all those who called his name.

Dōgen, the founder of the Sōtō Zen sect, asserted that the three trainings of Buddhism—ethics, meditation, and wisdom—were already fully present in the act of Zen meditation; he even accepted the view that to observe the Hīnayāna vows was to break the bodhisattva vows. This is not to suggest that Dōgen rejected all rules; he made the routines of the Zen monastery, instituted by the great patriarchs of China, the foundation of Sōtō monastic life. He followed the Tendai in basing monastic ordination on the *Brahmā's Net Sūtra* but made his own list of sixteen precepts.

MONASTIC LIFE

The primary abode of the monk was the monastery. Despite the presence of large monasteries throughout the Buddhist world, evidence suggests that most were quite small. In 1930 in China, for example, there were some five hundred thousand monks living in one hundred thousand monasteries and temples, with only about 5 percent living in larger monasteries that ranged in size from fifty to one hundred fifty monks. In the Indian monastic code there is discussion of monasteries being owned by laymen (suggesting that donors retained rights over lands they donated to the saṅgha) and of there being so few monks that they were constrained to occupy more than one monastery each day so that the owner could accrue the requisite merit. In such cases, it seems almost as if the monastery was a kind of tenant farm, leased to monks, which they cultivated in order to harvest merit rather than millet, merit duly provided to the landlord.

Monastic life was highly regulated. Monasteries had their own administration with officers of various ranks. In a large Chinese monastery, these included the guest prefect, the bath prefect, the water chief, the charcoal manager, the manager of the infirmary, the chief of the bell tower, and the abbot's quarters acolytes. The day, the month, and the year were marked by ceremonies that must be performed properly, and individual monks lived according to an elaborate etiquette, much of which was based on seniority, determined not by age but by the number of years one had been a monk. A twelfth-century Chinese vinaya text contains instructions on such things as the proper contents of the pack of a wandering monk, the procedures for staying overnight at a monastery, entering the abbot's quarters, entertaining distinguished visitors, inaugurating and ending the summer retreat, serving a meal provided by a donor, and performing the funeral for an abbot. There were also detailed instructions on how to serve tea in various ceremonies and services.

Much of the activity in a large Chinese training monastery took place in the saṅgha hall, a large rectangular structure, one end of which held an altar with an image of the bodhisattva of wisdom Mañjuśrī. Much of the hall was filled with low platforms, each large enough to accommodate the assigned space for several monks. The monks sat in meditation, took their morning and noon meals, and slept in these spaces. Rules prescribed how one was to rise in the morning (in some monasteries at 3 A.M.). Stepping down from the platform after waking up in the morning, and proceeding to the washstand, the monk was to mentally say, "From the hours of dawn straight through to dusk, I will make way for all living beings. If any of them should lose their bodily form under my feet [that is, be killed], I pray that they may immediately be born in the pure land." There were rules for washing one's face and brushing one's teeth, for folding one's blanket and putting on one's robes. There were rules for offering rice (not less than seven grains) to the hungry ghosts before each meal, eating the meal in silence, receiving a second helping, washing one's bowls, spoon, and chopsticks afterward. One was to sleep on the right side; lying on one's back or stomach was said to induce bad dreams. And there were detailed rules for using the toilet, an elaborate undertaking even though a simplified robe was worn for the purpose. All of these rules were to be followed in addition to the 250 vows of a monk.

In general, monks were to comport themselves in a discreet and dignified manner at all times, respecting the ranks of seniority in all situations and following precise rules of decorum, their activities punctuated by the mental recitation of verses that reminded them of the larger purpose of their routine. When a monk raised his bowl to receive food from the server, he was to recite silently, "Upon receiving this food, I pray that living beings shall have as food the bliss of meditation and be filled to satiation with joy in the dharma."

The degree to which Buddhist monks meditated differs, again, over time and across regions. The fact that monastic regulations refer to a special category of meditators suggests that this activity was considered a specialty of which not all monks partook. In the large and elite Chan training monasteries in the early decades of the twentieth century, monks would enroll in a five-month session during which there would be seven periods each day (with monks rising at 3 A.M. and going to bed at 10 P.M.) of combined seated and walking meditation, punctuated by four meals, three teas, and two naps. Even at such monasteries, those engaged in the full meditation regimen represented a minority of the monks of the monastery, who were engaged in all manner of other activities. At smaller monasteries, there may have been no formal schedule for meditation or chanting.

Monasteries supported themselves by different means in different countries. Some received support from the state. In Tibet and China, large monasteries often owned substantial lands (sometimes at a great distance from the monastery itself) that would be leased out to tenant farmers; monks were prohibited by the vinaya from tilling the soil because they might inadvertently kill insects. The Indian monastic codes contain instructions on how funds from permanent endowments to the monastery may be loaned at interest, a service that monasteries elsewhere in the Buddhist world also provided. Other monasteries supported themselves through performing services for the dead, while others, located on a sacred mountain or possessing a famous image, would benefit from the donations of pilgrims and tourists.

In addition to serving as sites of merit making, many Buddhist monasteries also served as centers of learning. Especially in largely illiterate societies, monasteries were important educational institutions. Some of the largest such centers in the Buddhist world were the great monasteries of Lhasa in Tibet. Just as the great monasteries of India had drawn students from many lands, so these Tibetan monasteries drew monks from China in the east, Kalmykia in the west, Mongolia in the north, and Nepal in the south. One of these monasteries was Drepung, the largest monastery in the world, with over ten thousand monks. A small percentage of these monks were engaged in a formidable scholastic curriculum that often took twenty years to complete. It was centered on the study of five Indian treatises, known simply as the "five texts." The first was the *Ornament of Realization (Abhisamayālaṃkāra)*, one of the works that Maitreya gave to Asaṅga. Studied for four to six years, this work is said to present the "hidden teaching" of the perfection of wisdom sūtras, that is, the intricate structure of the Hīnayāna and Mahāyāna paths to enlightenment. It is for the most part a list of terms, known as the "seventy topics," each of which has multiple subcategories. There are, for example, twenty varieties of the aspiration to buddhahood (bodhicitta). The second text was the *Introduction to the Middle Way* (*Madhyamakāvatāra*) by Candrakīrti, a work organized around the ten perfections of the bodhisattva path but the bulk of which is devoted to the sixth, the perfection of wisdom. This chapter served as the locus classicus for the Middle Way philosophy of Nāgārjuna. It was studied for two to four years. The third work was the *Commentary on Valid Knowledge* (*Pramāṇavarttika*) of Dharmakīrti. Monks of the three great monasteries of Lhasa would convene annually to debate about Dharmakīrti's text. This text contains arguments for the existence of rebirth, for liberation from rebirth, and for the omniscience of a buddha, discussions of the two valid sources of knowledge (direct perception and inference), classifications of logical proofs, and an analysis of the operations of thought. Written in a cryptic poetic style, this is considered one of the most difficult Indian treatises and thus is a particular favorite of the most scholarly monks. The fourth text was the *Treasury of Knowledge* (*Abhidharmakośa*) of Vasubandhu, a compendium of Hīnayāna doctrine, providing the basis for Buddhist cosmology and karma theory, among other topics. It was studied for four years. The final work, also studied for four years, was the *Discourse on Vinaya* (*Vinayasūtra*) of Guṇaprabha, setting forth the rules of monastic discipline according to the system practiced in Tibet.

The successful completion of the entire curriculum took some twenty years of study. During this time, the educational techniques were two: memorization and debate. It was customary for a monk over the course of his study to memorize the five Indian works, his college's textbooks on the Indian works, and some of the philosophical writings of the founder of the sect; consequently, it was not uncommon for an accomplished scholar to have over a thousand pages of Tibetan text committed to memory. This repository of doctrine was mined in the second educational technique of the monastic university, debate. Debate took place in a highly structured format in which one monk defended a position (often a memorized definition of a term or an interpretation of a passage of scripture) that was systematically attacked by his opponent. In answering the challenger's attacks, the defender was limited to four answers: "I agree," "Why?," "The reason is not proven," and "That does not follow." The defender of the position would be seated. His opponent would stand over him, his rosary draped over his left wrist. The challenger would clap his hands in the defender's face and then draw the rosary up his left arm. In the winter, the weather was often so cold that the monks' hands would crack and bleed as they slapped their palms together to punctuate a point, splashing blood in the opponent's face. Even this aggressive act was infused with Buddhist symbolism: the left hand was said to symbolize wisdom, the right, compassion. Bringing the hands together in a clap signified the union of method and wisdom required for the attainment of buddhahood. Drawing the rosary up the left arm symbolized pulling all beings out of saṃsāra and into nirvāṇa. Skill in debate was essential to progress to the highest rank of academic scholarship and was greatly admired. Particular fame was attached to those monks who were able to hold the position of one of the lower schools in the doxographical hierarchy against the higher. These debates were often quite spirited, and certain debates between highly skilled opponents are remembered with an affection not unlike that which some attach to important sporting events in the West. It was commonly the case that a monk, adept at the skills of memorization and debate, would achieve prominence as a scholar without ever writing a single word.

It would be misleading to conclude that all monks live in monasteries. There has long been the tradition of the wandering monk, a tradition that enjoyed a renaissance in twentieth-century Thailand. In 1902, the king of Thailand passed the Saṅgha Act in an effort to unite the various regional monastic traditions, with their local customs and dialects, under a single national system promulgated in the Thai language. The act prohibited local abbots from ordaining monks; the power to ordain was granted only to those monks who had been appointed by the Bangkok government. Local abbots who ignored the act and continued to ordain monks were arrested. The act required that monks remain in a monastery throughout the year; it prevented them from participating in local festivals; and it imposed a curriculum of study written in a language that many of the monks could not understand. Resistance to the reforms was widespread among both monks and laity.

Some monks sought to escape the scrutiny of the state saṅgha by adopting the ancient lifestyle of the wandering monk who lived in the forest and begged for alms in villages. They were called *thudong* monks because they adopted the thirteen practices of an ascetic (mentioned at the beginning of this chapter). These monks lived in the wild, each carrying on his shoulder a large umbrella with a mosquito net that served both for meditation and as a tent during the night. Their life stories are filled with encounters with tigers, wild elephants, pythons, and ghosts; one of their practices was to sleep in cremation grounds, something encouraged by laypeople who believed that the sanctity of the monks provided protection from vengeful spirits. Part of their power derived from their strong powers of concentration, often developed by focusing on the mantra *buddho*. These monks believed that ascetic practice was more efficacious than study and followed what they believed had been the practice of the Buddha himself.

As a result of a variety of factors, including deforestation, the concerns of the military, and the orders of the monastic hierarchy, the tradition of the wandering forest monk has largely died out. In 1987, the state Saṅgha Council issued an order that all forest monks leave the forest, except for those who reside in officially sanctioned forest monasteries. Since then, the Thai forest monks, once derided as uncivilized by educated urbanites, are now admired. Just as the tradition was dying out, popular monthly magazines began to be published that recounted the lives and teachings of the forest monks. The biographies of these monks are often reprinted and distributed at the funerals of laypeople.

NUNS

Shortly before the Buddha passed into nirvāṇṇa, Ānanda asked him how a monk should relate to women. "Do not look at them," the Buddha replied. But if we see one? "Do not speak to them," the Buddha replied. But if a woman speaks to us? "Maintain mindfulness and self-control," the Buddha replied.

The role of women in Buddhism may be traced back to the story of the Buddha's conception and birth. The bodhisattva, residing in the Joyous heaven, surveyed the world and chose King Śuddhodana and Queen Māyā as suitable parents for the next buddha. The queen dreamed that a white elephant had entered her womb and soon found that she was pregnant. Later texts, apparently concerned that the future Buddha could not abide in a foul-smelling womb, explained that Māyā's womb was transformed into a jeweled pavilion, resting on four pillars, containing a throne of lapis lazuli. Even then, after ten lunar months, the bodhisattva did not emerge via the usual route but instead from under his mother's right arm. And unlike other infants, he emerged immaculately clean and able to walk, taking seven steps (a lotus blooming at each) and announcing that this was his last birth. Queen Māyā died seven days later. The texts explain that a womb that has held the bodhisattva may not ever be polluted by sexual relations. The only alternative, apparently, was that the future buddha's mother must die.

Perhaps the most important text regarding women is the story of the foundation of the order of nuns. In the account, the Buddha's aunt and stepmother, Mahāprajāpatī, approached the Buddha and requested that women be allowed to go forth from the worldly life and enter the order. When the Buddha refused, Mahāprajāpatī and a number of other women shaved their heads, put on monks' robes, and followed the Buddha and his monks on their travels, their bare feet bloodied on the path. The Buddha had ruled that monks must receive the permission of their parents to go forth from the household life (this rule was requested by the Buddha's father, whose own son did not receive such permission) but not the permission of their wives. The women who followed the widow Mahāprajāpatī were the wives of men who had become monks. Feeling pity for them, Ānanda approached the Buddha and requested that the women be allowed to enter the order. The Buddha refused. Ānanda then asked whether women are capable of following the path to enlightenment, and the Buddha conceded that they are. Ānanda persisted, however, and after his third request, the Buddha relented, but only after prescribing a set of eight rules for nuns that establish their inferiority to monks. First, although seniority within the order of monks was based on length of ordination, a nun who had been ordained for one hundred years must rise and pay respects to all monks, even those who had been ordained for one day. Second, a nun must not spend the rains retreat in a place where there are no monks. Third, nuns must ask the order of monks for instruction in the dharma and for the appropriate time to hold the fortnightly confession assembly. Fourth, after the rains retreat, a nun should confess any infractions to both the order of monks and the order of nuns. Fifth, a nun who has committed an important infraction must submit to discipline from both the order of monks and the order of nuns. Sixth, a female novice must train for a probationary period of two years before seeking ordination from both the order of monks and the order of nuns. Seventh, a nun may never revile a monk in any way. Eighth, although a monk may criticize a nun, a nun may not criticize a monk.

The account closes with the Buddha predicting, with a certain resentment, that his admission of women to the order will drastically curtail the length of time that his teaching will remain in the world before it disappears completely. Had he not been compelled to admit them, his teaching would have lasted for one thousand years. Now it would remain for only five hundred. A Chinese Buddhist monk who made a pilgrimage to India in the fifth century observed that nuns paid particular obeisance to the stūpa of Ānanda because of his role in establishing the order, something that Ānanda was chastised for (along with allowing the body of the Buddha to be touched by women's tears) at the first council of monks convened shortly after the Buddha's death.

The story of the ordination of women has been widely interpreted. Read as a historical account, it presents clear difficulties for those who wish to present the Buddha as a protofeminist. In order to preserve such a picture, several scholars have pointed out that this account was written by monks after the Buddha's death and thus may not represent the events as they actually occurred. Such a view reflects a strong anticlerical attitude, in which anything that the Buddha says or does that does not conform with a particular image of him is ascribed to the work of monks. It is, in fact, a very Buddhist position to take, regarding the Buddha as the precursor who anticipates all that is good and true, postulating a lineage, and then equating that lineage with authority. The weight of the argument is diminished when it is recalled that everything that the Buddha is reported to have said or done was recorded by monks after the Buddha's death. What the Buddha actually said or did is inaccessible.

The Buddha's views on the dangers of women probably reflected those of the Indian society of his day. At the same time, unlike leaders of some other contemporary groups, he granted women admission to his order and confirmed their ability to follow the path to nirvāṇa. In traditional Indian society, a woman was said to be protected by her father in her youth, protected by her husband in midlife, and protected by her son in old age. It is noteworthy that the women seeking to become nuns are led by Mahāprajāpatī, the Buddha's stepmother. Now a widow, she turns to her son for protection. Indeed, it appears that the early members of the order of nuns were those widowed by the dharma. For although men did not require the consent of their wives in order to receive ordination, women did require the consent of their husbands. It is therefore not surprising that among the stories of illustrious female disciples of the Buddha, one finds a preponderance of widows, courtesans, and unwed daughters of kings as well as the wives of monks; the five hundred women who follow Mahāprajāpatī are all abandoned wives of monks. Aging courtesans used their lost looks as instructions in impermanence, describing in stark detail how their own full breasts had become like empty water bags, how their once-beautiful teeth were now broken and yellow. A beautiful young woman devoted to the Buddha would often convert her parents, servants, and fiancé to the dharma. For those who were too taken with their own beauty, the Buddha would conjure a woman even more beautiful, whom he would magically cause to age before her eyes, falling at her feet as a rotting corpse.

There are also stories of women who came to the order of nuns out of desperation, having undergone sufferings risible in their extremity. One well-known story tells of a wealthy young woman who refused to marry the man chosen for her by her parents. Instead, she escaped with a servant by whom she became pregnant. Some years later, she was returning with her husband to her parents' home in order to give birth to her second child, when a great storm arose. Her husband went into the woods to seek shelter for them and was stung by an adder and died. She gave birth to a son that night and continued on her journey, carrying one son and leading the other. Reaching a river, she left the older child on the riverbank and carried the baby across. Returning for the first child, she watched helplessly as he plunged into the river by himself and was swept away by the current. Turning back to the infant, she saw him being carried away by a hawk. Continuing on her journey, she encountered a neighbor who informed her that her parents perished when their house collapsed in the storm the previous night. Later, she remarried and had another child. One night, her husband returned home in a drunken rage, murdered the child, threw it into the fire, and made the woman eat the flesh. She left her husband and later met a young man whose wife had recently died. Sharing stories of their past misfortunes, they married, but the young man soon became sick and died. She learned that it was the custom of his country for the widow to be buried alive with her husband. She escaped death herself when thieves broke into the grave. At this point, she began to wonder what the source of her sorrows might be. She wandered naked, reviled as a crazy woman. One day, she happened to come upon the Buddha. His disciples tried to forbid her from approaching, but he saw that she had made a prayer to a buddha in a previous life to become a nun. In order to fulfill her prayer, the Buddha told her to return to her senses and taught her the dharma. After hearing his teaching, she asked to be admitted to the order of nuns and eventually became an arhat.

The Buddha's female lay disciples are often women of great wealth who generously provide the Buddha and his monks with requisites such as food, clothing, shelter, bedding, and medicine. He explains to them that a laywoman will be reborn as a god if she is an agreeable companion to her husband, honors his parents, is industrious in her housework, treats her servants properly, guards her husband's property and does not squander his wealth, takes refuge in the three jewels, observes the five precepts, and finds delight in generosity and renunciation. However, he is ultimately skeptical about the possibility of happiness in family life, saying that a person with a hundred loved ones has a hundred sorrows, but a person with no loved ones has none.

Regardless of what the attitude of the Buddha himself may have been, Buddhist texts are replete with negative portrayals of women, perhaps not surprisingly when one considers that these portrayals are the products of a community of celibate men. Women are presented as sites of danger and pollution, and the filth of the female body is cataloged in great detail. A text called the *Menstruation Sūtra* offered women salvation from a special hell in which they were chained in a lake of blood. They were doomed to this fate because their blood shed during childbirth had polluted the earth.

Further, when they had washed blood from their garments in a river, water downstream (and hence polluted by their menstrual blood) had been used to make tea that had been served to monks. The Buddha provides instructions on how to avoid being reborn in this hell. The *Sūtra in Forty-Two Sections,* renowned as the first Buddhist text to be translated into Chinese, says, "A deity presented a woman of pleasure to the Buddha, wanting to test the Buddha's will and examine the Buddha's way. The Buddha said, 'Why have you come here bearing this leather sack of filth? . . . Be gone! I have no use for her.'" In order to cure a monk of his infatuation with a beautiful courtesan named Sirimā, the Buddha ordered that she not be cremated when the young woman unexpectedly died but instead had the king have her body placed in the charnel grounds. When the body had reached a suitable level of putrefaction, the king ordered all in his kingdom to file past it. The Buddha and his monks also went, and the Buddha addressed the assembled populace, explaining that many would have paid a thousand gold coins just a few days ago to spend one night with Sirimā, but now no one would have her. The infatuated monk became an arhat upon hearing these words.

A text called the *Therīgāthā,* "Songs of the (Female) Elders," recounts the life stories of some of the Buddha's female disciples. The pregnant wife of a merchant was cast out of her home by her mother-in-law. She gave birth to a son while wandering; when she was bathing in a river the son was stolen. She was later kidnapped by a bandit chief to whom she bore a daughter but was able to escape, leaving the child behind. She became a courtesan and married a young man who, some years later, took a second, younger wife. The elder wife eventually determined that the younger wife was her own daughter and that they were married to her son. Repelled by their lot, the son became a monk and the mother became a nun. Apart from the gender of the protagonists, these works do not vary stylistically from another collection, the *Theragāthā,* "Songs of the (Male) Elders." It is difficult to discern a female voice in the *Therīgāthā,* and the work may have been written, once again, by monks, the products of a later monastic literary tradition rather than the autobiographical testimonials of nuns. The works present an uncompromising vision of the female form as foul. The question is whether this is the view of monks or whether it is the view of nuns, made to see themselves as monks are taught to see them.

Some changes in the attitude to women are evident in certain of the Mahāyāna sūtras, where the doctrine of emptiness calls into question the status of all categories, including male and female. In the *Vimalakīrti Sūtra,* a goddess turns Śāriputra into a woman momentarily, to his great chagrin. In another sūtra, an important exposition of the buddha nature is provided by the queen Śrīmālā. In the *Lotus Sūtra,* a serpent princess magically transforms herself into a human male and achieves perfect buddhahood in an instant. Despite the destabilization of the categories of male and female in these Mahāyāna sūtras, transformations tend to move in the male direction. Two of the great authors of the Mahāyāna, Nāgārjuna in his *Garland of Jewels* (*Ratnāvalī*) and Śāntideva in his *Entering the Path of Enlightenment* (*Bodhicaryāvatāra*) include stereotypical descriptions of the uncleanliness of the female body, and Śāntideva includes in the prayer that concludes his work the wish that women may be reborn as men. There is even the story in a Mahāyāna sūtra of a bodhisattva so handsome that upon seeing him women are overwhelmed by lust and drop dead, to be reborn in the more auspicious form of a male. The Buddha predicts that billions of women will suffer this happy fate.

The fact that the critique of the categories of male and female offered by the doctrine of emptiness did not appear to eliminate misogyny from Buddhist texts suggests that the influence of the doctrine of emptiness may not have been as pervasive as some have imagined. Whatever importance the critique may have had on the ultimate level, the socially constructed conventional world remained largely untouched by it, even by the most eloquent exponents of emptiness. Those who seek a refuge from misogyny in Buddhism must always choose their texts carefully and ignore the fact that, regardless of the textual resources that may be available, the presence of Buddhism in a given society has not materially improved the status of women, although nunneries have often provided a welcome refuge for women.

The order of nuns died out in Sri Lanka around the end of the tenth century. As a result of a protracted war with a South Indian king, Buddhist institutions were devastated to the point where there were not the requisite number of monks for the ordination of new monks. The king brought monks from Burma to revive the saṅgha of monks, but he did not make similar efforts for the saṅgha of nuns. During the Buddhist revival in Sri Lanka at the end of the nineteenth century, laywomen took the ten vows of a novice and wore robes of saffron (the color of monastic robes) and white (the color of lay dress), thereby indicating their ambivalent status.

Once the saṅgha of nuns declined in any Buddhist society, it was in severe jeopardy because the rules of discipline required that ten fully ordained nuns be present to confer ordination on a new nun, after which she was required to have a second ordination ceremony at which ten monks were present. It survives in China, Korea, and Vietnam. The ordination of nuns did not take place in Tibet.

The question of the status of women in Buddhism, a question to which the Buddha himself is seen as regarding with a certain ambivalence, remains an ongoing problem to which Buddhist women are responding in a variety of ways. The monastic community in the Theravāda traditions of Sri Lanka and Southeast Asia have generally responded negatively to proposals for the restoration of the order of fully ordained nuns. The order of nuns remains strong in Chinese Buddhism, and women from other Buddhist traditions, following the rule that ten fully ordained nuns must be present to ordain a female novice as a nun, have traveled to Hong Kong, Taiwan, and Korea to receive ordination. Such ordinations have met with a variety of responses. Because the lineage of ordination accepted in China is not accepted by the Theravāda tradition, it is not considered valid by Theravāda monks. The Dalai Lama, however, representing a society in which the full ordination of women never occurred, has encouraged women of the Tibetan Buddhist tradition to seek ordination from Chinese nuns.

Indeed, today the order of nuns is strongest in Taiwan, where over 60 percent of the some ten thousand ordained between 1952 and 1987 were women. The nun Cheng-yen founded in 1966 the Buddhist Compassion Relief Tzu-Chi Foundation, which collected pennies to provide medical fees for the poor. Today it is the largest civic organization in Taiwan with over four million members, the majority of whom are women. The organization has built a large hospital and medical college in Taiwan and has supported disaster relief around the world. Its founder made a vow at the age of twelve to the bodhisattva Guanyin that she would become a lay Buddhist if her mother recovered from an illness, which she did. After the death of her father she became a nun. She was moved to found her organization both out of pity for the plight of the poor who were unable to afford medical treatment and in response to the criticism of Catholic missionary nuns in Taiwan, who claimed that Buddhism cared only for individual salvation and ignored the plights of society.

Suggested Reading

Bodiford, William M. *Sōtō Zen in Medieval Japan.* Honolulu: University of Hawaii Press, 1993.

Buswell, Robert E., Jr. *The Zen Monastic Experience: Buddhist Practice in Contemporary Korea.* Princeton: Princeton University Press, 1992.

Dutt, Sukumar. *Buddhist Monks and Monasteries of India: Their History and Their Contribution to Indian Culture.* London: George Allen & Unwin, 1962.

Horner, Isabel B. *Women Under Primitive Buddhism: Lay Women and Alms Women.* New York: E. P. Dutton, 1930.

Schopen, Gregory. *Bones, Stones, and Buddhist Monks: Collected Papers on the Archaeology, Epigraphy, and Texts of Monastic Buddhism in India.* Honolulu: University of Hawaii Press, 1997.

Tiyavanich, Kamala. *Forest Recollections: Wandering Monks in Twentieth-Century Thailand.* Honolulu: University of Hawaii Press, 1997.

Warren, Henry Clarke. *Buddhism in Translations.* Cambridge: Harvard University Press, 1953.

Welch, Holmes. *The Practice of Chinese Buddhism: 1900–1950*. Cambridge: Harvard University Press, 1967.

Wilson, Liz. *Charming Cadavers: Horrific Figurations of the Feminine in Indian Buddhist Hagiographic Literature*. Chicago: University of Chicago Press, 1996.

5

LAY PRACTICE

A Buddhist is someone who says three times, "I go for refuge to the Buddha. I go for refuge to the dharma. I go for refuge to the saṅgha." This formula is repeated often, sometimes privately, sometimes publicly, in elaborate ceremonies and solitary moments. Within the general category of the Buddhist, of those who go for refuge to the three jewels, the fundamental division is between the monks and nuns on the one hand and the laity on the other. Laypeople may take up to five vows, promising for the rest of their lives (1) not to kill humans, (2) not to steal, (3) not to engage in sexual misconduct, (4) not to use intoxicants, (5) not to lie about spiritual attainments. It is possible to take one or any combination of these vows. These vows are sometimes administered individually and sometimes administered in large public ceremonies; as many as five thousand people attended such events in China during the Second World War.

From a doctrinal point of view, the purpose of a vow is to restrain nonvirtuous deeds of body and speech, thereby accumulating merit. According to Buddhist theory, once a vow is taken it assumes a subtle physical form inside the body and remains present until death or until the vow is broken. As long as the vow is present in the body, the person accumulates merit for maintaining the vow. For this reason, it is considered more virtuous (and hence more karmically efficacious) to take a vow not to steal, for example, and then not to steal, than simply not to steal without having taken a vow not to do so. At the same time, it is more damaging to commit a misdeed that one has vowed not to than it is to commit the deed without having taken a vow. Taking vows for short periods of time is also considered efficacious. Thus, in Sri Lanka and Southeast Asia, laypeople, especially laywomen, often maintain the five precepts (with restraint from sexual misconduct understood to mean celibacy) plus three others (not to eat after midday, not to attend musical performances or adorn their bodies, not to sleep in high beds) twice each month on the full moon and the new moon.

In medieval Japan, a tradition of the mass ordination of laypeople developed in the Zen sect. These ceremonies could last two or three days, often designed to coincide with a Buddhist holiday, such as the Buddha's birthday. Perhaps a hundred people from a wide range of social classes would gather at a temple, where they received teachings from a Zen master and followed some version of the monastic regimen. Special emphasis was placed on vows, which were said to be able to subdue evil in this life and confer enlightenment in the next. The physical embodiment of this power was a certificate called a *kechimyaku.* This was a lineage chart that began with the Buddha himself and listed in turn each generation of teacher and disciple, from India, to China, to Japan, and to the monk administering the vows to each layperson at the ceremony. The first name on the list was the Buddha, and the last name on the list was of the layperson, identified by a new Buddhist name received upon ordination. The layperson was thus linked by a direct line back to the Buddha. The kechimyaku was thus highly valued and was believed by many to possess extraordinary powers.

Such lay ordination indicates the power that is generally associated with monkhood, a power in which the laity sought to partake. Lay ordination is one of a number of conduits. More commonly, monks served as mediators of merit, merit that would bring happiness in this life and the next. The Buddha instructed laymen in the means of acquiring long life, beauty, happiness, fame, and rebirth in heaven, and he encouraged the accumulation of wealth acquired through honest effort. According to karmic theory, wealth is the direct result, and hence the sign, of past giving. The practice of generosity, particularly when it is directed toward a meritorious object such as the saṅgha, creates further wealth, which the Buddha praises for its capacity to allow the householder to give happiness to his family, to provide for his friends, to escape fire, thieves, and enemies, to honor guests and monarchs, and to make offerings to the saṅgha. The primary deed of the Buddhist layperson is therefore charity, but charity directed to a pure object, the saṅgha, which has the power to transmute the material wealth of the present into happiness in the future. This future certainly includes the present life but pertains particularly to the more mysterious world beyond death, a world in which the dharma has especial power.

The centrality of giving to lay practice is illustrated powerfully by perhaps the best-known story in all of Thai Buddhism. It tells of the arhat monk Phra Malai who one day encountered a poor grass cutter who presented him with eight lotuses, asking that the merit from his gift result in his never being reborn as a poor man again. In order to fulfill his request, Phra Malai took the eight lotuses and, using his supernormal powers, flew to the Heaven of the Thirty-Three on top of Mount Meru. When Prince Siddhārtha had gone forth from the world, he had cut off his topknot with his sword and thrown it into the air, saying that if he was to achieve his goal, the hair would not descend back to earth. The topknot was caught by Indra, the king of the gods, who enshrined it in a stūpa in the Heaven of the Thirty-Three, providing an object of worship, and thus merit making, for the gods, who otherwise would fall into a lower realm upon their death in heaven. Phra Malai offered the lotuses to the stūpa.

While at the stūpa, Phra Malai saw a deity approach with one hundred divine attendants. He was told that the deity had been reborn as a god as a result of feeding a starving crow. More gods arrived, one after another, each with a larger retinue than the last, and in each case Phra Malai was told of the act of charity that resulted in their divine station. A deity with twenty thousand attendants had given food to a monk. A deity with forty thousand attendants had given robes, food, shelter, and medicine to the saṅgha. A deity with eighty thousand attendants was a poor man who had caused his master to notice a monk on his alms-round. Eventually, Maitreya, the coming buddha, descended from the Joyous heaven to the Heaven of the Thirty-Three, where he also worshiped the stūpa. Maitreya asked Phra Malai how the people of Jambudvīpa made merit, and Phra Malai described their various practices, saying that the people of the world did so in order that they may be disciples of Maitreya when he becomes the next buddha. Maitreya explained that those who wished to do so should listen, in the course of a day and a night, to the story of the bodhisattva Vessantara, who gave away everything. They should also bring gifts, each numbering a thousand, to the temple where the story is recited. After describing how the conditions in the world would deteriorate and then improve before he came as the next buddha, Maitreya returned to his heaven, and Phra Malai returned to the world, where he reported Maitreya's teaching. The grass cutter who offered the eight lotuses eventually died and was reborn as a god in the Heaven of the Thirty-Three; a lotus bloomed under his feet with every step he took.

Much lay practice, not only in Thailand but throughout the Buddhist world, assumes that it is not possible for laypeople to complete the path to enlightenment during the present age, because they did not have the good fortune to benefit from the teachings of the Buddha during his lifetime. Much lay practice, therefore, has as its ultimate goal rebirth as a human at the time of Maitreya, with the good fortune of becoming a monk in his assembly and completing the path to nirvāṇa under his tutelage. One also hopes to accumulate sufficient merit to spend the intervening aeon as a god in one of the heavens.

As in other religions, death and death rituals are central concerns of Buddhist thought and practice, for monks and laity alike. Part of this importance derives from the doctrine of rebirth, according to which all beings in the universe have been born and died countless times in the past. Death then marks both an end and a beginning, but a beginning that is generally regarded with trepidation. According to the doctrine of impermanence, nothing lasts longer than an instant, and change, and hence death, is possible in the next moment. Until all the causes for rebirth have been destroyed through the practice of the path, death and rebirth will continue relentlessly. Human life, especially rebirth as a human with access to the Buddha's teachings, is regarded as a rare and precious opportunity. Gods are generally addicted to the pleasures of heaven and fail to seek liberation from rebirth. Animals, ghosts, and hell beings are overwhelmed by their particular sufferings and cannot turn to the path. Humans born in remote regions where Buddhism is unknown or who are born in an age when Buddhism has disappeared from the world have no chance to hear the dharma. Those with wrong views (such as the belief in the efficacy of animal sacrifice) or who have committed grave sins are also at a disadvantage. To be reborn as a human who has access to the Buddhist teaching is thus incredibly rare, an opportunity not to be lost in the pursuit of the ephemeral pleasures of the world. In a famous analogy, a single blind tortoise is said to swim in a vast ocean, surfacing for air only once every century. On the surface of the ocean floats a single golden yoke. It is rarer, said the Buddha, to be reborn as a human with the opportunity to practice the dharma than it is for the tortoise to surface for its centennial breath with its head through the hole in the golden yoke. It is also said that the number of beings in the realms of animals, ghosts, and the hells is equal to the number of stars seen on a clear night. The number of beings born as humans and gods is equal to the number of stars seen on a clear day. Thus, the death that Buddhist texts generally describe is the end of a life lived in easy access to dharma, a life but rarely lived and, once over, unlikely to be encountered in the near future because of the great store of negative karma accumulated over the beginningless course of saṃsāra.

Buddhist texts repeatedly warn that no matter who one might be or where one might hide, death cannot be escaped, not by strength or wealth or magic. If even the Buddha himself died, what hope is there for others? The human life span is rarely more than one hundred years, and this period wanes steadily with the passage of years, months, days, nights, mornings, and evenings. Much of life is already gone, and what remains cannot be extended. There is not an instant of life that does not move toward death. Hence, as one text warns, it is wrong to take pleasure in the misconception that we shall remain in this world, just as it would be inappropriate for a person who has fallen from a cliff to enjoy his descent to earth.

The uncertainty of the length of life is said to be a feature of the continent of Jambudvīpa, where humans reside, and is only exacerbated by the fact that in this world the causes of death are many, the causes of remaining alive few. Causes of death include enemies, demons, animals, and imbalances among the four elements (earth, water, fire, and wind) that constitute the physical body. The tenuous hold on life is further imperiled because those things upon which we depend for life are unreliable and can easily become causes of death. Food can poison, friends can deceive, roofs can collapse. Indeed, there are no causes of life that cannot become a cause of death. For these reasons it is said that, at the time of death, friends are of no benefit because they cannot prevent us from leaving this life and they cannot accompany us to the next. Wealth is of no benefit because it must be left behind. Not even the body can be taken along to the next life. At the time of death, nothing is said to be of benefit except the dharma, and a wide range of practices developed around the Buddhist world to that end, most prominently in funeral rites.

One of the chief functions of Buddhist monks is to perform rites for the dead. In contemporary Thailand, Buddhist monks often read summaries of the seven books of the Abhidharma at funerals. The Abhidharma is considered to be the most technical and difficult of all the teachings of the Buddha. Yet here the most scholastic of works is seen to have particular powers of salvation. One of the summaries declares, "Whoever is born or dies on Sunday and hears the *Dhammasaṅgaṇi* [one of the seven books] will be released from all demerit accrued through the eye. At death this person will not be reborn in hell but will enter heaven." The other six books of the Abhidharma provide for those who are born or die on the other days of the week.

The funerary function of Buddhist monks in China is suggested by the fact that during the Ming dynasty the government tried to incorporate the Buddhist clergy under the supervision of the Ministry of Rites. The most famous of the rites of the dead is the Ghost Festival, held during the seventh lunar month. The rite's textual source (whether of Indian or Chinese origin is unknown) is the *Ullambana Sūtra*, in which Maudgalyāyana, the disciple of the Buddha renowned for his supernormal powers, traveled through the realms of rebirth in search of his deceased mother. He was alarmed to find her as a hungry ghost and brought her a bowl of rice to satiate her starvation. However, it was his mother's fate that whatever food she tried to place in her mouth turned into flaming coals. He asked the Buddha what could be done. The Buddha explained that it was impossible to offer her food directly. He instructed Maudgalyāyana to prepare a great feast of food, water, incense, lamps, and bedding on the fifteenth day of the seventh month and offer it to the monks of the ten directions. At that time, all of the great bodhisattvas and arhats would appear in the form of ordinary monks. If the food was offered to them as they assembled at the end of their rains retreat, his parents, seven generations of ancestors, and various relatives would escape rebirth as an animal, ghost, or hell being for their next seven lives. If the parents were living at the time of the offering, they would live happily for one hundred years. The Buddha proclaimed that this offering would be efficacious not simply for Maudgalyāyana, but for anyone, of high station or low, who performed it. He advised, indeed, that it be performed annually.

The reciprocal nature of the relationship between the laity and the clergy is emphasized yet again here. The Buddha explains to Maudgalyāyana that his magical powers, although they surpass those of all other monks, are insufficient to the task of freeing his mother from her infernal fate. Only one means is effective: the laity must make offerings to the monastic community on behalf of their dead relatives. Only then can the dear departed be spared the tortures of the lower realms. It is a standard element of Buddhist doctrine, in fact, that laypeople are incapable of making offerings directly to the deceased relatives. Instead, they must make offerings to the saṅgha, who will, in turn, transfer the merit of their gift to the deceased. This mediation by monks has been one of the primary functions of the saṅgha, and the gifts given as raw materials by the laity have been a primary source of their sustenance. The practice carries a particular potency in China, where monks and nuns have traditionally been criticized for being unfilial; they have renounced the world and hence the family and have failed to continue the family line with their progeny. The *Ullambana Sūtra* makes clear that the traditional Chinese practice of making offerings to the ancestors is not efficacious. Instead, Buddhist monks are essential agents in the rituals, and hence the life, of the family.

Beginning in the eighth century, a related text appeared in China that would gain wide popularity. It was entitled *Sūtra for the Spell That Brought Deliverance to the Flaming Mouth Hungry Ghost* (*Fo shuo qiuba yankou egui tuoluoni jing*). In the text, Ānanda was sitting in contemplation when he was approached by a hungry ghost of horrifying visage named Flaming Mouth, who announced to Ānanda's great alarm that Ānanda would die three days hence and be reborn as a hungry ghost. When Ānanda asked whether there was anything he could do to avoid such a fate, the ghost informed him that the next day he must distribute one bushel of food and drink to hundreds of thousands of hungry ghosts and to hundreds of thousands of brahmins. By doing so, not only would Ānanda's life span be increased, but Flaming Mouth would be released from the realm of hungry ghosts and be reborn as a god. This remedy offered little solace to Ānanda; he had no wealth and so could not provide such extensive gifts. In despair, he went to the Buddha and was told that there was another method. He taught Ānanda a *dhāraṇī*, a kind of spell that, when recited, would magically provide forty-nine bushels of rice each to hungry ghosts and brahmins numerous as the sands of the Ganges. The spell would, in addition, cause hungry ghosts to be reborn as gods and would increase the life span of whoever recited it. (The spell, by the way, is *namo sarva tathāgata avalokita saṃvara saṃvara hūṃ.*) The Buddha recommended the practice to any and all who seek long life, merit, and prosperity. They need simply put a small amount of water and rice into a bowl, recite the spell seven times, recite the name mantras of four buddhas, snap their fingers seven times, and pour the water and rice on the ground. All the hungry ghosts in the four directions will thereby receive forty-nine bushels of rice, and those who make the offering will be protected from demons and attain limitless merit and a long life. By reciting the same spell fourteen times and casting the water and rice into flowing water, myriad brahmins will be fed. Anyone who even witnesses the ritual will be reborn as the great god Brahmā. Monks and nuns who wish to make similar offerings to the three jewels need only recite the spell twenty-one times. The *Sūtra for the Spell That Brought Deliverance to the Flaming Mouth Hungry Ghost* was put to wide use to feed hungry ghosts. The ceremony often took five hours to complete and was held in the evening, when hungry ghosts were said to be wandering. It could be performed for the benefit of a particular person and was performed often during the summer Festival of Hungry Ghosts.

The efficacy of the *Sūtra for the Spell That Brought Deliverance to the Flaming Mouth Hungry Ghost* made this text quite popular in China, especially as a mortuary text, and numerous rituals developed around it. One of the many forms that such rituals took was the "rite of water and land" (*shuilu fahui*), a grand ceremony usually lasting seven days and sometimes requiring the services of fifteen hundred monks. Although designed to relieve the sufferings of all beings who inhabit the water and land, this ritual, perhaps deriving from the Chinese tradition of making offerings to departed ancestors, generally took the form of an elaborate service for the dead, both ancestors who had been properly buried as well as the unidentified dead who had not—the victims of natural disaster, famine, and war who had none to mourn them or sustain them in the next world, wandering dangerously until they were sated. The purpose of the ritual was nothing less than freeing all beings from the torments of the six realms of rebirth. Such a rite entailed great expense, with food, incense, gems, and brocades offered to the living and the dead over the course of an entire week; its extravagance in both form and meaning drew throngs of spectators.

The basic structure of the ritual was that of a feast. First, the guest would be invited to the host's abode; second, the guest would be offered food; third, the guest would be sent on his way. In this case, there were two sets of guests and thus two main altars, an inner altar and an outer altar. The outer altar was the site of a wide range of efficacious activities. Indeed, there were several outer altars, with sites arranged for the recitation of particularly potent sūtras. Shorter sūtras could be recited in a single day. Hence, on the fourth day the *Lotus Sūtra* would be recited, on the seventh day, the *Diamond Sūtra.* At other altars, two monks would recite the *Avataṃsaka Sūtra* over the seven days of the ritual; at another eight monks would recite the name of Amitābha for seven days.

The inner altar was where the rite of water and land proper took place. It was in turn divided into an upper hall and a lower hall, providing seats for two sets of guests. The former was the more exalted, serving as the seat for buddhas, bodhisattvas, arhats, and various gods, immortals, monastic patriarchs, and past masters. A scroll would be hung on the walls for each of the categories of superior beings, along with a verse of praise. For each scroll a small altar was set up where incense and offerings were placed. This altar would serve as the guest's seat (complete with name card) at the banquet that would ensue. Outside the inner altar was a miniature bathing pavilion, with basin and towel, all connected to the inner altar by a long cloth, to serve as a passageway for the exalted guests.

The lower hall was reserved for those still sunk in saṃsāra, generally organized into the categories of members of the imperial government, gods, demigods, humans, ghosts, animals, hell beings, and those in the intermediate state between death and rebirth. Other lists added local gods, protector spirits, as well as departed monks and friends of the sponsoring monastery and departed relatives of the sponsoring patron. Scrolls and seats were similarly arranged for each of these groups.

Once all was in place, on the third day the officiating monks dispatched effigy emissaries to the heavens, atmosphere, earth, and underworld to invite the exalted guests from their respective abodes. They arrived the next day and were duly escorted to the bathing pavilion and then across the bolt of cloth to the inner altar, where they were requested to occupy their designated seats. Offerings were then presented to them. On the fifth day, emissaries were dispatched to the administrators of the celestial and terrestrial realms (including the hells), to whom they presented pardons granting permission to all the beings of saṃsāra to leave their homes, whether palaces or prisons, to attend the great feast. Upon their arrival they were offered a bath and a new set of clothes and given refuge in the three jewels. Thus purified, they were escorted into the presence of the buddhas and bodhisattvas in the inner altar and were escorted to their seats in the lower chamber. On the sixth day, the guests of the lower chamber were offered both material and spiritual sustenance, in the form of food and the recitation of sūtras and the buddha's name, converting them all to the dharma. The seventh day was taken up with rituals of completion, including the issuing of a document of verification, after which all the guests were invited to return to their homes. The guests of the lower chamber departed with the new knowledge that their final destination was the pure land.

Scholars have suggested that the popularity and persistence of

Buddhist services for the dead derives in part from their intersection, in motivation if not ideology, with traditional offerings to ancestors. In Sri Lanka, it is customary to invite monks to one's home to be fed and to receive offerings after the death of a parent. Such offerings are made typically seven days after the death, again three months after the death, and annually on the anniversary of the death thereafter. In order for this to be a gift to the saṅgha, at least five monks must be present. According to pre-Buddhist Chinese practice, family members must be properly buried and then sustained with regular offerings. The spirit of an ancestor so supported will send blessings to the family below. But a spirit neglected will become a demon or ghost and haunt the family. The introduction of the Buddhist doctrine of rebirth, in which the realm of ghosts was just one of three negative postmortem states, caused a certain confusion and conflation, and Buddhist clerics were constantly reminding the laity that not all ritually neglected ancestors had become hungry ghosts. Such conflations were strengthened by the fact that both pre-Buddhist and Buddhist rites entailed the offering of food to the departed. Again, Buddhist clerics had to remind their fold that such food should be regarded as an offering to all beings, an act of giving, rather than dispatched to a single departed relative. Whatever good fortune accrued from such good deeds should be regarded not as a blessing from above but as a result of the law of karma.

Mortuary rites in China often involved the use of so-called "spirit money," bank notes in different denominations, as well as silver and gold ingots (made of paper) that would be burned during the ceremony and thus transported to those awaiting the judgment of where they would be reborn next, who could then use it to make gifts to the various infernal bureaucrats. After the death of a family member, his or her name was inscribed on a stone tablet and installed on the family altar, where it would receive offerings of food. Those who could afford to do so would have another such tablet installed in a monastery, where monks would recite sūtras before it on the first and fifteenth day of each month, during the Festival of Hungry Ghosts, and on the winter solstice. More expensive arrangements could be made in which sūtras would be recited daily. Regardless, the recitation of the sūtra provided two services to the dead: it provided instruction in the dharma, and it provided merit, for the monks would transfer the merit they accrued through the recitation to the deceased. Many monasteries had a "hall of rebirth" where these tablets were installed. Others had a "hall of longevity" where tablets for the living were kept, the recitation of sūtras designed in this case to prolong life.

One of the chief functions of Buddhism in Japan has been to deal with death; the word *hotoke* in Japanese means both "buddha" and "dead person." In Japan, the deceased were generally placed into two categories: the near dead and the distant dead. The former included family members who had been dead for less than thirty-three years and who retained a specific identity within recent memory. The latter were family members who passed into the more generic category of ancestors. The dead who had no family to perform rituals on their behalf, regardless of how long they had been dead, fell into a third category, called "the dead lacking relations," and were regarded with both pity and fear. According to the funeral rites performed by the Shingon sect (and followed in somewhat different forms in other sects), rites for deceased relatives would be performed on the forty-ninth day after the death (with more elaborate versions calling for rites in each of the preceding weeks), and then on the first, third, seventh, thirteenth, and thirty-third anniversary of the death. Until the thirty-third year, these rites were performed on the behalf of the deceased individual. After the thirty-third anniversary, the deceased would become a member of the ancestral collective and would receive offerings in the annual Obon festival in late summer, where the ritual for feeding the Flaming Mouth hungry ghost would be performed. As in China, then, Buddhist funerals and memorial rituals were accepted in Japan as the most efficacious way of dealing with the dead, effectively transforming deceased relatives into beneficent ancestors who protected the living, and effectively placating the ghosts of "the dead lacking relations" who otherwise might afflict the living. In the always inexact accommodation of practice to doctrine, many of the ideas considered most classically Buddhist, such as no-self and the mechanisms of karma that lead to rebirth in one of the realms of samsāra, have been largely forgotten in Japan in favor of the cult of the ancestors.

In the decades since the Second World War, rituals have been developed for the welfare of aborted and miscarried fetuses. Although unborn children were not given funeral rites in premodern Japan, with the legalization of abortion in 1948 and its prevalence as a form of birth control, Buddhist temples began to invent memorial services for the unborn, modeled on the funeral ceremony, in which the unborn child was given a name, texts were recited in order to produce merit for the dead child and to prevent it from haunting the living, and a place was established as a site for offering and commemoration. The most visible of such sites are stone images of the bodhisattva Jizō, revered as a protector of children. Rows of identical statues of Jizō are found at Buddhist temples throughout Japan, distinguished by the bibs, knit caps, and sweaters in which they have been dressed and by the small toys placed at their feet.

SAṄGHA AND STATE

The appeal of Buddhism has not been limited to solitary yogins meditating on emptiness or simple peasants seeking a happy rebirth for their loved ones. Despite its characterization of the world as an ephemeral realm of relentless suffering, Buddhism has had strong relations with the state throughout its history. The Buddha counted among his patrons a number of kings, such as Bimbisāra, who first encountered the prince shortly after his renunciation, inviting him to return to his kingdom after his enlightenment. Bimbisāra donated a bamboo grove to the Buddha and his monks, where the Buddha spent several rain retreats. Eventually eighteen monasteries were provided to the saṅgha in his city of Rājagṛha and its environs.

The most famous of all Buddhist kings (although the extent to which he was Buddhist remains the subject of scholarly debate), regarded as the ideal Buddhist ruler throughout Asia, was Aśoka, who ascended to the throne of the Mauryan dynasty of northern India in 270 B.C.E. Soon after his ascension, Aśoka undertook a military conquest that brought almost the entire Indian subcontinent under his domain. As a result of a particularly bloody war in South India, he is said to have renounced violence in favor of the dharma, inaugurating a forty-year reign of peace and prosperity. The most enduring record of Aśoka's rule is the rock inscriptions he had carved on stone pillars, in which he sets forth a policy of rule according to the dharma. The question is whether *dharma* should be taken to mean the teachings of the Buddha or whether it should be understood in the more general sense of law or righteousness. Support for the former view derives from occasional references to the three jewels, his visit to the Buddha's birthplace, and the names of Buddhist texts in the edicts. According to Buddhist legend, however, there is no doubt about the king's allegiance.

In the most famous of these legends, in his previous life Aśoka had—as a young boy playing in the dirt—encountered the Buddha on his begging rounds. The boy had piously placed a handful of dirt into the Buddha's begging bowl, with the prayer that the merit of his deed would cause him to become a great king who would rule the earth and honor the Buddha. The Buddha smiled at the boy, and, as often occurred, rays of light in various colors emerged from his mouth, traveling in all directions, warming the cold hells and cooling the hot hells below, teaching impermanence to the gods above. When these rays of light were reabsorbed, the place in the Buddha's body to which they returned was significant. If the person he smiled upon was to be reborn as an animal, they vanished into the sole of his foot. If the person was to become a buddha, they disappeared into his crown protrusion. On this occasion, the rays of light vanished into his left hand, signifying that the boy would become an "armed *cakravartin.*"

The notion of the *cakravartin,* or wheel-turning king, predates the rise of Buddhism in India but was incorporated into Buddhist theories of kingship. According to one myth, during an ideal age before the present time of degeneration, the world was ruled by a king. His body bore the thirty-two marks of a superman; he was endowed with seven treasures (a wheel, a jewel, a queen, a minister, a general, an elephant, and a horse), the most important of which was a great wheel that conquered without conflict any region where it rolled. After bringing the four continents under the domain of the king, the wheel returned to his capital, where it hovered in the air above his palace. At the end of the king's reign, the wheel sunk to the ground. Later Buddhist texts distinguished four types of cakravartins, making it clear that their appearance in the world was not restricted to the past. A cakravartin with a golden wheel rules all four continents of the world. A cakravartin with a silver wheel rules three continents, and a cakravartin with a copper wheel rules two. The least of the kings is a cakravartin with an iron wheel, who rules only one continent, Jambudvīpa. Each of the four kings requires more disputation in order to secure dominion over this realm, with the cakravartin with an iron wheel resorting to the sword. This last category seems to correspond to the armed cakravartin mentioned in the legend of Aśoka; by filling the Buddha's begging bowl with earth (with good intention), he wins dominion over the earth. Throughout the history of Buddhism in Asia, all manner of kings and potentates would identify themselves, or be praised by others, as cakravartins. Some Japanese Buddhist apologists for the invasion of China in 1937 described Emperor Hirohito as a cakravartin with a golden wheel.

Aśoka began his next lifetime inauspiciously, being ugly in form (said to be a negative effect of offering dirt to the Buddha) and malicious in nature, delighting in torturing prisoners, building a prison modeled on the Buddhist hells—beautiful on the outside but horrible on the inside—condemning all who passed through its gates to death. One such unfortunate person was a Buddhist monk who became an arhat while imprisoned. When the time for his execution came, the jailer found it impossible to light the fire beneath the cauldron in which the monk was to be boiled. The king was summoned, at which point the monk displayed all manner of supernormal feats, converting the king to the dharma. Aśoka had the prison destroyed and began a construction project of another kind, gathering the relics of the Buddha to build eighty-four thousand stūpas. Aśoka devoted the rest of his life to the support of Buddhism, visiting the great pilgrimage sites, entertaining the saṅgha in a great festival, and finally, on his deathbed, giving away all of his wealth to Buddhist monks, until he was left with only half a fruit, which he had made into a soup and served to the saṅgha.

Such largesse was not merely legendary. There was a tradition of extravagant royal festivals in which all manner of gifts were given to the saṅgha. In some cases, the king would go so far as to offer his own ornaments and robes, donning the dress of a Buddhist monk to preach the dharma. But such transformations were only temporary, and his attendants would soon buy back the symbols of kingship and the king would return to his royal robes.

In the histories of many lands, the introduction of Buddhism is associated with a pious prince. In Japan, Prince Shōtoku (547–622) is regarded as both the founder of the Japanese state and the first patron of Buddhism. The dharma had been recommended to him by the Korean king of Paekche, who described it in a way in which it was perhaps regarded throughout Asia: as difficult to comprehend but capable of producing measureless merit such that every wish is fulfilled. The appeal of Buddhism, then, was not so much that it provided liberation from suffering as that, in the words of the *Lotus Sūtra,* it provided "peace and safety in the present life and good circumstances in future lives." This promise of happiness in this life and the next has contributed powerfully to the persistence of the dharma.

Prince Shōtoku is credited with building temples and writing commentaries on sūtras, putting the dharma into practice in support of his own rule and, by extension, of the nation. As in the case of many countries, images of Buddhist deities played an important role in the establishment of the dharma. In a battle with a rival (and anti-Buddhist) faction, the fourteen-year-old prince is said to have felled a tree, carved small statues of the kings of the four directions, and placed the statues in his topknot, vowing to build a temple in their honor when he emerged victorious. Another statue, still to be seen in Nara, was less effective. When Prince Shōtoku and his wife became ill, members of the court, in an effort to save him, vowed to have a statue of Śākyamuni Buddha made that resembled the prince. The prince died the next day, but the statue was completed and is enshrined in the Golden Hall of Hōryūji.

Another royal defender of the dharma is the Sri Lankan prince

Duṭṭhagāmaṇī, who defeated the other minor kingdoms of the island and briefly united them into a Buddhist kingdom in the second century B.C.E. His rather mythologized tale is told in the fifth-century chronicle of the island, the *Mahāvaṃsa.* Duṭṭhagāmaṇī had been a monk in his previous life; the monk had vowed to be reborn as a cakravartin. As king, he went to war against the enemies of the dharma, carrying a spear that bore a relic of the Buddha. The battle ended when he killed the enemy king, the pious but non-Buddhist Eḷāra. After his victory, he planted his spear in the earth. When he attempted to extract it, he failed and so decided to have a stūpa built around it, making the instrument of his victory a site for the making of merit. He is remembered for building important stūpas and for granting sovereignty over the island of Sri Lanka, not to any king, but to the relics of the Buddha, again suggesting the vitality and agency such relics were seen to possess. Like Aśoka, Duṭṭhagāmaṇī was troubled by the carnage he had caused with the deaths of sixty thousand. But he was assured by a delegation of arhats that, because among his victims there was only one Buddhist and one recent convert, he had only accrued the karma of killing one and one half persons. As a result of meritorious deeds, Duṭṭhagāmaṇī is said to have been reborn in the Joyous heaven, awaiting rebirth as a disciple of Maitreya. The story of Duṭṭhagāmaṇī continues to be told and has been deployed in recent years to defend the violence of Sinhalese Buddhists against non-Buddhist Tamils in Sri Lanka.

Sometimes the resistance to the introduction of Buddhism came not merely from rival factions but from the land itself. When a famous image of the Buddha was being transported from China to Tibet, where the dharma had recently been adopted by the king, all manner of obstacles prevented its successful transport to the royal capital. It was soon determined that the very land of Tibet, in the form of a great demoness, was objecting to the introduction of the new religion and was thus, through the movements of her body (which was also the surface of the state) attempting to impede its progress. The king then ordered that Buddhist temples be constructed around his land, each above a vital point in the demoness's body, effectively impaling her in a supine position and making his realm ready for the establishment of the dharma.

Images and relics of the Buddha thus play an important role in the histories of dynasties, serving as signs of righteousness and legitimation. The fifteenth-century *Legend of Queen Cāma* (*Cāmadevīvaṃsa*) tells how the Buddha visits northern Thailand and predicts that after he enters nirvāṇa one of his relics will appear there. An ascetic builds a great city in preparation for the discovery of the relic and invites a pregnant princess (whose husband has become a Buddhist monk) to be its ruler, Queen Cāma. She gives birth to twin sons, who in turn become forebears of a royal lineage. A pious Buddhist, her dying words are "suffering, impermanence, no-self." Twenty-eight kings and some four hundred years later, the relic is finally discovered buried beneath the king's latrine, its presence revealed by a white crow that preaches the dharma. It is only then that the true purpose of the dynasty, the protection of the relic and hence of the three jewels, is revealed.

Throughout much of Asia, Buddhist monks were supported by the state because of their abilities to predict the future, to bring timely rains, and to legitimate rule by identifying the king's past associations with the Buddha in previous lives. In China, in an apocryphal text called *The Perfection of Wisdom Sūtra for Humane Kings Who Wish to Protect Their States* (*Renwang hu guo banrou boluomiduo jing*), the Buddha explained that, during the time of the final dharma, rulers are entrusted with the preservation of Buddhism. And by performing the proper rituals (which entailed elaborate feasts for monks), their realms will be protected from drought, plague, floods, and invading armies. Across East Asia there thus developed the view of a symbiotic relationship between imperial rule and the saṅgha, between state law and Buddhist law. The ruler was responsible for protecting and maintaining the saṅgha. The saṅgha was responsible for maintaining moral rectitude, thus creating the merit that would sustain the state, and for instructing the populace in the virtuous behavior that would promote social order. Monks must maintain their vows, and the state must maintain monks in order for harmony to prevail. This twofold promotion of the dharma was meant to ensure the welfare of the state and its subjects in this life and the next.

In Japan, one of the ways in which Buddhist monks sought to

gain state support for their particular sect was to claim its efficacy in securing the welfare of the nation. For example, the Zen monk Eisai (1141–1215) returned from China to compose a *Treatise on Promoting Zen for the Protection of the Country* (*Kōzen gokokuron*), which he submitted to the new military dictatorship based in Kamakura. It was believed that the security and prosperity of Japan depended on a variety of deities, who had the power both to avert natural disasters and to protect the island from foreign invasion. In order to maintain the favor and support of these deities, the appropriate offerings and prayers had to be performed. The efficacy of such rituals depended, according to traditional Buddhist theory, on the purity of those who performed them. Eisai argued that the ethical discipline of Zen monks made them the most potent practitioners of the rituals for the protection of the state described in such works as the *Perfection of Wisdom Sūtra for Humane Kings Who Wish to Protect Their States.* In this sense Buddhism is not so much identified with a particular state as it is regarded as a power, of equal or perhaps greater importance, that can serve the state when properly propitiated. Such arguments for the reciprocal relation of saṅgha and state continued to be made in Japan during the twentieth century, used by many Buddhist sects to justify their strong support for the Japanese conquest of much of Asia.

Eisai was successful in gaining the patronage of the Kamakura shogunate. One of his near contemporaries, Nichiren (1222–1282), was not. He was the founder of one of the new movements of Kamakura Buddhism, which claimed that a single practice held the key to enlightenment. For Dōgen, it was "just sitting" in Zen meditation. Seated meditation, he claimed, is not just one of a variety of Buddhist practices or just the practice of the Zen sect, it is rather the essential practice of Buddhism. Zazen is not a method that results in buddhahood but rather is the most perfect expression of the buddhahood that pervades the universe. From this perspective, to sit in meditation is to be a buddha; it is a manifestation of one's true nature, present from the very beginning. For Hōnen, the single practice was chanting *namu amida butsu,* "homage to Amitābha Buddha," calling on him to deliver the faithful to his pure land upon their death. For Nichiren, it was chanting the great title of the

Lotus Sūtra, in Japanese *namu myōhō renge kyō.* Other sects in Japan, notably the Tendai, had championed the *Lotus* as the Buddha's true and final teaching, regarding other sūtras as examples of the Buddha's skillful methods. Nichiren went much further, declaring all other Buddhist texts to be utterly ineffectual during the degenerate age. He reinterpreted the Buddhist sin of "deprecating the dharma." Traditionally it had been taken to mean denying the efficacy of the Buddha's teaching, claiming a spurious text to be the word of the Buddha, or claiming an authentic text to be spurious (these latter two forms being commonly invoked in debates over the status of the Mahāyāna sūtras). Nichiren rather radically reinterpreted what it meant to deprecate the dharma; for him, it was a sin to promote any text other than the *Lotus,* with the sinner doomed to hell. He preached this view quite publicly, attracting the opprobrium of the other Buddhist sects of Japan. Nichiren declared, however, that such harsh rhetoric was required to turn the benighted toward the true teaching, and whatever persecution he suffered as a result served both as a further sign of the degenerate age when the devotees of the *Lotus* are persecuted (as the sūtra itself predicted) and as an opportunity for him to experience the effects of his own past karma. Like Eisai, Nichiren also wrote a treatise to the military dictator in Kamakura, predicting that Japan would suffer both natural disaster and foreign invasion if patronage of the other Buddhist sects was not suspended in favor of the *Lotus Sūtra.* Nichiren was arrested and sent into exile. His example of criticizing the government was emulated by many of his followers. While under arrest, Nisshin (1407–1488) was handed the bamboo saw with which he was to be beheaded (the sentence was apparently subsequently commuted). Nisshin struck the saw against the floor of his cell, explaining that he was dulling the blade so that he might suffer more for the sake of the *Lotus Sūtra.*

Relations between the saṅgha and the state have taken a wide variety of forms throughout the Buddhist world, often with questions over domains of authority. The Chinese monk Hui-yuan (334–417) refused to bow to the emperor, arguing that because Buddhist monks had renounced the world, they were not obliged to abide by its customs. The saṅgha has been regarded as essential to the good fortune of the state by some rulers, as a drain on the state treasury and a refuge of scoundrels by others. The most sweeping monastic reform of recent times occurred in 1872 in Japan, when the Meiji government removed any special status from monkhood. Henceforth, monks had to register in the household registry system and were subject to secular education, taxation, and military conscription. Most controversially, the government declared, "From now on Buddhist clerics will be free to eat meat, marry, grow their hair, and so on." Nuns were also allowed to eat meat, marry, and grow their hair, but they were not permitted to wear lay dress. Unlike most monks, Japanese nuns have chosen to remain celibate, despite the Meiji declaration. Since the seventeenth century, there had been laws, sporadically enforced, making meat eating and marriage criminal offenses for monks; during the Tokugawa period (1603–1868) the government enacted regulations requiring all monks to be celibate and making relations with a woman punishable by death. The fact that these activities had been criminalized by the government suggests that such acts were widespread, and this appears to have been the case. It was common, for example, for monks, despite vows of celibacy, to have wives and children. Indeed, the fate of the widows and orphans of monks appears to have been an embarrassment to the state.

The new regulations were met with alarm by the Buddhist sects of Japan, especially the regulation permitting marriage. It was feared that rescinding the law against clerical marriage would destroy the distinction between monk and layperson, bringing chaos to the state. In response to protests from Buddhist leaders, the government subsequently issued an addendum to the law, stating that although meat eating and marriage were no longer criminal offenses, the individual sects were free to regulate these activities as they saw fit. Most sects subsequently issued regulations either condemning or prohibiting marriage for their monks. Nonetheless, during the last century it became increasingly common for monks to marry, with less than 1 percent keeping the code of monastic discipline.

In other Buddhist lands the line between monk and state was blurred in other ways. Mongkut (Rama IV, 1806–1868) of Thailand was ordained at the age of twenty and spent twenty-seven years as a monk, becoming a distinguished scholar, before returning to lay life and ascending the throne. One of the purposes served by his long period of monkhood was the protection it afforded from attempts on his life that might be made by his elder brother, the king. As a monk, he founded a new sect called the Thammayut ("adhering to the dharma") that placed special emphasis on strict observance of the code of monastic discipline. He instituted a wide range of changes in monastic life, including the way that robes were worn. As with all reform movements, such changes were said to be a return to the practices of the original saṅgha. In his sect, the study of the sūtras was emphasized over meditation practice.

Sometimes the head of state was identified with a particular bodhisattva. In Tibet, the fifth Dalai Lama, a Buddhist monk, was installed on the throne of Tibet by his Mongol patrons in 1642. The Dalai Lama also consolidated his power mythologically, declaring himself to be the present incarnation of the bodhisattva Avalokiteśvara, the embodiment of compassion, who according to myth was the progenitor of the Tibetan people: Avalokiteśvara had taken the form of a monkey in order to mate with an ogress, their offspring being the first Tibetans. By identifying himself with Avalokiteśvara, the Dalai Lama became the human manifestation of the cosmic bodhisattva of compassion. He was at once a Buddhist monk, the human incarnation of a bodhisattva, and a divine king, combining saṅgha and state simultaneously in a single person.

THE ROLE OF THE BOOK

It is important to bear in mind that the vast majority of Buddhists across Asia have been illiterate. Thus, it is misleading to think of the Buddhist book solely as something to be read. Sūtras were placed on altars and worshiped with offerings of flowers and incense, as the sūtra itself often prescribed. Laypeople sought to accrue merit and avert misfortune by paying monks to come into their homes and chant sūtras. Regardless of whether the audience (or the reader) could understand the content, the word of the Buddha was being heard, and this carried the power of a magic spell. Those with sufficient resources would commission the copying of a sūtra, as the sūtra itself often prescribed, thereby not simply making a duplicate that someone else could read, but multiplying a sacred object that would serve as the focus of further meritorious devotions. In China, some monasteries had halls devoted exclusively to the recitation of sūtras. Laypeople could purchase certificates representing a given number of recitations of a sūtra. Those certificates could then be offered (through burning) in services for deceased relatives. Other monasteries had rooms for perusing scriptures, where monks would read, or simply glance at, the pages of scriptures. Whether or not the text was comprehended, this was considered a meritorious act. Indeed, in Tibet at the time of the new year or in the case of natural disasters such as droughts, it was common for the monks of a monastery to read the entire portion of the canon considered to be the word of the Buddha, traditionally contained in 108 volumes. In this massive undertaking, the volumes of the collection were divided among as many monks as possible, who simultaneously read each page aloud, creating a cacophony of the dharma. As an additional blessing, the volumes were then carried in a procession around the village. In East Asia, communal readings of the canon sometimes did not even entail the texts being read aloud; each text simply had to be unfolded. In addition to whatever merit this practice accrued, it also aired out texts to prevent damage from mold and insects.

The *Heart Sūtra* is perhaps the most famous of all Buddhist texts, chanted daily in Buddhist temples and monasteries throughout East Asia and Tibet, renowned for its terse expression of the perfection of wisdom, the knowledge whereby buddhahood is achieved. In part because of its brevity (it is only about one page long in translation), in part because of its potency (as the quintessence of the Buddha's wisdom), the *Heart Sūtra* has been put to a wide variety of ritual uses. The most common use to which the *Heart Sūtra* is put in Tibet is in a rite for turning away demons. This is a rite that laypeople will ask a monk or lama to perform in an effort to remove a present problem or avert a future danger.

The lama performing the rite (who may or may not be a monk) first places either a painting or statue of the Buddha in the center of a white cloth and arranges offerings in front of it. To the east (that is, in front of the Buddha image), he places seven images of dough stamped with the impression of the divine demon Māra, in the form of a white human on a white horse, with flowers in his right hand (the flowers of desire that Māra shoots at his victims) and a noose in his left. To the south he places seven images of the Demon of the Afflictions, a yellow human on a yellow horse. In his right hand is a sword, in his left a noose. To the west, he places seven images of the Demon of the Aggregates in the form of a red human on a red horse with a spear in his right hand and a noose in his left. To the north, the lama places seven images of the demon who is the Lord of Death in the form of a black human on a black horse. In his right hand he holds a club, in his left a noose.

It is then necessary to prepare an effigy of the person who has commissioned the performance of the rite, the patron, the person whom the rite is meant to benefit. The lama makes a dough statue of the patron, having first had the patron breathe on and spit on the dough. The effigy is then dressed in a garment made from clothing belonging to the patron and is placed in front of the Buddha image with its face turned toward the Buddha and its back toward the lama. In this position, the effigy stands as both a substitute and a protector for the patron, acting as his surrogate before the demons.

The lama then visualizes himself as the Buddha, seated in the midst of the four demons. The lama, as the Buddha, plays the role first of host to the demons, then of the agent who enters into a contract with the demons, and finally of their conqueror. He is surrounded by a retinue, with Avalokiteśvara on the right and eight bodhisattvas and eight monks on the left. The lama next visualizes the goddess Prajñāpāramitā ("Perfection of Wisdom") at his heart, seated on a moon disc, surrounded by buddhas and bodhisattvas. Moving to an even smaller scale, the meditator imagines that there is a moon disc in the center of her heart, upon which stands the letter *āḥ*. At an even more minute level, the lama is instructed to visualize the letters of the *Heart Sūtra* standing upright around the edge of the moon disc at the goddess's heart. The letters of the sūtra radiate both light and their own sound, serving as offerings to the buddhas and bodhisattvas, who in turn alleviate the sufferings and purify all those gathered for the performance of the rite (and all sentient beings) as the lama contemplates the meaning of emptiness.

The lama is then instructed to recite the *Heart Sūtra* as many times as possible and then make the standard offerings of ablution, flowers, incense, lamps, perfume, food, and music, with the appropriate mantras followed by verses praising Śākyamuni and Prajñāpāramitā. He then moistens the images and offerings with water and invites the four actual demons to come from their abodes, the four Formless Realms, and dissolve into their molded images. The four demons are presumably said to reside in the Formless Realms because they are invisible. The four demons are believed to be invisible, perniciously invading the human domain undetected but for the harm they inflict. In order that the demons be placated and turned back, they must be made visible and brought into physical presence. Hence, dough images are made for them, which they are then invited to enter and animate.

The *Heart Sūtra* is then repeated nine times. After each set of nine repetitions, the lama claps and turns one of the seven demons aligned to the east so that it faces outward. The sūtra is then recited nine more times and another image is turned, until the seven demons in the east have all been turned around, requiring sixty-three recitations of the sūtra. The same procedure is repeated for the demons in the other three directions, such that the sūtra must be repeated 252 times to complete the process. The four demons and their retinues have been turned away from the Buddha by the power of the *Heart Sūtra* so that they now face outward toward the effigy of the patron.

The lama is instructed to say different things, depending on whether the rite is being performed for a sick person, to destroy an enemy, or for some other purpose. If the rite is being performed in order to destroy an enemy, the lama is instructed to say, "By the power of the words of truth of the noble three jewels, may our enemy so-and-so today be summoned, liberated [that is, killed], and his flesh and blood eaten by the gods and demons of the world. May his consciousness be led into the sphere of reality."

Offerings are then made to the demons, with requests that they refrain from further harm. The demons, now residing physically in their dough images and facing toward the lama, are further brought under control by bringing them into a social relation, the position of the guest, to be offered hospitality, in the form of food and gifts, by the lama acting as host. For example, to the divine demon Māra the lama is instructed to say, "I offer this biscuit, endowed with a hundred flavors and a thousand potencies, to the assembled armies of the child of gods. May it turn into enjoyments, their exhaustion unknown, that agree with their individual thoughts. Having delighted and satisfied them all, I pray that all of the harm unleashed by the four demons will be cast aside."

The gift to be offered to the demons is the effigy of the patron. First, the person whom the effigy represents cleans the effigy with water that has been in his or her mouth. The lama then blesses the effigy. The effigy is repeatedly praised; it is described as being superior to the patron of whom it is a replica. In return for releasing the patron from their power, the demons will be given something of greater value, the effigy. Once the offering of the effigy has been made to the demons, the next step is the dispatching of the demons. The demons, as guests, have been fed and offered a gift. It is now time for them to depart. Here the demons are both cajoled and threatened, invited to return with the gifts they have received to their palaces in the Formless Realm. The offering of the effigy is thus a gift given in order to receive; in effect, the demons and the patron (with the lama acting as his agent) enter into a contract, agreeing to release the patron from their power in return for their taking possession of the effigy. The demons are to understand that any breach of this contract carries with it a penalty; should they not keep their part of the bargain and return to harm the patron, then the lama, through his surrogate, the Buddha, will visit them with punishment.

The next step is to take all of the images and offerings (with the exception of the Buddha image) to a safe distance and then place them facing away from the place where the rite was performed. The location, however, depends on the purpose of the rite that the lama has been asked to perform. For example, if the rite is for the welfare of a sick person, they are to be put in a cemetery. If a horoscope predicts that danger is approaching as a result of the "fourth year executioner," the inauspicious year that occurs four years after one's birth year in the twelve-year cycle, or as a result of the "conjunction of the seven," the ill fortune that results from a relationship with someone seven years apart in age, they are to be placed in the direction the harm is predicted to come from. If it is for bringing happiness, they are placed either above or below a crossroads. If a curse is being deflected, they are placed in the direction of the curse. If one is making a curse, they are placed in the direction of the enemy. If one has been harmed by the spirit king, they are placed at the base of a temple or a stūpa. If one has been harmed by a female devil, it is placed outside the town. If one has been harmed by a water deity, they are to be placed at a lake or a spring.

The rite then concludes with a blessing, calling upon the five buddhas and a sixth deity, the goddess of the earth. The usual offerings, prayers, and dedications are then made, with the lama reminded to keep in mind throughout that both he and the patron are by nature empty. The text concludes with a final testimony to the rite's potency: "By coming under the power of the four [demons] in this existence, one is bereft of happiness and tormented by millions of sufferings. Until one attains the vajra-like samādhi [the final moment of meditation before the achievement of buddhahood], this rite is an amazing method of exorcism."

Such rituals, in which the Buddha and his dharma are called upon to dispel the damage done by evil spirits, are repeated in myriad forms throughout the Buddhist world. The presence of these rites in Buddhist cultures was once regarded as evidence of "the little tradition," a concession made to the laity by monks who knew better than to believe in such things. In fact, Buddhism has always derived much of its support, from the most powerful kings to the local villagers, from its magical power to dispel evil and promote goodness. Monks, with their ability to read and recite the sūtras and mantras that possess such power, have often been the agents of this protection. From the time of the Buddha, this appears to have been a central means for their sustenance and a central element of their practice, forming an essential link to the laity.

KARMA

Whether they were seeking to dispel demons in this life or to find a fortunate rebirth in the next, Buddhists, both monks and laity, have remained preoccupied with karma, generally seeking a magical means of subverting the negative karma of the past and an efficient technique for amassing positive karma in the present. The law of karma as classically expounded, in which the misdeeds of the past must fructify as present and future suffering, unless one attains insight into no-self, was either unknown to or ignored by most Buddhists over the centuries and across Asia. This did not mean, however, that elaborate interventions into the workings of karma did not occur. Indeed, such interventions have constituted the practice of Buddhism.

The powers of the *Lotus Sūtra,* for example, are considered so great that its very title has miraculous power. A story from twelfth-century China tells of a depraved and evil man who once mocked a pious monk by making a face at him and sarcastically saying, "*Lotus Sutra.*" When the man died and was appropriately consigned to hell in accordance with his evil deeds in life, the Lord of Death declared that a mistake had been made, that despite his evil appearance the man had performed a deed of such goodness that he should return to the world. Indeed, no one who had ever chanted the name of the *Lotus Sūtra* even once had ever been reborn in hell.

In a Tang dynasty tale, a woman fishmonger was reborn in hell for having engaged in wrong livelihood. The Lord of Death determined that she had once listened to a lecture on the *Lotus Sūtra* and so allowed her to return to earth, but not before giving her a tour of the sufferings she avoided. In seeing the plight of denizens of the various hells, she spontaneously said, "Homage to the *Lotus Sutra*" (akin to someone remarking in disbelief, "Jesus Christ"), at which point all the hell beings who heard her were miraculously reborn in heaven.

In each of these cases, there is a mechanism at work referred to in China as "stimulation-response." Rather than a simple case of divine intercession or compassionate salvation by a bodhisattva, the pious person creates a kind of resonance through the recitation that first attracts the attention of the deity and then compels him or her to respond. It would be misleading, therefore, to regard these stories as somehow supernatural, in which the divine momentarily suspends the laws of nature to intervene in the human world. Instead, the salvations that occur are wholly natural, in the sense that when the appropriate cause is present, the effect must occur.

This rather mechanistic view found a somewhat different expression in the calculation of karma. The classical exposition of karmic theory saw all intentional deeds of the ignorant person, whether virtuous or evil, as producing karma and thus further binding the person in saṃsāra. Rebirth was not seen to be the result of weighing the deeds of the past life in a balance and moving up or down in the six realms, depending on the way the scales tipped. Rather, each complete deed from any past life was a potential cause of an entire lifetime, and a variety of factors, including one's state of mind at the time of death, determined which particular deed would fructify as the next lifetime. But such fine points seem to have been of little interest in most Buddhist societies, where one finds an enduring interest in the calculation of karma. This is nowhere more true than in China, where hell was transformed into an infernal bureaucracy, where the minions of the Lord of Death consulted ledgers of the deeds of the damned. In a Chinese text called the *Sūtra of the Ten Kings* (*Shiwang jing*), the fate of the dead in the world between death and rebirth is described. Ten times after death (at the end of each of the first seven weeks, one hundred days, one year, and three years) the deceased is escorted like a prisoner into the presence of a king who has before him a precise record of all the person's deeds of the past life. The dead are herded like sheep from court to court, pushed along by ox-headed guards wielding pitchforks. In the fourth court a scale weighs their good deeds against their sins. In the fifth court they are dragged by the hair and made to look into the mirror of karma, where they see their past misdeeds reflected. In the tenth court, reached after three years of suffering, the place of rebirth is decided. Among misdeeds, specific mention is made of the gravity of using money that rightfully belongs to the three jewels.

In the sūtra, the Buddha explains that if the family left behind on earth sends the appropriate offerings at the appropriate time, the deceased may be excused from the courts at various points along the journey and be granted a favorable rebirth. Those families who sponsor vegetarian feasts for monks and commission the making of images may create sufficient merit to have their loved one avoid the judicial system entirely and be reborn in heaven. Of particular efficacy is oneself copying or sponsoring the copying of the *Sūtra of the Ten Kings* and making pictures of the ten kings. Doing so for one's own benefit will be duly noted in the registry of one's deeds, and one will be spared the ordeal of judgment when one dies. Doing so on behalf of deceased loved ones will cause them to emerge from the ordeal and secure a happy rebirth. In testimony to the popularity of this practice, many copies of the scriptures, many with illustrations of the ten courts, have been discovered in manuscript collections.

Among the living, there was also a fascination with determining the merits and demerits of one's deeds, and works were composed prescribing some deeds and proscribing others. The prototype of such texts is the *Tract of the Most Exalted on Action and Response* (*Taishang ganying pian*), first published in 1164. An entire genre of ledgers of merit and demerit was spawned, works that drew eclectically from Confucian, Daoist, and Buddhist sources, with one tradition usually weighted against the others, depending on the allegiance of the author. These works list hundreds of meritorious and demeritorious deeds, assigning a certain number of positive and negative points to each. Readers were encouraged to pause before sleep each night to take account of the past day's activities, recording good deeds (and their respective merit) in one column and bad deeds (and their respective demerit) in another. Scholars have linked the popularity of these works with changes in the social and economic structures during the late Ming and early Qing dynasties.

A Buddhist work from 1604 assigns two merit points per day for serving one's stepmother with respect and one point per day for obeying the laws of the dynasty. Fifty points are earned for saving an infant from being drowned and raising it as one's own child. Trying to convince fishermen, hunters, and butchers to seek a more virtuous source for their livelihood earns three points, increased to fifty if one is successful. Giving a burial plot to a family that has none is worth thirty points. Among more specifically Buddhist activities, composing a commentary on a Mahāyāna text earns fifty points per work, to a maximum of fifteen hundred for prolific authors. A commentary on a Hīnayāna text is worth only one point, the same amount of merit earned by chanting the name of the Buddha one thousand times. Among negative deeds, talking back to one's parents results in ten negative points, making poison results in five negative points, and sentencing a person to death counts one hundred points. Killing animals during a period of the year in which killing animals is prohibited results in twice the negative points that would be incurred at other times. Among Buddhist practices, to slander the Buddha results in five negative points. Each character misread or omitted while chanting a sūtra counts one negative point. Rising to receive a guest while chanting a sūtra results in two negative points, unless the guest is a government official, in which case there is no penalty. Reciting a sūtra after eating garlic or onions results in one negative point. Illicit sexual intercourse with a person of good family results in ten negative points; two negative points are incurred for having sexual relations with a prostitute.

The concern with making merit and the ideal of the bodhisattva's compassion intersected in the practice of releasing animals. Refraining from killing and maintaining a vegetarian diet were themselves sources of merit, but they were, in a certain sense, passive deeds. An apocryphal Chinese sūtra, called *Brahmā's Net* (*Fan wang jing*), lists, in a long enumeration of things that a bodhisattva vows to avoid, "the nonpractice of releasing and saving." In Tibet, as a result of a bad omen or inauspicious horoscope, one might be advised to free some animals. This would involve purchasing a goat or a sheep that was destined to slaughter and protecting it from death. In China, the release of animals more commonly involved turtles and fish (although game birds and animals were also sometimes included) and was carried out on a grander, often imperial, scale. In 619, an imperial decree prohibited fishing, hunting, and the slaughter of animals during the first, fifth, and ninth months of the year. A decree of 759 established eighty-one ponds for the release and protection of fish. Sometimes public ceremonies for the release of creatures were held annually to commemorate the Buddha's birth. (Reports suggest that in medieval Japan the imperial government would order the capture of three times the number of fish needed to be released at a ceremony in order that the requisite number—often from one thousand to three thousand—be alive by the time the ceremony took place. In such cases, the practice of releasing animals resulted in the unfortunate death of many before they could be liberated.) At the local level, lay societies for releasing living beings were founded, often inspired by the preaching of a famous monk. In some, each member would bring an animal for release to the monthly meeting, in others members collected donations in order to purchase fish, birds, and domesticated animals doomed to the dinner table.

The locus classicus for the practice is a story in the *Sūtra of Golden Light* (*Suvarṇabhāsottama*). In a previous life, the Buddha was a merchant's son named Jalavāhana, who one day encountered a dried-up pond in the forest, filled with ten thousand dying fish. Summoning twenty elephants, he carried bags of water from a river into the forest and replenished the pond, saving the fish. He then sent for food with which to feed them. Finally, recalling that anyone who hears the name of the buddha Ratnaśikhin will be reborn in heaven, he waded into the pond and pronounced the buddha's name, followed by an exposition of dependent origination. When the fish died, they were reborn in the Heaven of the Thirty-Three. Recalling the reason for their happy fate, they visited the world of humans, where each offered a pearl necklace to Jalavāhana's head, foot, right side, and left side.

Among the benefits said to accrue from the practice of releasing animals were honor, longevity, prosperity, progeny, a successful career, recovery from mental illness, protection from natural disasters (such as drought), and rebirth in one of the heavenly realms. A tenth-century Japanese work tells of a devout woman who had chanted the name of Amitābha all her life. At the time of her death, she felt that some small karmic obstacle was preventing her rebirth in the pure land. She recalled that some time ago someone had given her some carp. Rather than eat them, she released them into a well. She now wondered whether the carp, so confined, longed to swim in a river. She had someone transport the carp to a river. Soon after, the fragrance of lotuses filled her room and she died painlessly facing the west, the direction of Amitābha's land. But there were benefits in this life as well. A winemaker who compassionately prevented flies from drowning in his casks was arrested and convicted for a crime he did not commit. As the judge was about to write his sentence, a swarm of flies covered his pen. The winemaker was released.

The physical release of fish and animals was not considered fully efficacious unless some attempt was made to ensure their spiritual release as well. Ceremonies to accompany the liberation of the animals were composed by eminent Buddhist monks. As in the rite of water and land, the model was one of salvation through hearing the dharma; a famous story tells of a frog who was accidentally stepped on while the Buddha was preaching the dharma and was reborn in the Heaven of the Thirty-Three. In some cases, the rite would be as simple as the chanting of a sūtra or the chanting of Amitābha's name. In more elaborate ceremonies, the fish would hear a sermon on the sufferings of saṃsāra. After that, the officiating priest would sprinkle them with water that would purify them of the mental defilements that prevented them from understanding what was being said. The priest would then bestow refuge in the three jewels, followed by a prayer for the animals to be reborn in their next life in the Heaven of the Thirty-Three and eventually achieve enlightenment. This would be followed by a lecture on the twelvefold chain of dependent origination, one of the most difficult of Buddhist doctrines even for bipeds, then a confession of the animals' sins, and finally a prayer for rebirth in the pure land. Eventually, almost every large monastery in China had a pool for releasing fish and pens for the care of livestock that had been rescued from the butcher. Because these animals had been given Buddhist precepts, they were encouraged to observe them, with males and females segregated and carnivorous fish kept separately. Birds, turtles, and fish were more popular for release than domesticated animals because they required no further assistance. The pious who delivered cows and pigs to the monastery, however, were required to contribute toward their sustenance.

PILGRIMAGE

In his final instructions before his death, the Buddha prescribed the practice of pilgrimage to sites where his relics would be enshrined. He declared that those who offer flowers, incense, or paint to one of his stūpas will derive merit from their good deed, and those who feel delight at the sight of a stūpa or who die while on pilgrimage will be reborn in heaven. Pilgrimage has been a major form of practice throughout the history of Buddhism and across the Buddhist world, with pilgrims journeying from around Asia to India in order to visit the sites important in the life of the Buddha, especially Bodhgaya, the place of his enlightenment. Accounts from the thirteenth century indicate that Bodhgaya was maintained by a delegation of Sri Lankan monks, who would retreat into the forest when Muslim troops passed through the area. In subsequent centuries, control of Bodhgaya was lost by Buddhists; it was only restored after Indian independence in the last century. Since that time, pilgrimage to Bodhgaya from across the Buddhist world has increased greatly.

Each region of the Buddhist world also has its own pilgrimage sites, whether they be temples, statues, monasteries, sacred mountains, or caves once occupied by saints. Pilgrimage provides a powerful technique for the "buddhification" of the landscape, with locales (often mountains) already important in local practice transformed into Buddhist sites by the identification of the mountain as the location of a relic of the Buddha or as the residence of a bodhisattva. At the summit of Adam's Peak in Sri Lanka there are footprints of the Buddha. In China, Mount Wutai was regarded as the abode of the bodhisattva of wisdom, Mañjuśrī, and was identified with a mountain mentioned in the *Flower Garland Sūtra* (*Avataṃsaka*). It became a major pilgrimage site, drawing pilgrims from as far away as Mongolia and Tibet. In some cases, mountains far beyond India were identified as mountains mentioned in Indian Buddhist sūtras as the place where the Buddha had delivered an important discourse or performed a famous miracle. In Tibet and Japan, certain sacred mountains were said to have originally been Indian peaks that had detached themselves from the earth and flown through the air and descended in another land, carrying their deities with them. These mountains contained hidden treasuries and secret caves, which were discovered by charismatic figures like the eighth-century Japanese figure En the Ascetic. Pilgrimage has served as an important conduit for various forms of exchange, both religious and commercial.

In Tibet, pilgrimage is often made to the abodes of deities known as protectors. Protectors play a central role in Tibetan Buddhism, for monks, nuns, and laypeople alike. Buddhas and bodhisattvas are distant and exalted enlightened beings of Indian origin. Their aid is not generally sought for the more mundane matters of life. Often of Tibetan origin, some dating from pre-Buddhist times, protectors are the formerly malignant spirits who animated and terrorized the Tibetan landscape. In order for Buddhism to take hold in Tibet, these spirits had to be defeated in magical battle by Indian masters such as Padmasambhava in the eighth century. Rather than be killed, the Tibetan spirits agreed to submit to the new faith and defend Buddhism. Unlike the foreign buddhas and bodhisattvas, protectors thus have strong local associations; they are ancestral guardians of a clan, a valley, a mountain, a monastery. A protector is thus a much more personal deity, like a big brother or a guardian angel or a godfather (in both senses of the term), someone who can help with financial or personal problems, who will protect you from danger and punish your enemies. It is common for Tibetans to credit their protector with everything from success in business to surviving an accident. Tibetans thus feel a great sense of allegiance and personal intimacy toward their protector.

A protector, although a local god, was often regarded, as often occurred throughout the Buddhist world, as a member of the retinue of a great buddha and bodhisattva. The abode of the local god was thereby incorporated into the Buddhist domain. Scholars have noted in the case of Tibet that many of the most important pilgrimage mountains are located in border regions that define the boundaries of a kingdom as a Buddhist realm. Pilgrimage to the abodes of these enlightened beings conferred a range of blessings, including fortunate rebirth and fortune and good health in this life. The mountain abodes of these deities were considered sacred spaces, often discovered or "opened" by a great lama in the past, who used his magical powers to wrest control of the place from malignant spirits, recognizing that, in reality, the mountain is a maṇḍala, with its peak serving as the seat of the central deity. As such, even to set foot on the mountain was considered efficacious. Circumambulation was thus a common practice in Tibetan Buddhism, made all the more potent if one could trace the circuit of the mountain not simply with one's footsteps but with one's entire body. Hence, the well-known image of Tibetan pilgrims performing "full prostrations," in which they bow down and stretch their bodies on the ground at full length, rise, walk forward a few steps, and then bow down again. Tibetan pilgrims commonly traverse pilgrimage routes of hundreds of miles in this fashion.

In northern Thailand, the practice of pilgrimage is associated with the life cycle of the individual. There, as in many parts of Asia, years are named after animals in a twelve-year cycle; one is said to have been born in the Year of the Dog, the Year of the Hare, the Year of the Monkey, and so forth. It is considered auspicious to make a pilgrimage to one of twelve sacred sites linked to one's birth year in order to worship the relic of the Buddha enshrined there. In most cases the relics are said to have been brought to Thailand by emissaries of Aśoka. Some of these shrines are of easier access than others; three of them are not located in Thailand. One of these is the Shwe Dagon in Rangoon; another is Bodhgaya in India. The third of the twelve sites is not in Thailand, nor is it on earth. After the time of the Buddha's cremation, Droṇa, the brahmin who distributed the relics, kept a tooth of the Buddha for himself and hid it in his hair. The tooth was taken by the god Indra and enshrined in the Heaven of the Thirty-Three. Those born in the Year of the Dog would be required to visit this most inaccessible of stūpas. However, they may instead visit the city of Chiang Mai and the shrine of Wat Ket, named after this tooth relic of the Buddha.

One of the most famous pilgrimage routes in Japan is the eighty-eight-stage pilgrimage route around the smallest of the main islands, Shikoku. Once accomplished on foot, this circuit today is most often traveled by bus, with most pilgrims stopping at each temple on the route to have the name of the site stamped on to a scroll or into a book. The pilgrimage is associated with the great Shingon master Kūkai (774–835, reverentially also known as Kōbō Daishi, "Great Teacher Who Spread the Dharma"). Kūkai is believed still to be present in the world. For according to his legend, Kūkai did not die on Mount Kōya in 835 but merely entered a state of eternal samādhi, awaiting, like Mahākāśyapa, the coming of Maitreya. Although memorial services were performed each week for seven weeks after his death, no funeral was performed. Kūkai appeared alive, and his hair and beard continued to grow. He was sealed inside a mausoleum, where priests continued to change his clothes. The vicinity of his tomb on Mount Kōya is filled with the ashes of the dead, who await with Kūkai the advent of Maitreya.

Kūkai was born on Shikoku, although the pilgrimage route as it is currently known did not take shape until the seventeenth century. He is said to accompany each pilgrim along the route around the island of Shikoku and often assumes the guise of a pilgrim himself, benefiting those who show him generosity and punishing those who do not. Performing the pilgrimage is said to offer many rewards, recounted in several collections of tales. A man who could not speak undertook the pilgrimage and began to speak fluently by the third day. A woman carrying water to her sick daughter encountered a pilgrim who asked for the water. She gave it to him freely. In gratitude, the pilgrim, who was in fact Kūkai, performed a tantric rite, and a river of pure water magically appeared. A leper performed the pilgrimage and was cured by the time he returned home. The most famous story, one of punishment and salvation, is about a greedy man named Emon Saburō, who refused to give alms to a pilgrim who came to his door. Instead, he struck him with a stick and broke his begging bowl into eight pieces. Emon had eight sons, and over the next eight days each son died. Emon realized that the pilgrim had been Kūkai and set out to ask his forgiveness. In an effort to find him, he traversed the Shikoku pilgrimage route in the reverse direction, making the circuit twenty-one times without meeting the master. As Emon lay dying at one of the temples, Kūkai appeared to him and absolved him of his misdeeds. Emon asked to be reborn into a good family so that he could perform good deeds. Kūkai wrote "Emon Saburō reborn" on a stone and placed it in his hand as he died. After the appointed time, a child was born clenching the same stone in his hand and grew up to restore a temple on the pilgrimage route where the stone is today enshrined.

Suggested Reading

Brereton, Bonnie. *Thai Tellings of Phra Malai: Texts and Rituals Concerning a Popular Buddhist Saint.* Tempe: Arizona State University Program for Southeast Asian Studies, 1995.

Gombrich, Richard F. *Precept and Practice: Traditional Buddhism in the Rural Highlands of Ceylon.* Oxford: Clarendon Press, 1971.

Groot, Jan J. M. de. *Sectarianism and Religious Persecution in China.* Taipei: Literature House, 1963.

Lopez, Donald S., Jr. *Elaborations on Emptiness: Uses of the Heart Sūtra.* Princeton: Princeton University Press, 1996.

———, ed. *Buddhism in Practice.* Princeton: Princeton University Press, 1995.

———. *Religions of China in Practice.* Princeton: Princeton University Press, 1996.

Reader, Ian, and George J. Tanabe Jr. *Practically Religious: Worldly Benefits and the Common Religion of Japan.* Honolulu: University of Hawaii Press, 1998.

Strong, John S. *The Legend of King Aśoka: A Study and Translation of the Aśokāvadāna.* Princeton: Princeton University Press, 1983.

Swearer, Donald K., and Sommai Premchit. *The Legend of Queen Cāma: Bodhiraṃsi's Cāmadevīvaṃsa, A Translation and Commentary.* Albany: State University of New York Press, 1998.

Tanabe, George J., Jr., ed. *Religions of Japan in Practice.* Princeton: Princeton University Press, 1999.

Teiser, Stephen F. *The Ghost Festival in Medieval China.* Princeton: Princeton University Press, 1988.

———. *The Scripture of the Ten Kings and the Making of Purgatory in Medieval Chinese Buddhism.* Honolulu: University of Hawaii Press, 1994.

Welch, Holmes. *The Practice of Chinese Buddhism: 1900–1950.* Cambridge: Harvard University Press, 1967.

Yü, Chün-fang. *The Renewal of Buddhism in China: Chu-hung and the Late Ming Synthesis.* New York: Columbia University Press, 1981.

6

ENLIGHTENMENT

The nature of enlightenment and the most efficient means to achieve it have been much discussed in Buddhist texts across Asia and across the centuries, often at some remove from those most devoted to its pursuit. Some claim that enlightenment can occur suddenly, brought about by something as simple as the ringing of a bell. Others set forth a detailed process of gradual perfection of the mind, proceeding over ten stages and ensuing over millions of lifetimes. Some claim that no one has become enlightened since the time of the Buddha. Others declare that all beings are already enlightened, they just need to recognize it. Buddhist sūtras regularly report the number of beings who achieved various states of enlightenment by simply listening to a discourse of the Buddha. The Buddha's first five disciples became arhats after hearing his second sermon, and all sixty of the Buddha's early disciples also became arhats. Śāriputra, the wisest of the Buddha's disciples, became an arhat while he stood behind the Buddha, fanning him, as the Buddha delivered a discourse to another monk. Ānanda, the Buddha's attendant, became an arhat after the Buddha's death as he lay down to go to sleep, just before his head touched the pillow.

The techniques for achieving enlightenment are equally varied. Some declare that intellectual analysis of the constituents of mind and body is essential. For others, there is no greater obstacle to enlightenment than the discursive activities of the mind. For some, the suppression of desire is required before progress can be made on the path. For others, desire, especially sexual desire, offers access to deep states of consciousness essential to the path. Whatever the technique, the measure of enlightenment is difficult to make. The state is rarely described as self-validating—even Śāriputra and Maudgalyāyana, the chief disciples of the Buddha, did not know that they had become arhats until the Buddha told them so—and, in the absence of the Buddha, who else is qualified to determine who has reached enlightenment? Two centuries after the Buddha's death, a controversy arose over whether arhats were subject to nocturnal emissions; although free from desire during the day, could they be seduced in their dreams? The ability to perform miracles is, as we shall see below, a side effect of relatively lesser states and hence cannot be taken as an indication of enlightenment. In the mainstream traditions, the final proof of enlightenment is to never be reborn again, something difficult to determine by those left behind. Yet many modern Theravāda teachers say that so much time has passed since the death of the Buddha that it is now impossible for anyone to become an arhat; we must await the coming of Maitreya. The Mahāyāna traditions either declare the immanence of enlightenment or predict it in the unimaginably distant future. What remain are the texts, texts that describe enlightenment and texts that tell how to get there.

In many Indian Buddhist texts, it is stated that a certain level of concentration is necessary in order for the knowledge of nirvāṇa to be salvific, that is, for the vision of nirvāṇa to be powerful enough to destroy all the seeds of future rebirth. In this sense, concentration serves as a prerequisite for insight into reality. But such concentration, called samādhi, also brings other benefits prior to the ultimate passage into nirvāṇa. These include not only rebirth in the heaven of Brahmā, but a wealth of supernormal abilities. Thus, because of his attainment of concentration, Śāriputra, while meditating one day, survived a blow on the head from a demon, a blow that would have felled an elephant or split a mountain. When a monk who observed the incident asked how he was feeling, Śāriputra responded that he was quite well but had a slight headache. Another monk survived immolation unburned, another was protected from robbers, a laywoman was unhurt by boiling oil, a queen repelled a poison arrow. Even more impressively, it is said that one who has attained a state of deep concentration is able to create multiple versions of himself or herself, to walk through walls and mountains, to dive in and out of the earth, to walk on water, and to fly through the sky in the lotus posture, touching the sun and the moon.

To achieve such powers, the mind must first be concentrated upon an object, and forty suitable objects of concentration are traditionally set forth in Theravāda literature. The first of the forty objects is called the earth device. The meditator is to stretch a piece of leather or cloth across a wooden frame and then smear a disc of dawn-colored clay, the size of a saucer, onto the surface, using a trowel to make it smooth. After sweeping the surrounding area and taking a bath, the meditator then sits down two and a half cubits from this earth device and stares at the disc, mentally repeating "earth," opening and shutting his eyes until the disc appears just as clearly with eyes shut as it does with eyes open. At this point, the meditator is to return to his dwelling and concentrate on the mental image, only going back to look at the clay disc should the image fade. After focusing on the mental image for some time, it will be replaced by a bright light, like the moon emerging from behind a cloud. This is the mark of the attainment of a state called "access concentration," the precursor to actual concentration.

For the water device, the meditator stares at a bowl of clean water and thinks "water, water." For the fire device, the meditator makes a four-finger-breadth hole in a woven mat or a cloth or a piece of leather, hangs it between himself and a fire, and stares at the center of the flame through the hole, thinking, "fire, fire." For the air device, the meditator should notice the tops of trees moving in the wind or feel the breeze on his skin and think, "air, air." For the blue device, the meditator should stare at a tray filled with morning glories or at a blue cloth and think, "blue, blue." (There are also yellow, red, and white devices.) For the light device, the meditator should focus on a circle of sunlight or moonlight on the ground or a circle of light cast on the wall by a lamp and think, "light, light." For the space device, the meditator is to look through a hole in the wall and think, "space, space." In each case, therefore, a visual (or in the case of wind, a tactile) image provides the basis from which a mental image is formed and then visualized, augmented by the mental repetition of its name.

Among the forty traditional objects for developing samādhi is the practice known as *buddhānusmṛti,* variously translated as "remembrance," "recollection," "commemoration," or "mindfulness" of the Buddha. In the Theravāda text *The Path of Purification* (*Visuddhimagga*), the meditator is instructed to call to mind the virtues of the Buddha through a formula of ten epithets: "Indeed this Bhagavān is the arhat, perfectly and fully enlightened, perfect in knowledge and deed, the Sugata, the knower of the world, the unsurpassed, the tamer of persons suitable to be tamed, the teacher of gods and humans, the Buddha, the Bhagavān." Sustained attention to these qualities of the Buddha leads to happiness, which leads to bliss, which, in turn, leads to samādhi. However, as was the case with the development of concentration through the devices, it has other effects. Those who recollect the Buddha are full of faith, understanding, mindfulness, and merit. They are happy and free from fear, feeling as if they are living in the presence of the Buddha. Indeed, the body of a person who is concentrating on the qualities of the Buddha becomes worthy of veneration. This sense of identification with the Buddha will be encountered again in tantric meditations.

Mindfulness of death is another of these forty topics. Among six types of person (the desirous, the hateful, the ignorant, the faithful, the intelligent, and the speculative), mindfulness of death is said to be a suitable object for persons of intelligent temperament. Elsewhere, however, it is said that only two among the forty are generally useful: the cultivation of love for the community of monks and the mindfulness of death.

In his specific exposition of how to cultivate mindfulness of death, the fifth-century Indian monk Buddhaghosa says that the meditator who wishes to take death as his object of concentration should go to a remote place and should simply repeatedly think, "Death will take place," or, "death, death." Should that not result in the development of concentration, Buddhaghosa provides eight ways of contemplating death.

The first of the eight is contemplation of death as a murderer, where one imagines that death will appear to deprive one of life. Death is certain from the moment of birth; beings move progressively toward their demise, never turning back, just as the sun never reverses its course through the sky. The second contemplation is to think of death as the ruin of all the accomplishments and fortune acquired in life. The third contemplation is to compare oneself to others who have suffered death yet who are greater than oneself in fame, merit, strength, supernormal power, or wisdom. Death will come to oneself just as it has come to these beings. The fourth contemplation is that the body is shared with many other creatures. Here one contemplates that the body is inhabited by the eighty families of worms, who may easily cause one's death, as may a variety of accidents. The fifth contemplation is of the tenuous nature of life, that life requires both inhalation and exhalation of breath, requires a balanced alternation of the four postures of standing, sitting, walking, and lying down. It requires moderation of hot and cold, a balance of the four physical constituents (earth, water, fire, and air), and nourishment at the proper time. The sixth contemplation is that there is no certainty about death; that is, there is no certainty as to the length of one's life, the type of illness of which one will die, when one will die, or where, and there is no certainty as to where one will be reborn. The seventh contemplation is that life is limited in length. In general, human life is short. Beyond that, there is no certainty that one will live as long as it takes "to chew and swallow four or five mouthfuls." The final contemplation is of the shortness of the moment, that is, that life is in fact just a series of moments of consciousness.

It is clear from this presentation, as from many others from across the Buddhist world, that meditation does not refer simply to a trance state free of all cognitive content. What Buddhaghosa describes is a series of reflections, a series of thoughts to be pondered, but while sitting in the formal posture. What is particularly noteworthy here is that such reflections are designed to induce not simply a mindfulness of death but a deep state of concentration that can be employed to understand the nature of reality. As already mentioned, Buddhist texts described three types of wisdom: the wisdom arising from hearing would include understanding derived from listening to teachings and reading texts; the wisdom arising from thinking refers to understanding developed in a process of sustained and systematic reflection in meditation, precisely the kind of understanding of death described above; the wisdom arising from meditation refers to the specific state of understanding that is conjoined with samādhi, that is, insight strengthened by a deep level of concentration.

But such concentration is just one of the benefits of cultivating mindfulness of death. A monk devoted to the mindfulness of death is diligent and disenchanted with the things of the world. He is neither acquisitive nor avaricious and is increasingly aware of impermanence, the first of three marks of mundane existence. From this develops an awareness of the other two marks, suffering and selflessness. He dies without confusion or fear. If he does not attain the deathless state of nirvāṇa in this lifetime, he will at least be reborn in an auspicious realm.

Such doctrinal points were also enunciated in tales that tell of a dispassion that challenges the credulity even of the gods. In a former life the Buddha was a simple farmer skilled in the mindfulness of death. While working in the fields, his son was bitten by a poisonous snake and died. Unmoved, the farmer carried his son's body to the foot of a tree and went back to his plowing until it was time for his noon meal. He sent word back to his wife to send only one meal instead of two. His wife understood immediately what had happened but was quite unperturbed and took perfume and flowers to her son's body, which was prepared for cremation. The family stood around the flaming pyre, without any display of emotion, causing Indra, the chief of the gods, who happened to be passing by, to ask whether they were roasting an animal. When he was told that it was a human body in the fire, Indra asked if he had been an enemy. Told that it was not an enemy but the farmer's son, Indra commented that the boy must not have been loved by his father. The farmer assured him that the boy had been very dear to him. When Indra asked why, then, he did not weep, the farmer replied that the boy had suffered his fate and that lamenting could not restore him. When asked why she did not weep, the mother said, "As children cry in vain to grasp the moon above, so mortals idly mourn the loss of those they love. No friends' lament can touch the ashes of the dead. Why should I grieve? He fares the way he had to tread."

One of the more lurid of Buddhist meditations is the famous "meditation on the foul," in which one is instructed to visualize a corpse in various stages of decay. Indeed, ten types of corpses are enumerated: the bloated, the livid, the cut up, the gnawed, the scattered, the hacked and scattered, the bleeding, the worm infested, and the skeleton. As with the earth device practice, the meditator is to contemplate the physical corpse until a clear mental image can be visualized. This practice was apparently widely prescribed by the Buddha until he left the community to go on retreat for several days and returned to find the ranks of his monks rather diminished. When he inquired of Ānanda the reason for the attrition, Ānanda explained that during his absence as many as thirty monks had committed suicide in a single day, so overcome were they by loathing of their own bodies as a result of meditating on the foul. The Buddha then substituted meditation on the breath as the standard practice. Indeed, the practice of suicide is discouraged by the Buddha because it can rarely be done without being motivated by either desire or hatred and thus would simply result in a negative rebirth. He permitted a monk who was suffering from a terrible disease to take his own life because the monk was already an arhat and would enter nirvāṇa upon death.

A somewhat more pristine version of the meditation on the foul, described by Vasubandhu, instructs the meditator to imagine a small circle of exposed bone between the eyes. This area of bone is then slowly extended until the entire cranium is imagined to be bone. The meditator eventually comes to visualize himself or herself as a skeleton. One's environs are then transformed into bone, beginning with one's own dwelling and extending eventually to the shore of the ocean, with the entire landscape and all of the dwellings and beings in it made only of bone. Having expanded this vision to its furthest extent, the meditator then moves back in the opposite direction, until just one skeleton remains. Concentration is contracted once more to the exposed cranium, and finally to the thumb-sized circle between the eyes.

It is again noteworthy that these meditations on the foul are codified within the context of developing concentration, with specific topics designed for a variety of human predilections and failings. The contemplation of the foul is offered as an antidote to desire, and there are numerous stories of monks who overcome the desire they feel for women they encounter by imagining them to be skeletons. In one case, the elder Mahātissa passed by a beautifully adorned woman but noticed only her teeth. Realizing the impurity of the body, he became an arhat at that moment. Meditation on the breath, practiced so widely in the Zen tradition, is here just one of forty topics suitable as the focus for the development of concentration; breath meditation is prescribed especially for those who suffer from an excess of thoughts.

TANTRA

Some five centuries after the rise of the Mahāyāna, another major movement occurred in Indian Buddhism, which was retrospectively designated as the Vajrayāna ("Thunderbolt" or "Diamond Vehicle"). It is referred to in Western scholarship as Buddhist tantra, named after the texts in which the teachings occur. The term *tantra* most commonly connotes a ritual manual or set of instructions and in the Buddhist context is used in contrast to the term *sūtra*, a discourse of the Buddha. The tantras are traditionally regarded as the teachings of the Buddha as well, distinguished from the sūtras because the Buddha is said to have delivered these teachings secretly to a select group of disciples.

The origins of the Vajrayāna are even less clearly understood than those of the Mahāyāna. Like Hīnayāna and Mahāyāna, Vajrayāna is a retrospective designation, in this case coined to describe a rather disparate set of practices by which the long path to buddhahood could be traversed more quickly than was possible via the Mahāyāna, a path on which various supernormal powers were gained in the process. Given the great attention paid to these supernormal powers in many tantric texts, it is unclear whether they were not often seen as the goal of the practice, with the lofty goal of buddhahood becoming tangential. Some of these practices, such as engaging in behaviors that transgressed caste prohibitions concerning diet and miscegenation, appear to have been borrowed from ascetic movements current in India at the time, in which abominations became obligations and prohibitions prescribed. Others were developments of themes long present in Buddhist texts, such as the possibility of coming into the presence of the Buddha through visualization practices. Despite the efforts of generations of Buddhist thinkers, it remains exceedingly difficult to identify precisely what it is that sets the Vajrayāna apart.

In the tenth century, Nāropa was renowned as one of the greatest Buddhist scholars in India. Having defeated many non-Buddhists in philosophical debate, he became abbot of the great monastery of Nālandā. One day, while walking outside the monastery, he encountered an old hag who laughed at him mockingly, claiming that his knowledge of the dharma was merely intellectual, that he had no true understanding of the path. Nāropa asked the woman who had authentic knowledge. She said that he should seek her brother, Tilopa. Nāropa resigned his position at the monastery and set out in search of Tilopa. After many adventures, he arrived in a village and asked a passer-by if he knew the whereabouts of the great scholar Tilopa. The man replied that there was no great scholar named Tilopa, but a beggar named Tilopa lived in a hut on the edge of the village. Approaching the hut, Nāropa observed a black-skinned man squatting by a fire with a kettle of fish. He would grab a live fish, snap his fingers, plunge it into the fire for a moment, and then eat the fish. Nāropa, a monk who had taken a vow not to kill any living being, was horrified. Yet he respectfully spoke to the beggar, asking Tilopa to accept him as his disciple.

So began what are known as the twelve trials of Nāropa. Tilopa and Nāropa came to a pond. Tilopa said, "If I had a loyal disciple, he would build a bridge across that pond." Nāropa tried to do so, but his body was soon covered with leeches and he fainted from loss of blood. Another time, they saw a wedding party pass, with a royal minister and his bride riding on an elephant. Tilopa said, "If I had a loyal disciple, he would drag them off the elephant and beat them." Nāropa did as his teacher said and was himself beaten within an inch of his life by the wedding party. These were two of the twelve trials. In each case, Tilopa would heal his disciple's wounds and then give him instructions in what came to be known as the six yogas of Nāropa, among the most famous of the tantric teachings. Together, they give a sense of the world envisioned by the Vajrayāna.

There are a number of configurations of the six yogas, in most cases involving some combination of eight practices: (1) inner heat, (2) clear light, (3) sexual union with a consort, (4) dream yoga, (5) illusory body, (6) consciousness transference, (7) the intermediate state, and (8) forceful entry. These various practices seem not to have originated with Nāropa or Tilopa but rather to represent a collection of tantric teachings current in Bengal in the eleventh century. They are all considered highly advanced teachings intended to result in the attainment of buddhahood.

The foundational practice for the six teachings is the first, the yoga of inner heat, which, like the other yogas, is based on a physiology in which winds or subtle energies serve as the vehicles for consciousness. These winds course through the body via a network of channels, making possible everything from the movement of the limbs to the movement of the mind. Among these, the most important is the central channel, which runs from the genitals upward to the crown of the head. Parallel to the central channel are the right and left channels, which wrap around it at several points, creating constrictions that prevent wind from moving through the central channel. At these points of constriction, there are also networks of smaller channels that radiate throughout the body. These points are called "wheels," or "cakras." Those located at the crown of the head, throat, heart, and slightly below the navel are emphasized in inner-heat yoga. The practice entails the visualization of radiant letters on top of lotuses in the cakras, combined with breath exercises that loosen the constrictions in the channels and cause the winds to enter into the central channel. Through the generation of heat at the navel cakra, essences called drops at the head, throat, and heart cakras are caused to melt, generating bliss.

The ability to cause the winds to enter the central channel provides the meditator with access to various profound states of consciousness essential to the attainment of buddhahood, most importantly, the mind of clear light, located in the heart cakra. It is this most profound state of consciousness that, upon the realization of emptiness, is transformed into the omniscience of a buddha. A related technique for causing the winds to enter the central channel and the mind of clear light to become manifest is provided by sexual union with a consort. The mind of clear light is said to become manifest briefly at the moment of orgasm.

When the mind of clear light can be identified during the waking state, it is possible then also to gain access to the clear light of sleep. The third of the six teachings, dream yoga, is dedicated specifically to finding and using the mind of clear light during sleep. In order to reach that point, there is a series of instructions designed to provide control over dreams. At the conclusion of the practices, the yogin creates an illusory body, an immortal body made of the most subtle wind and mind that, upon enlightenment, becomes the physical body of a buddha. Prior to that point, there is a series of practices involving the contemplation both of one's own form and then of the form of a buddha in a mirror, designed to induce insight into the illusory nature of the body. The first five of the teachings are intended to bestow buddhahood in this lifetime. If this is not possible, the last three provide means for doing so after death or in another body. The practice of consciousness transference is a technique for forcibly causing one's consciousness to travel up through the central channel, exit from an aperture in the crown of the head, and travel to a pure land, an ideal realm for the achievement of enlightenment.

If this is not possible, there is the practice of the intermediate state, in which the mind of clear light is identified and buddhahood attained in the period between death and rebirth. If this is not possible, there are instructions on how to find an auspicious rebirth. In Tibet, a genre of texts known as *Liberation in the Intermediate State Through Hearing* (*Bar do thos grol*)—a portion of one of which was translated as the famous *Tibetan Book of the Dead*—describes the process of death and rebirth in terms of three intermediate states, or "bardos" (*bar do*, a Tibetan term that literally means "between two"). The first, and briefest, is the bardo of the moment of death when, at the end of a process of sensory dissolution that presages physical death, a profound state of consciousness, called the clear light, dawns. If one is able to recognize the clear light as reality, one immediately achieves liberation from saṃsāra, the cycle of rebirth.

If the clear light is not recognized at that time, the consciousness of the deceased person moves into the second bardo (which appears to be a Tibetan innovation), called the bardo of reality. The disintegration of the personality brought on by death again reveals reality, but in this case not as the clear light but in the multicolored forms of a maṇḍala of forty-two peaceful deities and a maṇḍala of fifty-eight wrathful deities. These deities appear in sequence to the consciousness of the deceased in the days immediately following death. If reality is not recognized in this second bardo, then the third bardo, the bardo of mundane existence, dawns, during which one must again take rebirth in one of the six realms of gods, demigods, humans, animals, ghosts, or in hell; consciousness is blown to the appropriate place of rebirth by the winds of past karma.

The last of the yogas of Nāropa is known as forceful entry, a practice discussed more rarely than the others, preserved, it seems, for emergency situations. The most famous case of forceful entry in Tibetan literature is found in the biography of Marpa (1012–1096), the teacher of Tibet's great yogin, Milarepa (Mi la ras pa). Marpa's son, after fracturing his skull in an equestrian accident, transferred his consciousness into the body of a recently deceased pigeon, since no human corpse could be found at short notice. The bird was then given directions by Marpa for flying across the Himalayas to India, where it discovered the fresh corpse of a thirteen-year-old brahmin boy, into which the bird transferred its consciousness and then expired. The boy rose from the funeral pyre prior to his immolation and grew up to become a great yogin.

Tilopa and Nāropa were two of the famous eighty-four mahāsiddhas, or great adepts. As the arhat is the ideal of mainstream Buddhism and the bodhisattva is the ideal of the Mahāyāna, so the mahāsiddha is the ideal of Buddhist tantra in India. Although many of the hagiographies of the mahāsiddhas present the stories of princes who, like the Buddha, turned away from the world, others tell of enlightened masters who are neither virtuous monks nor gentle bodhisattvas but instead are drawn from the most base levels of Indian society: butchers, hunters, fishermen, blacksmiths, leathersmiths, pimps, involved in professions that are sources of pollution. If this were not enough, they also engage in activities that break taboos: they eat meat, they meditate sitting on top of corpses, they copulate with low-caste girls. If the power of the monk derives from the purity he acquires through abstaining from the things that laymen do, the power of the tantric yogin derives from his transgression of purity, engaging in acts that violate monastic vows as well as the prescriptions regarding purity and pollution of the caste system.

The mahāsiddhas also perform prodigious magical feats, flying through the air, turning base metals into gold, diving into the earth, restoring amputated limbs. They are regarded as enlightened beings, using what is prohibited in the path, transforming activities that would send others to hell into the deeds of a buddha. It is unclear how many of the mahāsiddhas were historical figures, and the accounts of their deeds are obviously rich in mythological detail. What is perhaps more important than their historicity is what their stories might tell us about Buddhist tantra. Their stories are replete with what we might regard as miracles, the performance of which the Buddha was said to have discouraged. On the philosophical level, such miracles demonstrate that those who have insight into the nature of reality are not bound by rules, their transgression of the conventions of society signifying their transcendence of the laws of nature. Those who understand the true nature of the world can manipulate it, unbound by the laws of gravity or the laws of karma. When Tilopa snapped his fingers before plunging the fish into the fire, he was transporting their consciousness into a pure land.

The stories of the mahāsiddhas also demonstrate the persistence of the worldly in the history of Buddhism, that the appeal of Buddhism has always been, at least in part, that it had potent magic. Tantric practice is said to produce two types of powers, called *siddhis*. There are mundane siddhis, such as the ability to turn base metals into gold, to find buried treasure, to gain the love of a woman, to curse an enemy, to paralyze an invading army, to stop the sun from moving across the sky. And there is the supramundane siddhi of buddhahood. Much of the tantric literature that survives is designed to provide mundane siddhis, generally divided into four categories of deeds: pacifying, increasing, controlling, and wrathful.

At some point, these disparate practices became sufficiently respectable to be identified as a separate "vehicle." And just as the

Mahāyāna had to establish its identity against the earlier tradition by declaring both its priority and superiority, so the scholastic devotees of tantra argue at length for the priority of the Vajrayāna. Here the Vajrayāna (or, as it was also called, the Mantrayāna) was not a separate vehicle but was an alternative form of the Mahāyāna, superior to the path set forth in the Mahāyāna sūtras, a path that the tantric exegetes referred to as the "Perfection Vehicle." In late Indian Buddhist literature we find the term *tantra* being defined relationally, specifically in contradistinction to the term *sūtra.* Authors distinguish tantra by enumerating the various ways in which it is superior to sūtra practices. But no two authors can seem to agree on the set of characteristics that distinguishes tantra. Furthermore, these characteristics appear invariably vague.

One of the most influential declarations of the superiority of tantra was that of Tripiṭakamāla in his *Lamp for the Three Modes* (*Nayatrayapradīpa*): "Even if the aim is the same, the Mantra Vehicle is superior due to nonobscuration, many skillful methods, nondifficulty, and being designed for those of sharp faculties." Tripiṭakamāla explains that followers of the Perfection Vehicle are not entirely deluded with regard to method because they practice the six perfections but are nonetheless somewhat deluded because, in attempting to perfect the practice of giving, they do such extreme things as give away parts of their bodies, notably their heads. This, he argues, is not the way that the perfection of giving is fulfilled. Followers of the Mantrayāna look down upon such practices and fulfill all six perfections in a samādhi that unites method and wisdom. Tripiṭakamāla argues furthermore that the Mantrayāna has more methods than the exclusively peaceful practices of asceticism and vow-keeping found in the Perfection Vehicle; practitioners of mantra have techniques for transmuting the five poisons (desire, hatred, envy, pride, and delusion) into the five buddha lineages. The Mantrayāna is also easier than the Perfection Vehicle because in the Mantrayāna one uses the bliss of desire to achieve the bliss of enlightenment. He sets forth a hierarchy of tantric practitioners, the lowest of whom achieve enlightenment through the bliss achieved in union with an actual consort. The practitioners of an intermediate level consort with an imagined woman, and the best, already free from desire, have no consort and know the *mahāmudrā,* the wisdom of nonduality. Finally, Tripiṭakamāla argues that followers of the Mantrayāna have greater intelligence than others. Followers of the Hīnayāna are confused about the nature of reality. Followers of the exoteric Mahāyāna understand emptiness but are confused about the method for achieving buddhahood, whereas the followers of the Mantrayāna are not confused about anything and can perform deeds that would cause others to fall into an unfortunate realm of rebirth.

But this was just one view. The Tibetan scholar Tsong kha pa (1357–1419) argued, armed with copious citations from Indian texts, that there is only one factor that distinguishes tantra from sūtra. This is the practice of deity yoga, in which one visualizes oneself as being a buddha. He notes that buddhahood has two aspects, the truth body, which is a buddha's omniscient mind, and a form body, which is a buddha's magnificent form that appears on earth and in pure lands. Although the two bodies cannot be achieved separately, it is said that the truth body is the product of wisdom and the form body is the product of method. In the Perfection Vehicle, the wisdom is acquired through meditation on emptiness, while method entails the practice of limitless forms of the six perfections. Tsong kha pa argues that there is no reality higher than the emptiness taught in the Perfection of Wisdom sūtras and delineated by Nāgārjuna. Furthermore, to meditate on emptiness is to emulate the truth body of a buddha, the omniscient mind eternally cognizant of emptiness. Therefore, the superiority of tantra is not to be found in the realm of wisdom. The Perfection Vehicle's technique for the acquisition of a form body, however, is deficient, because the cause—the practice of the six perfections—does not simulate the effect: the magnificent body of a buddha endowed with thirty-two major marks and eighty minor marks of a superman. Bodhisattvas of the Mantra Vehicle also practice the six perfections, but they have an additional method that bodhisattvas of the Perfection Vehicle lack: they visualize themselves as having the body, speech, mind, and activities of a buddha now. As one Indian tantra, the *Vajrapañjara,* states, "The method is to bear the Teacher's form." Tsong kha pa explains that in the practice of deity yoga, the meditator first meditates on emptiness and then (in visualization) causes the consciousness that contemplates emptiness to appear in the form of a compassionate buddha. In this way, the bodhisattva simultaneously accumulates method and wisdom and unites method and wisdom in a single consciousness, indivisibly, like a diamond (*vajra*).

Tsong kha pa's elegant argument does not describe the majority of tantric practices, yet it demonstrates the degree of scholastic sophistication that eventually was brought to bear on practices that may have had much more humble origins. It also demonstrates the degree to which tantra became incorporated into the scholastic discourse concerning the various vehicles to liberation.

Indian tantric exegetes (and their Tibetan and East Asian descendants) employed a number of strategies to legitimate the tantras as authentic and authoritative teachings, strategies in many cases already familiar from the Mahāyāna sūtras. Hence, as with certain Mahāyāṇa sūtras, the late appearance of the tantras is explained by the fact that they were hidden at the time of the Buddha, to be discovered and revealed at a more appropriate time. As mentioned earlier, some tantras were said to have been spoken by the bodhisattva Vajrapāṇi on a mountain in Sri Lanka (considered a place of mystery in much Indian literature) to five sages, one of whom, a kind of demon known as a rākṣasa, inscribed them in malachite ink on pages of gold. Or, as with the claim of the *Lotus* that all arhats will eventually enter the bodhisattva path and become buddhas, so in certain exegetical systems of what is called Highest Yoga Tantra, we find the claim that only through its path has buddhahood ever been attained. In this scheme, the tantric path is seen as the necessary extension of the bodhisattva's path as set forth in the Mahāyāna sūtras, just as the *Lotus* portrayed the bodhisattva's path as the necessary extension of the arhat's path set forth in the earlier tradition.

The tantric path is thus represented as the supplement to the sūtra path, providing what is essential for the goal of the sūtra path, buddhahood, to be fulfilled. Those who remain on the sūtra path only prolong their time in saṃsāra, which, for the most extraordinary bodhisattvas, can be reduced from three periods of countless aeons to three years and three months by the practice of Highest Yoga Tantra. Indeed, the claim is made that Śākyamuni himself entered the tantric path and achieved enlightenment in the highest pure land. It was this practice of the tantric path that provided Śākyamuni with the method to become a buddha and then to set forth the sūtra path for those unsuited for tantra.

It is important, however, to consider not simply what tantric masters have said about tantra, but what they do. In order to be permitted to engage in tantric practice, some kind of initiation is generally required. These ceremonies may be very simple or very elaborate, involving a small group of disciples or hundreds of thousands, as when the Dalai Lama gives the Kālacakra initiation. Prior to the initiation, the tantric guru will prepare the initiation site, dispelling demons and creating a magical circle of protection to keep evil forces away. He will then create a maṇḍala, sometimes using a painted image, a drawing, or an elaborate sand diagram. The maṇḍala, representing the perfect world the initiates are to enter, will be kept hidden from them until the appropriate moment. Prior to the actual initiation, the initiates are given the bodhisattva vows (described in chapter 4), since their tantric practice is considered an advanced form of the Mahāyāna path.

The guru plays the role of the Buddha in the initiation. Indeed, in Buddhist tantras in general, one is instructed to regard the guru as the Buddha himself, and an elaborate etiquette is set forth to this end. There is a traditional list of thirty infractions regarding the guru that tantric initiates vow to avoid. These include neglecting to make obeisance and offerings to the guru six times each day; scorning and slandering the guru; disturbing the mind of the guru; imagining the guru and the buddha Vajradhara to be different; stepping on the guru's shadow, shoes, or seat; sitting on the bed or seat where he is present; walking in front of him without receiving permission to do so; leaning against pillars and cracking one's knuckles in the presence of the guru; not stopping others from bowing to oneself in the presence of one's guru; and so forth. There are also various sets of tantric vows associated with different tantric texts and deities. Some of the infractions, such as maintaining the ten virtues (that is, not committing one of the ten nonvirtuous deeds), are shared with the ethics both of monks and laypeople. Some of the infractions, such as abandoning the aspiration to enlightenment, are shared with the bodhisattva vows. Other infractions, such as despising one's own body, reflect the view of the body as the locus of enlightenment in this very lifetime. Yet other infractions, such as sexual union with an unqualified consort, neglecting to meditate on emptiness when in sexual union, and emitting semen during the act, derive from the sexual practices of Highest Yoga Tantra.

The actual initiation may be a simple or elaborate process, referred to as entering the maṇḍala. Here, the maṇḍala is regarded as the sanctified space of enlightenment, presided over by the teacher, regarded as a buddha. The initiation is meant to help ensure the achievement of buddhahood, but it is not certain which buddha one will become. In order to predict this, the initiate will sometimes throw a flower onto a smaller maṇḍala where five buddhas are represented. The buddha upon whom the flower lands identifies the buddha whom the initiate will become. In several of the initiations of Highest Yoga Tantra, the initiate, sitting outside the maṇḍala, imagines that rays of light emerge from the heart of the teacher (visualized as a buddha, seated in sexual union with his consort), drawing the initiate into his mouth, through his body, and out through his penis into the womb of the consort, where the initiate melts into a drop of light and then into emptiness. This emptiness turns into the letter and sounds of a mantra, then into a lotus, then into a buddha. Rays of light from the heart of the teacher make offerings to all the male and female buddhas and bodhisattvas, who enter into sexual union, melting into an ambrosia (called bodhicitta, the mind of enlightenment) that enters into the mouth of the teacher and passes into the womb of the consort, where it confers initiation upon the initiate, who now appears in the form of a buddha. This buddha emerges from the womb of the consort and is set on the initiation seat. After this "internal initiation," there are elaborate rites to cleanse and purify the body, speech, and mind of the initiate.

Much of the practice described in tantric initiation and practice involves the embodiment and enactment of a world, the fantastic jewel-encrusted world of the Mahāyāna sūtras (or the horrific world of the charnel ground). In the sūtras, these worlds appear before the audience of the sūtra at the command of the Buddha. In the tantras, it is the practitioner who manifests that world through visualization, through a process of invitation, descent, and identification. In tantric practice, it is the practitioner who manifests the world that the sūtras declare to be immanent yet only describe. Tantric practice is, in this sense, the making of the world of the Mahāyāna sūtras.

Despite the ubiquity of the doctrine of emptiness and the declaration of the ultimate unreality of all worlds, there is nonetheless a sense in much tantric practice (as there is in many Mahāyāna sūtras) that some worlds are more real than others. An important segment of tantric practice, therefore, often classed as the "stage of generation," is taken up with techniques for replacing one world with another, an ordinary world with an extraordinary world, called the maṇḍala. Tantric practice provides access to a reality that is more real than the real world, a world that is accessible to the enlightened. Nāgārjuna's emptiness provides much of the conceptual foundation for this view; it is freedom from the limitations of I and mine that bestows access to a higher reality as well as control over ordinary reality; hence the "supernatural" powers of the tantric yogin. In this vision of reality, the world is a maṇḍala, a palace, with a buddha seated at its center. To the extent that the world appears to a buddha, it appears as a bejeweled maṇḍala. In this sense, it can be said that within the conventional, which includes even the body of the buddha, some appearances are more true than others. Indeed what, according to some, sets tantric practice apart from "lower" forms is that the perfected world of the maṇḍala, which is the goal, also becomes the path. By visualizing oneself as already possessing the body, speech, mind, and resources of a buddha now, one will more quickly actually come to possess them in the future. The goal becomes the path. When this maṇḍala no longer needs to be simulated, when the visualization becomes objectified, then buddhahood is achieved. Ironically, at that point the meditator, now a buddha, no longer has any need to appear in the maṇḍala that has now been made real but continues to do so out of compassion, displaying to others the perfected world that awaits at the end of the path. The subjective visualization of the meditator becomes the objective projection of the buddha.

Daily tantra practices, called *sādhanas* ("methods of achievement"), tend to follow a fairly set sequence, whether they are simple and brief or more detailed and prolix. More elaborate sādhanas may include the recitation of a lineage of gurus; the creation of a protection wheel guarded by wrathful deities to subjugate enemies; the creation of a body maṇḍala, in which a pantheon of deities takes residence at various parts of the meditator's body; and so forth.

In many sādhanas, the meditator is instructed to imagine light radiating from the body, inviting buddhas and bodhisattvas from throughout the universe. Visualizing them arrayed in the space before him or her, the meditator then performs a series of standard preliminary practices called the sevenfold service, a standard component of sādhanas and prayers that developed from an Indian Mahāyāna rite called the three-part liturgy. Prior to the actual sevenfold service, the assembled deities are offered (again, in visualization) a bath and new clothing, treated just as an honored guest would be in India. The sevenfold service would then be performed. The first of the seven elements is obeisance, an expression of homage to the assembled deities. Next comes offering, usually the longest section of the seven parts. Here fantastic gifts are imagined to be arrayed before the buddhas and bodhisattvas, offerings to please each of their five senses: beautiful forms for the eye, music for the ears, fragrances for the nose, delicacies for the tongue, sensuous silks for the body. The offering often concludes with a gift of the entire physical universe with all its marvels. The third step is confession of misdeeds. Despite the apparent inexorability of the law of karma, it is nonetheless believed that by sincerely confessing a sin to the buddhas and bodhisattvas, promising not to commit it again in the future, and performing some kind of purificatory penance (usually the recitation of a mantra) as an antidote to the sin, the eventual negative karmic effect of the negative deed can be avoided. The fourth step, admiration, is also related to the law of karma. It is believed that acknowledging, praising, and otherwise taking pleasure in the virtuous deeds of others causes the taker of such pleasure to accumulate the same merit as that accrued by the person who actually performed the good deed.

The fifth step is an entreaty to the buddhas not to pass into nirvāṇa. As discussed in chapter 2, a buddha is said to have the ability to live for aeons but will do so only if he is asked; otherwise, he will disappear from the world, pretending to die and pass into nirvāṇa. The sixth of the seven branches follows naturally from the entreaty to remain in the world; it is a supplication of the buddhas and bodhisattvas to teach the dharma. The final step is the dedication of the merit of performing the preceding toward the enlightenment of all beings. It is noteworthy that each of these steps is a Buddhist practice found, either in full form or in resonance, in mainstream Buddhist practice; there is nothing aberrant in the tantric form.

The meditator then goes for refuge to the three jewels, creates the aspiration to enlightenment, the promise to achieve buddhahood in order to liberate all beings in the universe from suffering, and then dedicates the merit from the foregoing and subsequent practices toward that end. The meditator next cultivates the four attitudes of love, compassion, joy, and equanimity, before meditating on emptiness and reciting the purificatory mantra, *oṃ svabhāvaśuddhāḥ sarvadharmāḥ svabhāvaśuddho 'haṃ,* "Oṃ, naturally pure are all phenomena, naturally pure am I," understanding that emptiness is the primordial nature of everything, the unmoving world and the beings who move upon it. Out of this emptiness, the meditator next creates the maṇḍala.

The meditator here creates an imaginary universe out of emptiness. The foundation is provided by the four elements, wind, fire, water, and earth (represented by Sanskrit syllables). On top of these, the meditator visualizes the maṇḍala. The Sanskrit term *maṇḍala* simply means circle, but in this context, within a tantric sādhana, a maṇḍala is the residence of a buddha, an extraordinary palace inhabited by buddhas and their consorts, by bodhisattvas and protectors. A maṇḍala may be quite spare, an undescribed palace with only five deities, one deity in the center and one in each of the cardinal directions. But usually maṇḍalas are much more elaborate. The maṇḍala of the buddha Guhyasamāja, for example, is articulated in great detail, with five layers of walls of white, yellow, red, green, and blue. It has a jeweled molding, archways, a quadruple colonnade; it is festooned with jewels and pendants; and it is populated by thirty-one deities, each on its own throne, arrayed on two levels. The maṇḍala is the perfected world that the meditator seeks to manifest and then inhabit, either by identifying with the central deity or by making offerings to him or her. It was said to be essential for the meditator to imagine the fantastic palace of the buddha, the maṇḍala that he or she inhabits, noting the particular bodhisattvas, protectors, gods, and goddesses located throughout the multistoried dwelling, with each item of silk clothing and gold ornament appearing clearly. Part of this visualization was accomplished through the description of the details in the tantric text itself. However, meditators were typically advised to study a visual image of the particular buddha and maṇḍala, and this was one of the uses to which paintings and statues were put by those involved in meditation practice.

The next step in the sādhana is for the meditator to animate the residents of the maṇḍala by causing the actual buddhas and bodhisattvas, referred to as "wisdom beings," to descend and merge with their imagined doubles, the "pledge beings." Light radiates from the meditator's heart, drawing the wisdom beings to the maṇḍala, where, through offerings and the recitation of the mantra *jaḥ hūṃ baṃ hoḥ*, they are caused to enter the residents of the maṇḍala. The residents are then often blessed with the three syllables: a white *oṃ* at the crown of the head, a red *āḥ* at the throat, and a blue *hūṃ* at the heart.

With the preliminary visualization now complete, the stage is set for the central meditation of the sādhana, and this varies depending upon the purpose of the sādhana. Generally, offerings and prayers are made to a sequence of deities, and boons are requested from them, each time accompanied with the recitation of an appropriate mantra. At the end of the session, the meditator makes mental offerings to the assembly before inviting them to leave, at which point the entire visualization, the palace and its residents, dissolves into emptiness. The sādhana ends with a dedication of the merit accrued from the performance of the sādhana to the welfare of all beings.

Tantra has often been described as "the yoga of sex," causing despair for scholars of the nineteenth century and delight for seekers in the twentieth. There are the famous *yab yum* (father and mother) images of Tibetan Buddhism, depicting buddhas in sexual union with beautiful female consorts; the *Guhyasamāja Tantra* begins, "Thus did I hear. At one time the Bhagavan was abiding in the vaginas of the vajra-maidens, the essence of the body, speech, and mind of all the buddhas." There are numerous tantric texts describing the symbolic meaning of such statements. The male, for example, is said to represent method, the female, wisdom—the two factors that must be united in order to achieve buddhahood. However, there is much to suggest that such statements were often taken literally, with a variety of motivations. A Tibetan king of the eleventh century complained that if tantric practice resulted in buddhahood, as its adherents claimed, then butchers, hunters, and prostitutes would have been enlightened long ago.

With the elaboration of the tantric systems, profound meanings were found in passion. The *Saṃputa Tantra* states, "Looking, laughing, holding hands, the two embracing, the four tantras abide in the manner of insects." In the systemization of tantra in India, different groups of tantras were set forth, starting with Action Tantra at the bottom and ascending to Performance Tantra, Yoga Tantra, and Highest Yoga Tantra. Such a hierarchy was obviously devised by the proponents of Highest Yoga Tantra, but the presence of such a system suggests that enough tantric literature and competing schools existed in India for such a ranking, artificial as it might have been, to be advanced. According to the quotation from the *Saṃputa Tantra,* the four classes of tantras are divided according to the ascending ability of their initiates to use desire in the path. Followers of Action Tantra were able to handle the desire that arises from looking at a lover; those of Performance Tantra could also employ the desire of sharing a smile with the beloved. The physical contact of holding hands was permitted to those of Yoga Tantra. Only the most advanced of tantric practitioners, those of Highest Yoga Tantra, could use the most intense form of desire, that of sexual embrace. In ancient India, it was believed that the insects that one found when a log was split open had been born from the wood that they in turn consumed. To say that "the four tantras abide in the manner of insects" means that the desire born from sexual passion can be used to destroy the desire that binds beings in saṃsāra, like using a thorn to remove a thorn. Sexual intercourse and the powerful feelings it engenders becomes, for those who are capable of using it, a potent method for attaining enlightenment. This is called "bringing desire to the path." In the final initiations of Highest Yoga Tantra, the guru engages in ritual union with a consort and then places a drop of the fluid resulting from their union, called here bodhicitta, on the initiate's tongue. The initiate then sits in ritual embrace with a consort in order to achieve the state of innate bliss. The tantric vows specify that one must not forget the ultimate reality at this time. Indeed, this mind of profound bliss is to be used to understand emptiness, the ultimate reality.

But much tantric practice made no mention of the union of male and female or made any mention of desire, relying instead on imagery of a more horrific nature. A well-known example is the practice called *chö* (*gcod*) in Tibetan Buddhism. The *chö* practitioner is expected to frequent cemeteries and other sites fraught with danger, where he or she will pitch a tent, perform a dance, beat a drum, and blow on a trumpet made from a human thigh bone.

The full name of the practice is "the demon to be severed." There is a long tradition in Buddhism of regarding demons as the projections of the desire, hatred, and ignorance that are the root cause of suffering and that must be eliminated on the path to buddhahood. Indeed, according to an Indian enumeration by Asaṅga, one's own mind and body are regarded as "the demon of the aggregates," and one of the demons to be eliminated in *chö* practice is attachment to one's own body. In the *chö* literature, four demons are enumerated: tangible demons, the harmful forces that exist in the external world; intangible demons, the negative mental states resulting from desire, hatred, and ignorance; the demon of delight, which takes false pride in the superiority of one's teacher or premature pleasure in the results of one's meditation practice; and the demon of conceit, the belief in self. In keeping with classical Buddhist doctrine, if this last demon can be destroyed through the understanding that there is no self, that the person and indeed all phenomena are devoid of any intrinsic nature, then the other three types of demons will also be eliminated. Indeed, the perfection of wisdom literature, with its exposition of the doctrine of emptiness, is highly revered in the *chö* tradition as the ultimate means of cutting through the webs of ignorance.

In the *chö* practice, the meditator imagines his or her consciousness in the form of the goddess Vajrayoginī, abiding in the central channel. She exits from the aperture at the crown of the head, at which point the meditator's body is imagined to collapse. Vajrayoginī cuts off the crown of the skull of the prostrate body and transforms it into a huge cauldron, into which the body is thrown. The boiling of the body produces an elixir that is offered to all the buddhas and bodhisattvas and to all sentient beings and spirits, both benevolent and malevolent. These offerings are referred to as the four feasts: the white, variegated, red, and black. The Mahāyāna dyad of wisdom and compassion are represented here. By severing the skull from the body, one cuts attachment to the body, resulting in wisdom. Among the deeds of the bodhisattva is the perfection of giving. Because the body is the object of such great attachment, the gift of the body is often praised as the highest form of the perfection of giving. This compassionate deed produces a great store of merit for the meditator. Indeed, because the practitioner of *chö* is often a wandering mendicant who has nothing other than his or her own body to offer in order to accumulate the necessary store of merit to progress on the path, *chö* is sometimes called "a beggar's collection of merit." Thus, even here, in a practice that an earlier generation of scholars regarded as a remnant of Tibetan shamanism, clear continuities with more "classical" forms of Buddhist practice may be discerned. From the mainstream traditions of India there is the emphasis on the accumulation of merit, the central practice of lay Buddhists. From the Mahāyāna of India, there is the practice of the perfection of giving, with the motivation of leading all beings to buddhahood. And from the example of the Buddha himself, there is the practice of cutting off attachment to the body, embodied in the life of the beggar, the literal meaning of *bhikṣu,* the Sanskrit term for the Buddhist monk.

THE PURE LAND

It is common Buddhist doctrine that buddhas come and buddhas go, with a new buddha appearing in the world only when the teachings of the previous buddha have disappeared from the world. Thus,

Śākyamuni only appeared when the teachings of the previous buddha, Kāśyapa, had disappeared, and Maitreya will only appear when Śākyamuni's teachings are gone. There are various formulas for calculating when this will occur, but the consensus seems to be that Maitreya will not arrive soon. This has led to various millennial movements in Buddhist history awaiting Maitreya. Some of those who see nirvāṇa as the utter extinction of the aggregates have sought to postpone their entry into nirvāṇa so that they may be reborn at the time of Maitreya. Others have developed alchemical practices designed vastly to prolong their lives so that they may live long enough to greet the advent of Maitreya.

But for much of the Buddhist world, the question of the disappearance of the dharma has been a cause for anxiety and hence doctrinal innovation. For who can say precisely when the dharma will disappear? The final signs will be clear enough. In the last stages of disappearance of the dharma, it is said, all Buddhist texts will disappear (the last to go will be those on monastic discipline), the saffron robes of the monks will turn white (the color of the robes of the laymen), and, in the end (when the human life span is seventy thousand years), all of the relics of the cremated Buddha—the teeth, the bones, the fingernails, the hair—will break free from their reliquaries, the stūpas and pagodas, and magically travel to Bodhgaya, where the sixteen arhats who have protected the dharma since the Buddha's passage will gather the relics into a stūpa beneath the tree where the Buddha achieved enlightenment. There they will be worshiped one last time by the arhats and gods before they fly into the air, burst into flames, and vanish. The arhats will do the same.

This obviously has not occurred yet, but what is the efficacy of Buddhist practice as the world declines, moving further and further from the time of the Buddha and closer and closer to the utter disappearance of his teaching? The prophecies concerning how long the dharma will remain after the death of the Buddha vary; some say only five hundred years, some say two thousand. But all describe a gradual process of decline, not in the quality of the teaching but in the quality of the disciples; the monks will be lax in their maintenance of their vows, the laypeople will be complacent, and the general fortitude and intelligence of practitioners will decline. In India, the disappearance of the dharma was used to promote the efficacy of tantric practice, specifically designed for beings of the degenerate age.

In China, Buddhists often despaired of their ability to make sense of the mass of disparate texts, doctrines, and practices that reached them from India, and from the fifth century onward the decline of the dharma became a consistent concern of Buddhist thought and practice. Rather than ascribing the problem to competing schools and variant translations, Buddhist monks in China often blamed themselves, concluding that they were living in the last stage of the decline of the dharma and thus were constitutionally incapable of making progress on the path that the Buddha had set forth. This led in turn to the composition of a large number of apocryphal texts that set forth specific remedies to the problem; in China some texts called for charity directed not to monks, but to the poor, the old, and the sick. This led in one case to the establishment of the Inexhaustible Treasury at a temple in Changan, which gathered donations that were then distributed to the needy.

Some of the texts that set forth the decline of the dharma described what must have been contemporary events—inadequate support of the saṅgha, state regulation of Buddhist institutions, the taxation of monastic property—in the form of prophecies of the Buddha, suggesting that the decline that the Buddha had prophesied was already at hand and that disaster was imminent unless the remedy, set forth in the sūtra, was taken immediately. The prophesied evils, however, were not limited to the state. Also commonly mentioned are corrupt and greedy monks who violate their vows and laypeople who allow temples to fall into disrepair and sell images of the Buddha.

But perhaps the most important response to the disappearance of the dharma in East Asia was Pure Land practice. While devotion to Amitābha and the prayer to be reborn in his pure land began (and to a certain extent remained) a common component of the practices of many Chinese Buddhist schools, beginning in the sixth century it began to be argued that, in the time of the decline of the dharma, it is impossible to follow the path traversed by the great arhats and bodhisattvas of the past. Humans of this age were simply lacking in the requisite intelligence and effort. For this reason, the only recourse available was to rely on the powers of Amitābha, who in his eighteenth vow had promised to deliver all who called his name into the Land of Bliss upon their death. Pure Land practice never became institutionalized as an independent school in China, as it would in Japan, but the influence of the Pure Land was pervasive, extending from eminent scholars such as Hui-yuan (334–416), who formed a group that made a collective vow to be reborn in the pure land, to popular preachers such as Shandao (613–681), who organized mass recitations of Amitābha's name in the capital; from members of the monastic and lay élite to the unlettered; from exegetical treatises to devotional tracts; from the public officials of the court to the women of the inner household. Hardly the simple practice suited to the unsophisticated (although often so promoted), the Pure Land has proved a compelling aspiration for Chinese from all strata of society for many centuries.

Pure Land practice is more variegated than the simple recitation of the name. It is accurate to say, however, that its central practice is *nianfo,* a term that means "buddha contemplation," "buddha intonation," and "buddha invocation." It is a translation of the Sanskrit term *buddhanusmṛti,* literally "mindfulness of the Buddha." In the early Indian tradition and in the Theravāda of Sri Lanka and Southeast Asia, this seems to have been a form of meditation in which one called to mind in a designated sequence the good qualities of the Buddha. Mindfulness of the Buddha was, however, simply one of the traditional list of forty suitable topics for inducing a state of deep concentration. In Indian Mahāyāna texts, recollection of the Buddha evolved into a visualization practice of the Buddha's magnificent form—adorned with thirty-two major marks and eighty minor marks—a practice that was still used to develop concentration but also served more visionary purposes, designed to bring one face-to-face with the Buddha himself. One of the buddhas to be encountered in this way was Amitābha.

In China as in India, visions of Amitābha and his pure land remained central goals of the practice, certifying that one would be born in the Land of Bliss after death. A particularly efficacious technique for inducing such visions was the intonation of his name; in Chinese Amitābha was A-mi-tuo-fuo. Such practices clearly have

Indian antecedents but received special emphasis in China. The *Sūtra on the Meditation of the Buddha of Infinite Life* (*Guan wu liang shou jing*) presents itself as being an Indian sūtra but is in fact of Chinese or Central Asian origin. It prescribes "ten moments of single-minded and sustained recitation of the Buddha's name." This phrase would receive particular emphasis in China, with one manual explaining that every morning after having bathed and dressed, one should stand facing the west, with palms joined in reverence, and recite the name of Amitābha ten times, neither too loud nor too soft, too fast nor too slow, with each recitation taking a single exhalation of the breath.

It is important to recall, however, that such recitation most often occurred within a designated ritual structure, where it was accompanied by prostrations, the burning of incense, confession of sins, the chanting of scriptures, and visualization practice. Even in large popular movements such as that of Shandao, where less emphasis was placed on the efforts of the devotee and more emphasis was placed on Amitābha's salvific power, meditative visions were both sought and praised as reliable signs (more reliable than dreams, for example) of one's imminent birth in the retinue of the Buddha of Infinite Light. It is not the case, therefore, that we find in China an inexorable movement from an élite and scholarly Pure Land practice, in which private meditation is the key, to a popular practice of communal chanting by the unlettered.

Pure Land practice in China is typically performed in a purified space before an altar where an image of the Buddha has been installed. The ceremony begins with the offering of incense and the prayer that the smoke of the incense will spread through the ten directions and the limitless buddha lands, being transformed into offerings to the three jewels and perfuming all beings in the universe, inspiring them to seek rebirth in the pure land. The three jewels are then invited to enter the sanctuary in the form of buddhas, sūtras, and the inhabitants of the pure land, especially Amitābha and his two attending bodhisattvas, Avalokiteśvara and Mahāsthāmaprāpta. Each of the invited buddhas and bodhisattvas is then worshiped individually with prostrations and praise. The members of the congregation then visualize themselves as standing before Amitābha and all the other buddhas and recite a prayer of repentance, which reads in part, "May he cause the grave sins committed by me and other beings to be completely purified—regardless of whether they were done in the beginningless past, in the present life, or are yet to be done in the future; whether they were committed by me or urged on others, passively witnessed or [actively] celebrated, remembered or forgotten, committed knowingly or not, doubtful or certain, hidden or revealed." Next, the merit accumulated through the performance of the rite is dedicated to the welfare of all beings, and all pledge to be reborn in the pure land in order to complete the bodhisattva path quickly and liberate all beings from suffering. The refuge formula is then recited, after which each person should recite from memory one of the pure land sūtras or single-mindedly intone the name of Amitābha.

A popular form of this rite for both monks and laity was extended over seven days. During this period, the practitioners ate only one meal of plain food each day. Throughout the period, they were not allowed to lie down or sleep, with every moment dedicated to the constant contemplation of Amitābha's qualities and the constant recitation of his name, while visualizing Amitābha standing before them, his golden body radiant with light. Speaking was prohibited, except to announce their intentions for rebirth in the pure land, to confess their sins, to recite the *Sūtra of the Land of Bliss,* or to recite Amitābha's name. There were various techniques for intoning Amitābha's name, such as the famous "five-tempo recitation" of the ninth-century monk Fazhao, where the five tempos were said to harmonize with the heavenly music that resounded naturally through the pure land. A more elaborate form of Pure Land practice, generally limited to monastics because of its length, involved a ninety-day retreat in a specially constructed buddha-mindfulness sanctuary. During this time the practitioner would constantly circumambulate an altar with an image of Amitābha while reciting his name and visualizing his form. The goal was eventually to achieve a state of samādhi in which Amitābha and his pure land would appear in a vision.

Given the goal of rebirth in the pure land, it is not surprising to find that particular attention is given to the moment of death. It is standard Buddhist doctrine that death, which may come at any moment, is a time of both great opportunity and great danger. Each being carries the store of all of his or her past deeds, any one of which can serve as the cause of the next lifetime. Which one of these seeds will fructify as the next life is determined by one's state of mind at the time of death. A virtuous state of mind will bring a seed for a happy rebirth to the fore, a nonvirtuous state of mind, such as fear of death, greed for one's possessions, or attachment to family members, will bring forward the cause of a miserable rebirth. Great pains are therefore taken in trying to promote a virtuous state of mind at the time of death by such traditional means as having sūtras chanted and placing an image of a buddha in the room. But a virtuous state of mind is not so easily ensured. It is said that the time of death is so traumatic that the dying person is unable to turn his or her mind to something unfamiliar; at death the mind reverts to what it knows. Hence the necessity that Pure Land practitioners always have the name of Amitābha on their lips. Even then, the situation is always volatile. A Chinese text warns against allowing into the presence of a dying person anyone who consumes meat, wine, or the five pungent herbs. Otherwise, the person will become confused by demons and will be reborn as an animal, ghost, or hell being.

In the Pure Land tradition, what is deemed essential is some sign that the dying person has successfully forged "the connection to the pure land," certifying that rebirth is assured in the Land of Bliss. Some of the signs are derived from the Pure Land sūtras themselves: paintings commonly depict the scene from the *Sūtra on the Meditation on the Buddha of Infinite Life* of Amitābha and his retinue appearing before the deathbed bearing the lotus pedestal where the devotee will soon be enthroned in the pure land. Other signs include a peaceful death while seated upright in the meditative posture. Those in attendance may hear otherworldly music, detect rare fragrances, or perceive supernal lights. If the corpse is cremated, it may yield crystal beads; if it is to be buried, it may be naturally preserved from decay. A somewhat more mundane sign had to do with the temperature of the body. Every corpse was said to have a warm spot that indicated the point at which the soul had exited. If the feet were warm, it meant that one would be reborn in hell. Warm knees meant that one would be reborn as an animal. A warm chest meant rebirth as a human. A warm spot on the crown of the head was proof that the deceased had gone on to the pure land. After death, the deceased may visit friends and family members in dreams and conduct them on a tour of the pure land. In one account, the Lady of Yueguo is led to the pure land by her recently departed maidservant, who shows her a lotus pond. Yet some of the lotuses are in full and glorious bloom while others are wilting. The maid explains that whenever someone on earth vows to be reborn in the pure land, a lotus takes root. It will grow and blossom as long as the person's practice remains strong; if their diligence falters, it will wither. Those who remain dedicated in their devotions will upon death be reborn in the pure land in the center of their lotus blossom. When the lady asks where she herself will be reborn, she is led to a resplendent altar encircled by rainbows. Such stories serve as testimonies to the efficacy of Amitābha's vow.

But the efficacy of the vow also raised questions. If one simply had to call upon Amitābha once, even at the last moment of life, why not live a profligate life and then appeal to the Buddha at the moment of death, knowing that he is bound by his vow to appear and deliver one to the pure land? Why participate in seven-week retreats of intensive contemplation or devote one's waking moments to the recitation of the name? The answer provided by several Chinese clerics was that, although rebirth in the pure land was assured to all who called on Amitābha without distinction, once in the pure land there were distinctions of time and place that were directly related to one's deeds in life. A hierarchy of the saved, with nine grades of devotees, was elaborated, from the most pious to the most depraved, ranging from devout practitioners of the Mahāyāna, who maintained the Buddhist precepts throughout their lives, to moral persons who called upon Amitābha at the time of death to parricides saved by a deathbed conversion. As with the law of karma, which Amitābha's vows seemed somehow to subvert, one's deeds in the past life determined one's status in the next. In the pure land, lifelong practitioners were reborn in lotuses located close to Amitābha's seat, and their lotuses blossomed quickly. The less pious would find themselves in lotuses that bloomed more slowly—the greatest sinners waiting twelve aeons—and were located at some remove from Amitābha.

In the first centuries of Buddhism in Japan, the recitation of the homage to Amitābha, in Japanese *namu amida butsu,* was used primarily as a means of protecting the living by sending the spirits of the dead to the pure land and thus was regarded as inauspicious. It was employed as one of a number of practices in the Tendai and Shingon schools. The itinerant monk Kūya (903–972) is credited with spreading the practice of chanting the nembutsu as a means for the living to gain birth in the pure land at death. He would chant the nembutsu in the marketplace of Kyoto, beating a gong and dancing. In the temple called Rokuharamitsuji in Kyoto there is today a famous statue depicting Kūya dressed in rags, with a gong suspended around his neck, carrying a hammer in one hand and a staff topped with antlers in the other. His mouth is open, and from it protrudes a wire to which are attached what appear to be six cylinders. On closer inspection, they are seen to be six identical standing buddhas, one for each of the syllables: *na-mu-a-mi-da-butsu* (Homage to Amitābha Buddha).

Perhaps the most famous of the deathbed instructions is a work by the Japanese Tendai monk Genshin (942–1017) entitled *Essentials for Rebirth in the Pure Land* (*Ojōyōshū*). According to the *Sūtra of the Land of Bliss,* Amitābha would appear at the deathbed of any and all who called upon him and would escort them to the pure land. Genshin designed a ritual to ensure that this would happen. It entailed providing a proper setting for death as well as a series of ten reflections for the dying person. The person should be placed in a separate room, if possible, away from his or her possessions, the sight of which may induce nostalgia for and attachment to the things of this world. A golden image should be installed, facing the west, the direction of Amitābha's pure land. The left hand of the image should hold a five-colored pennant, the end of which should be grasped by the dying person, who should be placed behind the Buddha image, ready to be led to the pure land. The dying person should chant the nembutsu and imagine the arrival of Amitābha and his hosts, bearing a lotus throne to transport the person to the pure land. Family members who have recently partaken of meat, alcohol, garlic, or onions should not be allowed to visit. Only fellow devotees should be present to offer encouragement to the dying person to perform the ten moments of reflection stipulated in the eighteenth vow of Dharmākara as the means of gaining entry into the pure land. To that end, the dying person should be exhorted to see only the Buddha, hear only the dharma, speak only the teachings of the Buddha, and think of nothing except birth in the pure land.

Recognizing that ten uninterrupted moments of the aspiration to be reborn in the pure land are difficult for unenlightened beings whose minds are like an untamed horse, Genshin provides a sequence of ten different reflections, each of which is to be accompanied by chanting *namu amida butsu*. He begins with a rather sophisticated point of Mahāyāna doctrine. First, one should reflect on the ultimate nonduality of nirvāṇa and saṃsāra, such that ignorance arises ultimately from the mind of all the buddhas. Thus, chanting *namu amida butsu,* one should reflect on the qualities of the three jewels, regarding the Buddha as the doctor, the dharma as the medicine, and the saṅgha as the nurse. Second, the dying person should feel a sense of weariness with the world and the cycle of birth, aging, sickness, and death, seeing in Amitābha the power to destroy the karma that would otherwise bind one in saṃsāra for eight billion aeons. One should therefore long for Amitābha to appear and should chant *namu amida butsu.* Third, realizing that if one is not born in the pure land now, one will be reborn as an animal, ghost, or hell being and thus lose the opportunity to hear the dharma and be reborn in the pure land, one should therefore aspire to be reborn in the pure land and chant *namu amida butsu.* Fourth, one should reflect on all the good deeds that one has performed in the past and dedicate all of the resulting merit to a single aim: rebirth in the pure land. With that dedication, one should chant *namu amida butsu.* Fifth, the purpose of being reborn in the pure land is to eventually become a buddha in order to be able to benefit all sentient beings. Affirming the vow of the bodhisattva, one should chant *namu amida butsu.* Sixth, the virtues of Amitābha are beyond description. All of the buddhas of the ten directions, as numerous as the grains of sand of the Ganges, constantly extol the virtues of Amitābha. Therefore, one should take refuge single-mindedly in Amitābha, rather than another buddha, and chant *namu amida butsu.* Seventh, one should visualize Amitābha in all his splendor, focusing specifically on the small curl between his eyebrows (called the *ūrṇā*), which radiates seven billion fifty-six million rays of light throughout the universe. To reflect on the ūrṇā for just an instant destroys the evil karma accumulated over billions of aeons in saṃsāra. Focusing on the ūrṇā, one should chant *namu amida butsu.* Eighth, one should reflect that the minds of all those who are touched by the light radiating from the ūrṇā overcome attachment to objects, to self, and to rebirth, and focus on the nembutsu meditation, thereby attaining birth in the pure land. With this in mind, one should chant *namu amida butsu.* Ninth, one must know that, even though it may not be visible to the dying person, Amitābha is emitting light from his ūrṇā and is at that very moment on his way to the deathbed, accompanied by his two chief bodhisattvas. Wishing for his arrival, one should chant *namu amida butsu.* Genshin considered the seventh, eighth, and ninth reflections to be the most important. Finally, the dying person should be reminded that he or she is about to have his or her last thought, the most important thought of the lifetime, more weighty than all the deeds of the past century. If one can think now of Amitābha, one will be born in the pure land. If not, one will plunge again into the ocean of saṃsāra. With faith in the power of Amitābha's vow and the wish that he guide one to the pure land, chant *namu amida butsu.*

During the Kamakura period in Japan, the Tendai monk Hōnen read the entire Buddhist canon three times before concluding that during the degenerate age (which according to the calculations of the day had begun in 1052), faith in chanting the name of Amitābha was the only path to salvation; all other routes ended in failure. He reported that his own teacher, not realizing this, had concluded that the only means of salvation was to await the coming of Maitreya and to that end had vowed to be reborn in a lake as a particularly long-lived serpent. Hōnen's views gained popularity, even attracting the attention of the emperor. But he also gained the enmity of the established sects of Japanese Buddhism. When two of his monks, known for their beautiful chanting, were invited to court and ended up spending the night in the ladies' quarters, the monks were executed and Hōnen was sent into exile.

Hōnen had continued to emphasize ethical behavior, declaring that if the wicked person could be reborn in the pure land, how much greater were the chances of the good person. He urged his followers to repeat the name of Amitābha as much as possible. He himself repeated it seventy thousand times each day. His disciple Shinran followed him into exile and came to hold more radical views. Like Hōnen, he believed that any attempt to rely on one's own powers to achieve freedom from saṃsāra was futile. The only possible course of action was to rely on the power of Amitābha. But for Shinran, this power was pervasive. To even make the effort to say silently, *namu amida butsu*, "Homage to Amitābha Buddha," was a futile act of hubris. The very presence of the sounds of Amitābha's name in one's heart was due to Amitābha's compassionate power. It was therefore redundant to repeat the name more than once in one's life; all subsequent recitation should be regarded as a form of thanksgiving. Shinran therefore reversed Hōnen's dictum to say that if the good person can be reborn in the pure land, how much greater were the chances of the wicked person, who had no delusions about his ability to effect his own welfare, to achieve his own salvation. The enlightened activity of Amitābha is present everywhere, and it is only ignorant striving after self-gratification that obstructs the fulfillment of Amitābha's vow. Once one abandons the conceit that one can achieve happiness, either in this life or the next, through one's own willful deeds, and instead entrusts oneself to the power of Amitābha, one is instantaneously freed from the bonds of saṃsāra (although still subject to its afflictions) in this life and will be born in the pure land at death. Salvation in this sense occurs not at death but at the initial moment of faith in Amitābha. This moment of faith, again, occurs not through an act of will. It is, in fact, a manifestation of the mind of Amitābha. With this immediate and irreversible confirmation, there is no reason to be concerned with elaborate deathbed rituals and contemplations, such as that designed by Genshin. In fact, Shinran argued that performing such practices in the hope of being delivered into the pure land was simply another manifestation of futile self-power; he thus rejected all prayers and rituals designed to provide happiness in this life or the next. Yet the moment of faith does not imply permission to engage in unethical behavior, secure in the belief that, whatever one might do, one will be born in the pure land at death. Shinran emphasized that even to make such an assumption was to again succumb to the ignorance of self-power.

The salvation of the most depraved sinner from hell and his deliverance into the pure land was not a dictum unique to Hōnen and his disciples. The question was rather the means of deliverance. Myōe, one of Hōnen's harshest critics, advocated a technique called the mantra of light, in which pure sand infused with the power of a mantra was sprinkled on the grave. Even if the person had committed the five deeds of immediate retribution and was abiding in the most torturous hell, the light from the sand would reach them, instantly purifying their misdeeds and causing them to be reborn in the Land of Bliss.

In a certain sense, the reliance on Amitābha's grace that became the hallmark of Pure Land practice in Japan changed the status of Śākyamuni Buddha. No longer a model to be emulated or a teacher to be followed, he became instead a messenger, proclaiming to the world the presence of Amitābha's pure land and the potency of his vows. We should not conclude, however, that such a view of the Buddha carried the day. There were those who sought to duplicate the experience of the master, seated beneath the tree.

ZEN

There is no historical evidence for a Zen school in India. Yet Zen, like all Buddhist traditions, traces its origins back to the Buddha. It is said that the Buddha was seated before a large audience on Vulture Peak. He drew a flower from one of the bouquets placed in offering before him and held it up. No one understood except the monk Mahākāśyapa, who said nothing; he simply smiled. The Buddha said to him, "I possess the treasure of the true eye of the dharma, the wondrous mind of nirvāṇa, the subtle entry to the dharma, born from the formlessness of true form, not relying on words and letters, a special transmission outside the teachings. I bequeath it to Mahākāśyapa." This teaching beyond words, this mind-to-mind transmission, was passed down from master to disciple in a lineage that included such illustrious figures as Nāgārjuna, until it reached one Bodhidharma, who in the late fifth century left India and traveled to China. According to a famous story first recorded in 758, the Emperor Wu of Liang was delighted to learn of the presence of the Indian master in his realm and summoned him to court. The emperor was known as a devoted patron of the dharma, having sponsored the construction of monasteries and the printing of sūtras. He was therefore eager to ask the Indian monk how much merit he accumulated through these good deeds. Bodhidharma answered, "None whatsoever." The emperor then asked exactly who Bodhidharma was. He answered that he did not know. Bodhidharma is said to have retreated into the mountains, where he spent nine years in meditation, gazing at the wall of a cave. When he was unable to keep his eyes open, he cut off his eyelids and threw them aside, where they grew into the first tea plants in China. According to a story that first appears some four centuries after the event it describes, he was eventually approached by a Chinese man who stood silently waiting for his presence to be acknowledged by Bodhidharma. The Indian monk continued to ignore him, even as snow fell and drifted against his feet. Finally, the man drew a sword, cut off his left arm, and presented it to Bodhidharma, asking the master to calm his mind. Bodhidharma told him that he would calm his mind if the man would first show it to him. The man said that he had looked for his mind for many years but had been unable to grasp it. Bodhidharma replied, "There, it is calmed." The Chinese scholar thus became the first Chinese patriarch of the Chan tradition in China, a tradition that became famous for its four phrases:

a special transmission outside the teachings
not relying upon words and letters
pointing directly at the human mind
seeing one's own nature and becoming a buddha

The most famous of the patriarchs was the sixth, Huineng. According to the story, he was a poor boy who sold firewood to support his mother. One day he heard a monk reciting the *Diamond Sūtra* in the market and experienced a moment of insight. He asked the monk who his master was. The monk replied that he was a disciple of the patriarch Hungren. Huineng left home to become his disciple. When he arrived at the monastery, Hungren asked how Huineng, being a barbarian from the south, could ever become a buddha. Huineng answered that there was no north or south in the buddha nature. Impressed by his answer, the master put the boy to work pounding rice in the kitchen.

One day he heard that the master had decided it was time to choose his successor, the student who would become the next patriarch and receive the signs of office, Bodhidharma's robe and bowl. Hungren told each student to write a poem expressing his understanding. The author of the best poem would be chosen as the sixth patriarch. All of the monks assumed that Hungren's leading disciple, a monk named Shenxiu, would succeed the master and so did not bother to compose poems. Shenxiu's poem was:

The body is the Bodhi tree;
The mind a bright mirror's stand.
We must always try to polish it.
Do not let dust collect.

Huineng overheard one of the monks reciting the poem and composed his own. But since he was illiterate, he could not write it down himself. Instead, he asked one of his friends to write his poem on one of the walls of the monastery at night, when no one would see. His poem responded to that of Shenxiu. It read:

Bodhi originally has no tree.
The mirror also has no stand.
Buddha nature is ever clear and pure.
Where is there room for dust?

The poem was noticed the next day, and the master himself came to read it. He announced publicly that although worthy, it did not display full understanding. But that night he secretly summoned Huineng to his room and presented him with Bodhidharma's robe and bowl, conferring on him the signs of the sixth patriarch. He told him that many would be upset by his selection, so he should leave the monastery immediately.

This is the story told by Huineng's followers, and recent scholarship has suggested that it is not a historical account but rather a story told for polemical purposes. Nonetheless, it points to an important paradigm of two models of enlightenment. The first might be referred to as the purification model, in which the afflictions of desire, hatred, and ignorance, and the karma that they produce, are viewed as pollutants. Precisely what it is that is polluted is often difficult to identify, sometimes simply referred to as the mind. The image here is of something pure that is obscured by dirt. In the first poem, the mind is compared to a mirror that, when clean, reflects things exactly as they are, without distortion or obscuration. Yet dust settles on the surface of the mirror, diminishing its clarity. The path to enlightenment therefore entails a process of purification in which the mind is cleansed of its impurities. That process takes place in the here and now, in this very body, which is likened to the tree under which the Buddha achieved enlightenment.

The second poem might be taken as an example of the second model, which might be referred to as the recognition model. The claim here is that if something is naturally pure, it cannot be polluted. There is thus no need to clean the mirror. Furthermore, this pure nature is not limited to any particular physical locus, present here, absent there, but is universal. Enlightenment, then, entails the recognition of what has always been the case. The mind is naturally enlightened; all beings are already buddhas.

This apparently simple dichotomy, more commonly known as the gradual and sudden paths, received extensive commentary and elaboration in China, often in the service of polemics. The master Zongmi (780–841) examined the categories in their various combinations. Gradual cultivation followed by sudden enlightenment was like gradually chopping down a tree until it suddenly falls; sudden cultivation followed by gradual enlightenment was like immediately discerning the target and then gradually learning how to hit it with an arrow; gradual cultivation and gradual enlightenment was like ascending a nine-story tower, one's vista expanding with each upward step; sudden enlightenment and sudden cultivation was the most rare of cases and depended on having practiced gradual cultivation in a previous life; sudden enlightenment followed by gradual cultivation was like the birth of an infant that has all its limbs but must slowly learn how to use them. This final model was preferred by Zongmi.

Zongmi's considered examination of the categories was unknown in Tibet, where a debate over sudden and gradual took place in the late eighth century. Here, the rivals were not two Chinese monks but a Chinese monk and an Indian monk. And this time the gradual position was said to carry the day. A conflict seems to have developed between the Indian and Chinese partisans (and their allies in the Tibetan court) over the question of the nature of enlightenment, with the Indians holding that enlightenment takes place as the culmination of a gradual process of purification, the result of combining virtuous action, meditational serenity, and philosophical insight. The Chinese spoke against this view, holding that enlightenment was the intrinsic nature of the mind rather than the goal of a protracted path, such that one need simply recognize the presence of this innate nature of enlightenment by entering what they deemed a nonconceptual state beyond distinctions; all other practices were superfluous. According to both Chinese and Tibetan records, a debate was held between the Indian scholar Kamalaśīla and the Chan monk Heshang Moheyan at Samye (Bsam yas) circa 797, with King Tisong Detsen (Khri srong lde btsan) himself serving as judge. Kamalaśīla was declared the winner, and Moheyan and his party were banished from Tibet, with the king proclaiming that thereafter the Madhyamaka position of Nāgārjuna would be followed in Tibet. It is unlikely that a face-to-face debate took place or that the outcome of the controversy was so unequivocal. Nonetheless, from this point Tibet turned for its Buddhism toward India and away from China; no school of Chinese Buddhism had any further influence in Tibet. Indeed, the identification of one's opponent with the Chinese monk Moheyan was to become a stock device in polemical literature in Tibet. Chan would remain one of the most enduring forms of Buddhism in China, spreading also to Korea, where it is known as Son, and Japan, where it is known as Zen. Contrary to the way Zen has been characterized in the West, in China, Korea, and Japan it is known for its strong and strict monastic training, its commitment to the study of Buddhist literature, and its disciplined lifestyle.

Since it claimed to be a special transmission outside the conventional Buddhist teachings, Zen developed its own scriptures through a literary tradition of collecting and commenting upon the statements of enlightened teachers, drawn from biographies and other records. These works of literature gathered what were purported to be reports of conversations between enlightened masters and their disciples, gnomic exchanges that often mocked traditional monastic practices such as memorizing and reciting sūtras and engaging in scriptural exegesis. These "recorded sayings" and "encounter dialogues" contained brief exchanges that seemed nonsensical: (Q: What is the Buddha? A: Three pounds of flax.) or outrageous (Q: What is the Buddha? A: A dried piece of shit.) These exchanges came to be known as "public cases" (*kung-an*), a term borrowed from Chinese jurisprudence that literally means "judge's bench" and referred to a legal precedent, a standard of judgment. These public cases have become famous in the West by the Japanese form of *kung-an,* kōan. Generally represented in modern times as logical puzzles designed to break through the barriers of thought, they in fact constitute Zen scriptures and are memorized, recited, analyzed, and expounded upon like any other Buddhist text, having their own traditional forms of commentary and exegesis and providing standards for the regulation of practice. A monk's ability to comment on these kōans became a means of testing his insight. Kōans, which seem to have begun as objects of study and commentary, eventually also became the focus of formal meditation practice.

To consider one of the most famous kōans to come from China, the monk Zhaozhou was asked whether or not a dog had the buddha nature. It is important to note that dogs are generally not kept as pets in China but are considered unclean creatures that eat garbage and ordure. We must also recall that it is a standard doctrine in Mahāyāna Buddhism, and especially in China, that all sentient beings possess the buddha nature. The question, then, is whether even one of the most disgusting forms of sentient life is endowed with the buddha nature. Zhaozhou answered, "Not" (*wu* in Chinese, *mu* in Japanese). Zhaozhou's unexpected answer may be understood within the larger context of the perennial debate in the Mahāyāna over whether all things have the buddha nature. Thus, the kōan provided for the Chan tradition, which claimed to have renounced reliance on words and letters, a literary form in which the fundamental truths of Buddhism could be both expressed and debated. The unusual form of the kōan, with its use of direct and sometimes even rude speech, allowed Chan at the same time to remain true to its rhetoric of immediacy.

Kōans were eventually transformed into a device for cultivating concentration, as a means of stopping thought and focusing the mind, much like the earth device. Indeed, the Chinese term *Chan* (*Zen* in Japanese) derives from an attempt to render in Chinese the sound of the Sanskrit term *dhyāna,* meaning concentration. One is often instructed to focus the mind on the word *mu.* The stoppage of thought—brought about by such questions as, "Two hands clapping make a sound. What is the sound of one hand?" and, "Why did Bodhidharma come from the west?"—is meant to freeze the mind in a ball of doubt, followed by a flood of understanding, so often described in Zen literature. Precisely what the nature of that understanding is, however, is more difficult to describe. It was customary for Japanese monks who visited China to submit an official report on what teachings they had acquired. Upon his return, the Zen monk Dōgen (1200–1253) reported that he had learned that eyes are horizontal and noses are vertical.

MEDITATION ON EMPTINESS

In the Chan and Zen traditions, the process of meditating on a kōan often follows a sequence of two steps: one first concentrates on the kōan in an effort to stop all thought, following which the "meaning" of the kōan is revealed in a flash of insight. Some scholars have noted a parallel between this process and the traditional Indian Buddhist practice of developing a deep state of concentration called serenity (*śamatha*) in which discursive thought is brought firmly under control, and then using that concentrated mind to develop insight (*vipaśyanā*) into the nature of reality, described often as no-self or as emptiness. But whereas the Zen insight is described in terms of spontaneity and immediacy, several of the Indian and Tibetan schools set forth a process that relies on reasoned analysis.

It is a common Buddhist tenet that direct perception of reality is necessary for the achievement of liberation from rebirth, whether it be the liberation of an arhat or of a buddha. For the Madhyamaka school in India and Tibet, this reality is referred to as emptiness or the selflessness of phenomena. It is emptiness that must be directly perceived by the mind in order to destroy desire, hatred, and ignorance and the karma of the deeds they have motivated over countless lifetimes. Emptiness is not immediately accessible to direct perception; its presence must first be understood conceptually, must be inferred, by using reasoned analysis. Numerous reasonings are set forth in Madhyamaka texts, two of which we might examine here. According to the Madhyamaka claim, we ordinarily conceive of things as if they existed in and of themselves, thinking that when we point to what we call a chariot, in the classical example, or a chair, there is a chariot or a chair there. It would seem to follow, then, that when we examined the chair more carefully, we would find the chair. If we were to take a set of tools and disassemble the chair, we would find four legs, a seat, and a back. None of these individually is the chair. This is not particularly surprising, since we consider the chair to be these parts assembled in a specific way. We might say, therefore, that the collection of the parts arranged accordingly is the chair. But where is the collection? It also cannot be found among its parts. The parts, even when properly assembled, are not the objectively existent chair that we pointed to. That chair is absent. This absence is the emptiness of the chair.

Another argument states that if something exists in and of itself, that is, if it exists intrinsically, it must be either intrinsically one or intrinsically many. Any gross object that is chosen cannot be intrinsically one because it will have parts, either physical parts or temporal parts (moments of duration). Even the smallest particle must logically have physical extension if it is to serve as a component of a larger object. If they had no size, then all such particles would occupy the same space and there would be no extension. Therefore, one can conclude that there is nothing that is intrinsically one. And because whatever is many must be composed of a number of ones, intrinsic manyness is also refuted. Even nirvāṇa, the state of the absence of the afflictions, is not immune from the critique. Nirvāṇa is permanent and does not change. Yet, because it is only known by consciousness over a series of moments, it can be shown to have parts and therefore is not intrinsically one.

The Madhyamaka claim is that nothing is ultimately findable under analysis. Everything is empty, even emptiness. This is not to deny that one can sit on a chair. The emptiness critique is not directed at functional efficacy. It targets instead the false nature of independence, the self, that we ignorantly project onto ourselves and the objects of our experience.

A twenty-dollar bill or a ten-pound note is a piece of paper of a particular shape with words and pictures printed on it in a particular arrangement. By common consent, the citizens of a particular region decide to project value onto the piece of paper, a value far beyond that of the paper and the ink. Although the paper and ink are of little worth, a piece of paper currency can provoke greed and jealousy, sometimes resulting in theft in which one person may be physically injured and another person might be imprisoned. If the note is torn in half, it ceases to have value. What an instant before was sufficient to purchase a meal is now two worthless pieces of paper. One half of a ten-pound note cannot be used to purchase a five-pound movie ticket. Yet if one were to carefully join the two halves together with transparent tape, the value of the bill would be magically restored. It is clear that the ten-pound note is nowhere to be found in the paper and the ink; its very existence as a ten-pound note arises entirely in dependence on the projection of value by the human minds of the members of a local society. The Madhyamaka claim is that nothing in the universe possesses intrinsic value, that all characteristics, both those deemed most essential and those deemed most trivial, are subjective projections and do not inhere in the object. The reasoned scrutiny that searches for the object among its parts is designed to demonstrate this fact and thereby overcome attachment and aversion, desire and hatred, for these illusory objects, illusory in the sense that they do not exist as they appear.

To meditate on emptiness is to perform this kind of analysis. To seek the self, one must first have a clear idea of what one is looking for. Thus, some meditation manuals advise actively cultivating the sense of self, despite the fact that this sense is the target of the analysis. Our sense of identity is often vaguely felt. Sometimes, for example, we identify with the body, saying, "I am sick." At other times, one is the owner of the body, "My stomach hurts." It is said that by imagining a moment of great pride or imagining a false accusation, a strong and palpable sense of the "I" appears in the center of the chest: "I did it," or, "I did not do that." This sense of self is to be carefully cultivated, until one is convinced of its reality. One then sets out to find this self, reasoning that, if it exists, it must be located somewhere in the mind or the body. A standard Buddhist list employed in this case gives the six constituents: earth, water, fire, wind, space, and consciousness. Earth includes all of the obstructive parts of the body: bones, teeth, fingernails, hair, internal organs, muscle, sinew. One is instructed to go through each of these individually and ask, "Is the hair on the head the I?," "Is the cranium the I?," "Is the right upper incisor the I?," "Is the left ring finger the I?," presumably answering no in each case. One then moves to water, all of the liquid parts of the body, the blood, the bile, the phlegm, the urine, lymph, the semen, the menstrual fluid, asking in each case whether any of these is the I. Fire refers to the warmth of the body, described in the Indian medical systems as residing in the belly. Is this heat the I? Space includes all of the empty cavities in the body, in the lungs, the stomach, the mouth. Are any of these the I?

The last of the six constituents, consciousness, is of six types. One asks whether the consciousness of the eye that sees forms, of the ear that hears sounds, of the nose that smells fragrances, of the tongue that tastes flavors, or of the body that feels sensations is the I. Perhaps the most likely candidate for the I is the mental consciousness, the process of thought and memory. But an observation of the mind reveals its inconstancy, moving without apparent reason from one object to another. It lacks the permanence and autonomy that the I seems to possess. At the conclusion of the process of detailed investigation, it is expected that the I will not be found. And because one reasoned in the first place that, if the I exists, it must be locatable somewhere in the mind or the body, one is left only with a sense of the absence of the I, of the lack of self, of emptiness. This is an intellectual understanding of emptiness, too weak to destroy the afflictions or past karma. This process must be repeated again and again until one's idea of emptiness becomes clearer and clearer. This conceptual understanding of emptiness, when combined with the strength of concentration similar to that gained by using the earth device described above, can be deepened further until what began as an idea becomes a direct perception in which the mind and emptiness seem to be mixed, like pure water poured into pure water. Concepts and logic can thus be employed to move to a nonconceptual state. As the *Kāśyapa Chapter Sūtra* (*Kāśyapaparivarta*) says, "Kāśyapa, it is thus. For example, fire arises when the wind rubs two branches together. Once the fire has started, the two branches are burned. Just so, Kāśyapa, if you have the correct analytical intellect, noble wisdom is created. Through its creation, the analytical intellect is consumed."

Suggested Reading

Abhayadatta. *Buddha's Lions: The Lives of the Eighty-Four Siddhas*. Translated by James B. Robinson. Berkeley: Dharma Publishing, 1979.

Buddhaghosa. *The Path of Purification* (*Visuddhimagga*). Translated by Bhikkhu Ñyaṇamoli [sic]. 2nd edition. Colombo, Sri Lanka: A. Semage, 1964.

Dalai Lama and Jeffrey Hopkins. *Kalachakra Tantra: Rite of Initiation*. 2nd revised edition. London: Wisdom Publications, 1989.

Faure, Bernard. *The Rhetoric of Immediacy: A Cultural Critique of Chan/Zen Buddhism*. Princeton: Princeton University Press, 1991.

Gregory, Peter. *Tsung-mi and the Sinification of Buddhism*. Princeton: Princeton University Press, 1991.

Guenther, Herbert V. *The Life and Teachings of Nāropa.* Oxford: Oxford University Press, 1963.

Heine, Steven, and Dale S. Wright, eds. *The Kōan: Texts and Contexts in Zen Buddhism.* New York: Oxford University Press, 2000.

Hopkins, Jeffrey. *Meditation on Emptiness.* London: Wisdom Publications, 1983.

Lopez, Donald S., Jr. *Elaborations on Emptiness: Uses of the Heart Sūtra.* Princeton: Princeton University Press, 1996.

———, ed. *Buddhism in Practice.* Princeton: Princeton University Press, 1995.

———. *Religions of China in Practice.* Princeton: Princeton University Press, 1996.

McRae, John R. *The Northern School and the Formation of Early Ch'an Buddhism.* Honolulu: University of Hawaii Press, 1986.

Snellgrove, David. *Indo-Tibetan Buddhism: Indian Buddhists and Their Tibetan Successors.* Boston: Shambhala, 1987.

Tanabe, George J., Jr., ed. *Religions of Japan in Practice.* Princeton: Princeton University Press, 1999.

Tsong-ka-pa. *Tantra in Tibet: The Great Exposition of Secret Mantra.* London: George Allen & Unwin, 1977.

White, David Gordon, ed. *Tantra in Practice.* Princeton: Princeton University Press, 2000.

CONCLUSION

Let us conclude with stories of statues. The first occurs not in an ancient Sanskrit text but in a modern English tale, told not by a Buddhist monk but by Oscar Wilde. In "The Happy Prince," Wilde tells of a prince who lived his life in the Palace of Sans-Souci, playing with his companions during the day and dancing in the Great Hall at night. "Round the garden ran a very lofty wall, but I never cared to ask what lay beyond it, everything about me was so beautiful." The prince lived and died without ever leaving the city. After his death, the people erected a gilded statue of the prince on a tall column that stood high above the city. Only then, as a statue, did the prince see the miseries of the world. And though his heart was made of lead, he could not help but weep.

With the help of a swallow, the prince does what he can to relieve the sufferings he surveys. He has the swallow remove the ruby from the hilt of his sword and bring it to a poor woman caring for her son, sick with fever. Next, the prince has the swallow pluck out one of his sapphire eyes and carry it to a young writer, so hungry and cold that he cannot finish his play. The other eye is delivered to a little match girl so that her father will not beat her. Finally, the prince has the swallow peck off the gold that covers his statue, leaf by leaf, and give it to the poor. Eventually, the swallow dies of the cold and the shabby statue of the prince is removed from the column and melted down. All that is left is a broken heart of lead, which will not melt in the furnace.

One does not know whether Wilde was providing an ironic twist on the story of Prince Siddhārtha here. The life of the Buddha was well known in England through such works as Sir Edwin Arnold's *The Light of Asia*. The story does cause one to wonder what might have happened had the Indian prince not succumbed to his curiosity about the world outside the walls, had not taken his chariot rides outside the city and beheld the four sights: of an old man, a sick man, a corpse, and a meditating mendicant. It was this stark confrontation with aging, sickness, death, and the possibility of a state beyond that sent the prince out in search of that state, a state that he claimed to have found six years hence. This, according to the story, is how Buddhism began, at least the Buddhism taught by the Buddha of our age.

Wilde's story provides a further parallel, one that he perhaps did not consider. The happy prince was able to alleviate suffering only after his death when he surveyed the world as a statue. The Buddha continued to live after his death, not as one image but as countless images. What remained of his body after it was burned, his relics, are enshrined throughout Asia and, like the jeweled eyes of the prince, are said to be able to dispel all manner of sorrow and bestow all manner of blessing. His statues, now multiplied around the world, are regarded as his living presence, approached daily to grant all manner of prayers.

The second statue can be seen today in Japan. In Kyoto stands the temple of Sanjūsangendō, built in 1266. It is a long and largely undistinguished structure. Inside, arrayed in five rows of almost four hundred feet each, are one thousand golden statues of the bodhisattva of compassion, Kannon, each five feet five inches in height. Each statue has eleven faces and one thousand arms (although only forty-two arms are visible to ordinary sight). Each of the statues appears to the untutored eye to be identical to all of the others. But we are told that each is slightly different. They all look the same, but they are different.

The bodhisattvas of Sanjūsangendō challenge the viewer to perceive difference. The student of Buddhism faces a different challenge. For Buddhism is renowned as a religion of adaptation and assimilation, shaping and reshaping itself to accommodate new cultures and circumstances. But such a characterization assumes that there is some self, some Buddhism, to change and to adapt in the first place. Where is the borderline between a local practice—be it Indian, Tibetan, Korean, Laotian, or Thai—and Buddhism? What makes something—a text, an image, a practice—Buddhist? These are admittedly questions that have only occasionally vexed Buddhists in the premodern period of the history of Asia. But they become pertinent when we come to regard Buddhism as a "world religion." The challenge, then, is not to see the minute differences in the dazzling array of statues in Kyoto but to survey all the people and texts and practices that appear so different and to identify among them something, no matter how elusive, that is the same and that might be called Buddhism, to detect an essence in a tradition that famously proclaims that there is no essence, that there is no self.

But there is also another challenge, the challenge provided by the dharma, which makes the remarkable claim that it is possible to live a life untainted by what are called the eight worldly concerns: gain and loss, fame and disgrace, praise and blame, happiness and sorrow.

GLOSSARY

Abhidharma (Sanskrit): literally, the "higher teaching," a category of scriptures that provide systematic analyses of the constituents of the person, the process of perception, the nature of enlightenment, and other issues of a scholastic nature.

Amitābha (Sanskrit): literally, "Infinite Light," the buddha who presides over the western pure land of Sukhāvatī, the Land of Bliss. Amitābha's vow to deliver the faithful to his pure land serves as the foundation of much Mahāyāna practice, especially in East Asia.

arhat (Sanskrit): literally, "one who is worthy," one who has followed the path and destroyed all causes for future rebirth and will enter nirvāṇa upon death. Regarded as the ideal in the mainstream traditions, where the Buddha is also described as an arhat, in the Mahāyāna the attainment of an arhat is negatively compared to that of a buddha. Certain arhats were selected by the Buddha to remain in the world until the coming of Maitreya. These arhats (called *lohans* in Chinese) were objects of particular devotion in East Asian Buddhism.

Avalokiteśvara (Sanskrit): literally, "the lord who looks down," the bodhisattva of compassion, often called upon for salvation in times of danger. A male bodhisattva in India and Tibet, Avalokiteśvara (known as Guanyin in Chinese, Kannon in Japanese) assumed a female form in East Asia. The Dalai Lamas of Tibet are considered human embodiments of Avalokiteśvara.

bodhicitta (Sanskrit): literally, "mind of enlightenment," it is the compassionate aspiration to achieve buddhahood in order to liberate all beings in the universe from suffering. The development of bodhicitta makes one a bodhisattva.

bodhisattva (Sanskrit): often glossed as "one who has the intention to achieve enlightenment," a bodhisattva is a person who has compassionately vowed to achieve buddhahood but has not yet done so. All forms of Buddhism set forth the path of the bodhisattva, who works for the welfare of others. In the Mahāyāna, the bodhisattva is presented as the ideal.

cakravartin (Sanskrit): literally, "wheel turner," an ideal monarch who rules according to the teachings of the Buddha. The Indian emperor Aśoka is often described as a cakravartin.

Chan (Chinese): the "meditation" school of Chinese Buddhism, which traces its lineage back to the Indian master Bodhidharma (who is said to have come to China in the late fifth century) and back to the Buddha himself. The school's name is pronounced "Zen" in Japanese.

Desire Realm (Sanskrit: *kāmadhātu*): the lowest of the three realms in Buddhist cosmology, populated (in ascending order) by hell beings, ghosts, animals, humans, demigods, and gods.

dharma (Sanskrit): although difficult to translate, the term has two general meanings in Buddhism. The first is the teaching or doctrine of the Buddha, both as expounded and as manifested in practice. The second, perhaps to be rendered as "phenomena," refers to the basic constituents of mind and matter.

dharmakāya (Sanskrit): literally, "dharma body," the term used to refer to the transcendent qualities of the Buddha. In the Mahāyāna doctrine of the three bodies of the Buddha, the dharmakāya is sometimes presented as the ultimate reality from which the other forms of the Buddha derive.

emptiness (Sanskrit: *śūnyatā*): the absence of substantial nature or intrinsic existence in any phenomenon in the universe. In the Madhyamaka philosophy of Nāgārjuna, emptiness is the final nature of reality, and the understanding of emptiness is essential for the achievement of enlightenment.

Form Realm (Sanskrit: *rūpadhātu*): in Buddhist cosmology, a realm of heavens above the Desire Realm reserved for those who attain certain states of deep concentration in their previous life.

Formless Realm (Sanskrit: *ārūpyadhātu*): in Buddhist cosmology, the highest realm within the cycle of rebirth where beings exist as deep states of concentration. Like the Form Realm, it is reserved for those who achieve those states in their previous life.

Gautama (Sanskrit): the clan name of the historical Buddha. His given name was Siddhārtha, "he who achieves his goal."

Jambudvīpa (Sanskrit): literally, "Rose Apple Island," the southern continent in traditional Buddhist cosmology. It is regarded as the world that we inhabit.

Hīnayāna (Sanskrit): literally, "low vehicle," a pejorative term used by proponents of the Mahāyāna to describe those who do not accept the Mahāyāna sūtras as authentic words of the Buddha. In Mahāyāna texts, those who follow the Hīnayāna seek to become arhats by following the path of the śrāvaka or pratyekabuddha rather than by following the superior path of the bodhisattva to buddhahood. In modern scholarship, Hīnayāna is also sometimes used in a nonpejorative sense to refer to the many non-Mahāyāna schools of Indian Buddhism.

Jātaka (Sanskrit): literally, "birth," a story of one of the Buddha's previous lives as a bodhisattva. Among the most popular of Buddhist stories, the tales relate the virtuous deeds of the bodhisattva, often when he was an animal.

karma (Sanskrit): literally, "action," the law of the cause and effect of actions according to which virtuous deeds result in happiness in the future and nonvirtuous deeds result in suffering. Karma is accumulated over many lifetimes and fructifies to create present experience.

kōan (Japanese): often rendered as "public case," the Japanese pronunciation of the Chinese legal term *kung-an*, referring to a standard of judgment. A kōan is commonly a short statement or exchange drawn from accounts of Chinese Chan masters. These statements served both as the basis for commentaries by Chan and Zen teachers and as objects of contemplation.

lama (Tibetan: *bla ma*): a religious teacher. The term is often used to denote an "incarnate lama," that is, a teacher who has been identified as the present incarnation of a great teacher of the past.

lohan (Chinese): *see* arhat.

Madhyamaka (Sanskrit): literally, "middle way," a philosophical school associated with Nāgārjuna that set forth a middle way between the extremes of existence and nonexistence. According to the Madhyamaka, the ultimate reality is emptiness.

Mahākāśyapa (Sanskrit): one of the disciples of the Buddha, Mahākāśyapa is said to have called the saṅgha together after the Buddha's death in order to compile his teachings. He is said to remain in samādhi inside a mountain, awaiting the coming of Maitreya.

Mahāyāna (Sanskrit): literally, "Great Vehicle," a term used by proponents of sūtras that began to appear some four centuries after the death of the Buddha and that were regarded by them as the word of the Buddha. The term has come to mean by extension those forms of Buddhism (today located for the most part in Tibet, China, Korea, and Japan) that base their practice on these sūtras.

Maitreya (Sanskrit): literally, "Kindness," the next buddha to appear in the world after Śākyamuni. Maitreya is currently a bodhisattva residing in a heaven, awaiting the appropriate time to appear.

maṇḍala (Sanskrit): literally, "circle," in tantric Buddhism a representation (in both two- and three-dimensional forms) of the palace of a buddha. Such representations are particularly important in initiation rites, in which the initiate is said to "enter the maṇḍala."

Mañjuśrī (Sanskrit): literally, "Gentle Glory," the bodhisattva of wisdom, often depicted holding aloft a sword, with which he cuts through the webs of ignorance.

mappō (Japanese): literally, "decay of the dharma," the third and final period of the Buddha's teaching before it disappears entirely from the world. A belief that humanity had entered this degenerate age provided the motivation for much Buddhist practice in East Asia, particularly directed at rebirth in the pure land.

Meru (Sanskrit): in Buddhist cosmology, the mountain in the center of the universe. Gods inhabit its surface and summit.

method (Sanskrit: *upāya*): (1) the expedient means by which the Buddha leads beings to enlightenment by teaching them what is not ultimately true until they are prepared for the definitive teaching; (2) practices (such as giving, ethics, and patience) whereby the bodhisattva accumulates the requisite store of merit required to achieve buddhahood.

Nāgārjuna (Sanskrit): Indian monk of the second century regarded as the chief proponent of the doctrine of emptiness and as the founder of the Madhyamaka school. In traditional biographies, he is credited with retrieving the perfection of wisdom sūtras from the ocean realm of the serpent king.

nembutsu (Japanese): literally, "buddha recitation," the practice of reciting the phrase, "Homage to Amitābha Buddha." A general Mahāyāna practice in China (and possibly in India), it became the central practice of the Pure Land (Shinshū) schools of Japan.

nirmāṇakāya (Sanskrit): literally, "emanation body," the third of the three bodies of the Buddha. It is this body that appears in the realm of humans and teaches the dharma. According to this Mahāyāna view, the Buddha who appeared on earth was the magical display of a buddha enlightened long before.

nirvāṇa (Sanskrit): literally, "blowing out," the cessation of suffering and hence the goal of Buddhist practice. The nature of nirvāṇa is widely interpreted in Buddhist literature, with distinctions made between the vision of nirvāṇa, which destroys the seeds of future rebirth, and the final nirvāṇa entered upon death. Mahāyāna texts also distinguished between the nirvāṇa of an arhat and the enlightenment of a buddha.

perfection (Sanskrit: *pāṛaṃiṭā*): the deeds performed by a bodhisattva on the path to buddhahood, commonly enumerated as six: giving, ethics, patience, effort, concentration, and wisdom.

perfection of wisdom: *see* prajñāpāramitā.

prajñāpāramitā (Sanskrit): literally, "perfection of wisdom," the understanding of reality required to achieve buddhahood, according to many Mahāyāna sūtras. The term also describes a genre of Mahāyāna sūtras devoted to the exposition of emptiness and the bodhisattva path.

pratyekabuddha (Sanskrit): literally, "individually enlightened one," a disciple of the Buddha devoted to solitary practice who achieves the state of an arhat without relying on the teachings of a buddha in his last lifetime. According to Mahāyāna exegetes, the path of the pratyekabuddha along with the path of the śrāvaka constitute the Hīnayāna.

pure land: also referred to as a buddha field, the domain that a buddha creates as an ideal setting for the practice of the dharma. Functioning in the Mahāyāna as a form of paradise, rebirth in a pure land, especially the pure land of Amitābha, was the focus of various practices, especially in East Asia.

Śākyamuni (Sanskrit): literally, "Sage of the Śākya Clan," an epithet of the historical Buddha.

samādhi (Sanskrit): a state of deep concentration developed through meditation practice. One of the three trainings (along with ethics and wisdom), samādhi, especially a specific level known as serenity (*śamatha*), is regarded as a prerequisite for liberating wisdom.

saṃbhogakāya (Sanskrit): literally, "enjoyment body," one of the three bodies of the Buddha. The saṃbhogakāya appears to bodhisattvas in pure lands.

saṃsāra (Sanskrit): literally, "wandering," the beginningless cycle of birth, death, and rebirth, composed of the realms of gods, demigods, humans, animals, ghosts, and hell beings. The ultimate goal of Buddhism is liberation from saṃsāra.

saṅgha (Sanskrit): literally "community," a term most commonly used to refer to the order of Buddhist monks and nuns, it can be used more generally for any community of Buddhists, including fully ordained monks, fully ordained nuns, male novices, female novices, laymen, and laywomen.

siddhi (Sanskrit): literally "achievement," a siddhi is a power gained through yogic practice. The term is especially important in Buddhist tantras, where there are two types of siddhis: (1) the mundane or worldly, such as the power to fly, walk through walls, and transmute base metals into gold; and (2) the supramundane or transcendent siddhi of buddhahood. One who possesses siddhi is called a siddha, hence the mahāsiddhas, or great adepts, of Indian tantric literature.

skandhas (Sanskrit): literally, "aggregates," one of the terms used to describe the physical and mental constituents of the person, among which there is no self. The five constituents are form, feeling, discrimination, conditioning factors, and consciousness.

śrāvaka (Sanskrit): literally, "listener," a general term for a disciple of the Buddha, interpreted in the Mahāyāna to designate those who follow the path in order to become an arhat. According to Mahāyāna exegetes, the path of the pratyekabuddha along with the path of the śrāvaka constitute the Hīnayāna.

stūpa (Sanskrit): a reliquary containing the remains or possessions of the Buddha or a Buddhist saint. Initially taking the form of a hemisphere in India, stūpas developed into a variety of architectural forms across Asia, including the pagoda in East Asia. Stūpas have served as important places of pilgrimage throughout the history of Buddhism.

Sukhāvatī (Sanskrit): literally, "the Land of Bliss," the pure land presided over by the buddha Amitābha. It is also known as the Western Paradise.

sūtra (Sanskrit): literally, "aphorism," a discourse traditionally regarded as having been spoken by the Buddha or spoken with his sanction.

tantra (Sanskrit): literally, "continuum." Tantra in its most general sense means a manual or handbook. In Buddhism it refers to a text that contains esoteric teachings, often ascribed to the Buddha. These texts provide techniques for gaining siddhis, both mundane and supramundane.

tathāgata (Sanskrit): literally, "one who has thus come" or "one who has thus gone," an epithet of a buddha.

tathāgatagarbha (Sanskrit): literally, "embryo" or "essence" "of the tathāgata," it is the buddha nature, which, according to some schools of Mahāyāna Buddhism, exists in all sentient beings.

Theravāda (Pali): literally, "School of the Elders," a branch of the Indian Sthāviravāda that was established in Sri Lanka in the third century B.C.E. In the eleventh century C.E. the Theravāda became the dominant form of Buddhism in Sri Lanka and Southeast Asia. As the last remaining school of the many Indian non-Mahāyāna schools, "Theravāda" is often mistakenly regarded as a synonym of "Hīnayāna."

three jewels (Sanskrit: *triratna*): the Buddha, the dharma, and the saṅgha, to whom a Buddhist goes for refuge from the sufferings of saṃsāra.

tripiṭaka (Sanskrit): literally, "three baskets," one of the traditional schemes for organizing Buddhist discourses into three: sūtra, vinaya, and abhidharma.

Vajrayāna (Sanskrit): literally, "Diamond Vehicle" or "Thunderbolt Vehicle," a term used to designate esoteric or tantric Buddhism, traditionally regarded as a form of the Mahāyāna capable of leading to buddhahood more quickly than the conventional bodhisattva path.

vinaya (Sanskrit): literally, "taming," the code of monastic conduct.

Yogācāra (Sanskrit): literally, "practitioners of yoga," a philosophical school originating in India and associated with the fourth-century monk Asaṅga. Among its many tenets, it is best known for the doctrine of "mind-only," which describes the world as a projection of consciousness.

Zen (Japanese): *see* Chan.

BIBLIOGRAPHY OF WORKS CONSULTED

Abhayadatta. *Buddha's Lions: The Lives of the Eighty-Four Siddhas*. Translated by James B. Robinson. Berkeley: Dharma Publishing, 1979.

Bielefeldt, Carl. *Dōgen's Manuals of Zen Meditation*. Berkeley: University of California Press, 1988.

Bodiford, William M. *Sōtō Zen in Medieval Japan*. Honolulu: University of Hawaii Press, 1993.

Brereton, Bonnie. *Thai Tellings of Phra Malai: Texts and Rituals Concerning a Popular Buddhist Saint*. Tempe: Arizona State University Program for Southeast Asian Studies, 1995.

Buddhaghosa. *The Path of Purification (Visuddhimagga)*. Translated by Bhikkhu Ñyaṇamoli [sic]. 2nd edition. Colombo, Sri Lanka: A. Semage, 1964.

Burlingame, Eugene Watson. *Buddhist Legends*. Cambridge: Harvard University Press, 1921.

Buswell, Robert E., Jr. *The Zen Monastic Experience: Buddhist Practice in Contemporary Korea*. Princeton: Princeton University Press, 1992.

———, ed. *Chinese Buddhist Apocrypha*. Honolulu: University of Hawaii Press, 1990.

Buswell, Robert E., Jr., and Robert Gimello, eds. *Paths to Liberation: The Mārga and Its Transformations in Buddhist Thought*. Honolulu: University of Hawaii Press, 1992.

Chang, Garma C. C., ed. *A Treasury of Mahāyāna Sūtras: Selections from the Mahāratnakūṭa Sūtra*. University Park: Pennsylvania State University Press, 1983.

Collins, Steven. *Nirvāṇa and Other Buddhist Felicities: Utopias of the Pali Imaginaire*. Cambridge: Cambridge University Press, 1998.

Cowell, E. B. *The Jātaka, or Stories of the Buddha's Former Births*. London: Pali Text Society, 1957.

Cox, Collett. *Disputed Dharmas: Early Buddhist Theories of Existence*. Tokyo: International Institute for Buddhist Studies, 1995.

Dalai Lama and Jeffrey Hopkins. *Kalachakra Tantra: Rite of Initiation*. 2nd revised edition London: Wisdom Publications, 1989.

Dharmasena Thera. *Jewels of the Doctrine: Stories of the Saddharma Ratnāvaliya*. Translated by Ranjini Obeyesekere. Albany: State University of New York Press, 1991.

Dutt, Sukumar. *Buddhist Monks and Monasteries of India: Their History and Their Contribution to Indian Culture*. London: George Allen & Unwin, 1962.

Emmerick, R. E. *The Sūtra of Golden Light: Being a Translation of the Suvarṇabhāsottamasūtra*. London: Luzac, 1970.

Faure, Bernard. *The Red Thread: Buddhist Approaches to Sexuality*. Princeton: Princeton University Press, 1998.

———. *The Rhetoric of Immediacy: A Cultural Critique of Chan/Zen Buddhism*. Princeton: Princeton University Press, 1991.

Gombrich, Richard F. *Precept and Practice: Traditional Buddhism in the Rural Highlands of Ceylon*. Oxford: Clarendon Press, 1971.

Gómez, Luis O. *Land of Bliss: The Paradise of the Buddha of Measureless Light: Sanskrit and Chinese Versions of the Sukhāvatīvyūha Sūtras*. Honolulu: University of Hawaii Press, 1996.

Gómez, Luis O., and Jonathan A. Silk, eds. *The Great Vehicle: Three Mahāyāna Buddhist Texts*. Ann Arbor: Collegiate Institute for the Study of Buddhist Literature and the Center for South and Southeast Asian Studies, 1989.

Gregory, Peter. *Tsung-mi and the Sinification of Buddhism*. Princeton: Princeton University Press, 1991.

Groot, Jan J. M. de. *Sectarianism and Religious Persecution in China*. Taipei: Literature House, 1963.

Guenther, Herbert V. *The Life and Teachings of Nāropa*. Oxford: Oxford University Press, 1963.

Hakeda, Yoshito S. *Kūkai: Major Works*. New York: Columbia University Press, 1972.

Harrison, Paul. *The Samādhi of Direct Encounter with the Buddhas of the Present: An Annotated English Translation of the Tibetan Translation of the Pratyupanna-Buddha-Saṃmukhāvasthita-Samādhi-Sūtra*. Tokyo: International Institute for Buddhist Studies, 1990.

Heine, Steven, and Dale S. Wright, eds. *The Kōan: Texts and Contexts in Zen Buddhism*. New York: Oxford University Press, 2000.

Hirakawa Akira. *A History of Indian Buddhism: From Śākyamuni to Early Mahāyāna*. Honolulu: University of Hawaii Press, 1990.

Hopkins, Jeffrey. *Meditation on Emptiness*. London: Wisdom Publications, 1983.

Horner, Isabel B. *Women Under Primitive Buddhism: Lay Women and Alms Women*. New York: E. P. Dutton, 1930.

Huber, Toni. *The Cult of Pure Crystal Mountain: Popular Pilgrimage and Visionary Landscape in Southeast Tibet*. Oxford: Oxford University Press, 1999.

Hurvitz, Leon. *Scripture of the Lotus Blossom of the Fine Dharma (The Lotus Sūtra)*. New York: Columbia University Press, 1976.

Jamgön Kongtrul Lodrö Tayé. *Myriad Worlds: Buddhist Cosmology in Abhidharma, Kālacakra, and Dzog-chen*. Ithaca: Snow Lion Publications, 1995.

Jayawickrama, N. A., trans. *The Story of Gotama Buddha: The Nidāna-kathā of the Jātakaṭṭhakathā*. Oxford: Pali Text Society, 1990.

Kalupahana, David J. *Mūlamadhyamakakārikā of Nāgārjuna*. Albany: State University of New York Press, 1986.

Kieschnick, John. *The Eminent Monk: Buddhist Ideals in Medieval Chinese Hagiography*. Honolulu: University of Hawaii Press, 1997.

Kitagawa, Joseph, and Mark D. Cummings. *Buddhism and Asian History*. New York: Macmillan, 1989.

Kloppenberg, Ria. *The Paccekabuddha: A Buddhist Ascetic*. Leiden, Belgium: E. J. Brill, 1974.

Lamotte, Étienne. *History of Indian Buddhism*. Louvain: Peeters Press, 1988.

———, trans. *The Teaching of Vimalakirti (Vimalakīrtinirdeśa)*. London: Pali Text Society, 1976.

Lindtner, Christian. *Nagarjuniana: Studies in the Writings and Philosophy of Nāgārjuna.* Copenhagen: Akademisk Forlag, 1982.

Lobsang Gyatso. *Memoirs of a Tibetan Lama.* Edited and translated by Gareth Sparham. Ithaca: Snow Lion Publications, 1998.

Lopez, Donald S., Jr. *Elaborations on Emptiness: Uses of the Heart Sūtra.* Princeton: Princeton University Press, 1996.

———. *The Heart Sūtra Explained: Indian and Tibetan Commentaries.* Albany: State University of New York Press, 1988.

———, ed. *Buddhism in Practice.* Princeton: Princeton University Press, 1995.

———. *Buddhist Hermeneutics.* Honolulu: University of Hawaii Press, 1998.

———. *Curators of the Buddha: The Study of Buddhism under Colonialism.* Chicago: University of Chicago Press, 1995.

———. *Religions of China in Practice.* Princeton: Princeton University Press, 1996.

———. *Religions of Tibet in Practice.* Princeton: Princeton University Press, 1997.

Matsunaga, Daigan, and Alicia Matsunaga. *The Buddhist Concept of Hell.* New York: Philosophical Library, 1972.

Mayer, Robert. *A Scripture of the Ancient Tantra Collection: The Phur-pa bcu-gnyis.* Oxford: Kicsadale Publications, 1996.

McRae, John R. *The Northern School and the Formation of Early Ch'an Buddhism.* Honolulu: University of Hawaii Press, 1986.

Mizuno, Kōgen. *Buddhist Sūtras: Origin, Development, Transmission.* Tokyo: Kōsei Publishing Company, 1982.

Narada Maha Thera. *The Buddha and His Teachings.* Colombo, Sri Lanka: Lever Brothers Cultural Conservation Trust, 1987.

Nattier, Jan. *Once Upon a Future Time: Studies in a Buddhist Prophecy of Decline.* Berkeley: Asian Humanities Press, 1991.

Nguyen, Cuong Tu. *Zen in Medieval Vietnam.* Honolulu: University of Hawaii Press, 1997.

Nyanaponika Thera and Hellmuth Hecker. *Great Disciples of the Buddha: Their Lives, Their Works, Their Legacy.* Boston: Wisdom Publications, 1997.

Patrul Rinpoche. *The Words of My Perfect Teacher.* San Francisco: HarperSanFrancisco, 1994.

Payne, Richard ed. *Re-Visioning "Kamakura" Buddhism.* Honolulu: University of Hawaii Press, 1998.

Reader, Ian, and George J. Tanabe Jr. *Practically Religious: Worldly Benefits and the Common Religion of Japan.* Honolulu: University of Hawaii Press, 1998.

Robinson, Richard H., and Willard L. Johnson. *The Buddhist Religion: A Historical Introduction.* 4th edition. Belmont, CA: Wadsworth, 1997.

Sadakata, Akira. *Buddhist Cosmology: Philosophy and Origins.* Tokyo: Kōsei Publishing, 1997.

Salomon, Richard. *Ancient Buddhist Scrolls from Gandhāra: The British Library Kharoṣṭhī Fragments.* Seattle: University of Washington Press, 1999.

Śāntideva. *The Bodhicaryāvatāra.* Translated by Kate Crosby and Andrew Stilton. Oxford: Oxford University Press, 1998.

Schober, Juliane, ed. *Sacred Biography and Buddhist Traditions of South and Southeast Asia.* Honolulu: University of Hawaii Press, 1997.

Schopen, Gregory. *Bones, Stones, and Buddhist Monks: Collected Papers on the Archaeology, Epigraphy, and Texts of Monastic Buddhism in India.* Honolulu: University of Hawaii Press, 1997.

Snellgrove, D. L. *The Hevajra Tantra: A Critical Study.* London: Oxford University Press, 1959.

Snellgrove, David. *Indo-Tibetan Buddhism: Indian Buddhists and Their Tibetan Successors.* Boston: Shambhala, 1987.

Stevens, John. *The Marathon Monks of Mount Hiei.* Boston: Shambhala, 1988.

Strong, John S. *The Legend of King Aśoka: A Study and Translation of the Aśokāvadāna.* Princeton: Princeton University Press, 1983.

———, ed. *The Experience of Buddhism: Sources and Interpretations.* Belmont, CA: Wadsworth, 1995.

Swearer, Donald K., and Sommai Premchit. *The Legend of Queen Cāma: Bodhiraṃsi's Cāmadevīvaṃsa, A Translation and Commentary.* Albany: State University of New York Press, 1998.

Tanabe, George J., Jr., ed. *Religions of Japan in Practice.* Princeton: Princeton University Press, 1999.

Teiser, Stephen F. *The Ghost Festival in Medieval China*. Princeton: Princeton University Press, 1988.

———. *The Scripture of the Ten Kings and the Making of Purgatory in Medieval Chinese Buddhism*. Honolulu: University of Hawaii Press, 1994.

Tiyavanich, Kamala. *Forest Recollections: Wandering Monks in Twentieth-Century Thailand*. Honolulu: University of Hawaii Press, 1997.

Tsong-ka-pa. *Tantra in Tibet: The Great Exposition of Secret Mantra*. London: George Allen & Unwin, 1977.

Tucker, Mary Evelyn, and Duncan Ryuken Williams. *Buddhism and Ecology: The Interconnection of Dharma and Deeds*. Cambridge: Harvard University Press, 1997.

Voice of the Buddha, The Beauty of Compassion: The Lalitavistara Sūtra. Berkeley: Dharma Publishing, 1983.

Wallace, B. Alan, trans. and ed. *The Life and Teachings of Geshé Rabten*. London: George Allen & Unwin, 1980.

Wangyal, Geshe. *The Door of Liberation: Essential Teachings of the Tibetan Buddhist Tradition*. Boston: Wisdom Publications, 1995.

Ward, Tim. *What the Buddha Never Taught*. Berkeley: Celestial Arts, 1993.

Warren, Henry Clarke. *Buddhism in Translations*. Cambridge: Harvard University Press, 1953.

Welch, Holmes. *The Practice of Chinese Buddhism: 1900–1950*. Cambridge: Harvard University Press, 1967.

White, David Gordon, ed. *Tantra in Practice*. Princeton: Princeton University Press, 2000.

Wilson, Liz. *Charming Cadavers: Horrific Figurations of the Feminine in Indian Buddhist Hagiographic Literature*. Chicago: University of Chicago Press, 1996.

Wisdom of the Buddha: The Saṁdhinirmocana Mahāyāna Sūtra. Translated by John Powers. Berkeley: Wisdom Publications, 1995.

Yü, Chün-fang. *The Renewal of Buddhism in China: Chu-hung and the Late Ming Synthesis*. New York: Columbia University Press, 1981.

INDEX